THE
YEAR
OF THE
HARE

FRANCIS X. WINTERS

AMERICA IN VIETNAM

January 25, 1963–February 15, 1964

The University of Georgia Press

Athens & London

University of Georgia Press
paperback edition, 1999
© 1997 by the
University of Georgia Press
Athens, Georgia 30602
All rights reserved
Designed by Richard Hendel
Set in Janson
by G&S Typesetters
Printed and bound by Thomson-Shore, Inc.
The paper in this book meets
the guidelines for permanence
and durability of the Committee on
Production Guidelines for Book
Longevity of the Council
on Library Resources.

Printed in the
United States of America
03 02 01 00 99 P 5 4 3 2 1

The Library of Congress has cataloged
the cloth edition of this book as follows:
Library of Congress
Cataloging in Publication Data
Winters, Francis X.
The year of the hare : America in Vietnam,
January 25, 1963–February 15, 1964 /
Francis X. Winters.
p.   cm.
Includes bibliographical references and index.
ISBN 0-8203-1874-4 (alk. paper)
1. Vietnam—Politics and government—
1945–1975.
2. United States—Foreign relations—
Vietnam.
3. Vietnam—Foreign relations—
United States.
4. United States—Foreign relations—
1963–1969.   I. Title.
DS556.9.W57 1997
327.730597—dc20   96-12163
ISBN 0-8203-2121-4 (pbk. : alk. paper)

British Library Cataloging in Publication
Data available

CONTENTS

• • • • • • • • • • •

PART III: AN AMERICAN MORALITY TALE

PREFACE

This study originated, while the war was still raging in Vietnam and at home, with a naive American question and a patient Vietnamese reply. Late in 1972 I made the acquaintance of a gifted Vietnamese graduate student at the School of Foreign Service at Georgetown University, Pham Bao Thien. I asked Thien what he thought of the American engagement in his country, now near its conclusion. Thien's answer was unhesitating: "It was fine until you killed our president." Thien had identified a turning point in the war then not seriously studied by specialists or criticized by antiwar activists, the coup directed by President John F. Kennedy against his ally, the nine-year premier and later president of South Vietnam, Ngo Dinh Diem.

At the time, I was intellectually preoccupied by another, and apparently more urgent, dimension of the Cold War, the nuclear deterrence standoff between the superpowers. Reluctantly I had to delay my study of Vietnam, an inquiry that would trace the dynamics and consequences of Kennedy's decision to overthrow Diem. This deferral lasted much longer than anticipated because of the layered complexity of the puzzle of nuclear deterrence, a puzzle compounded by my professional focus on the relationship between ethics and foreign policy. Making ethical sense of the American-NATO policy of "mutual assured destruction" was not the work of a fortnight.

Inquiry into the logic and risks of nuclear deterrence turned out, however, not to be merely a detour around the urgent issue of the morality of the war in Vietnam but rather the unexpected key that unlocked the complementary Cold War puzzle of Vietnam. For I was to discover, during interviews in the late 1980s and early 1990s, that President Kennedy and Secretary of State Dean Rusk had raised the American ante in Vietnam precisely in order to lower the risks of a nuclear confrontation in a European war. For they correctly believed that nuclear war was likely to lead to the annihilation of the Northern Hemisphere.

The modest contribution of the present study, finally concluded following the close of the Cold War era, is to underline this link between nuclear deterrence and America's Vietnam intervention. The study challenges a dominant stream of analysis of that war — one that has rested largely on a meticulous investigation of U.S.-Vietnamese bilateral relations while virtually ignoring the global concerns of the United States, especially the perilous status of its 1960s European containment policies. One of the many unexpected conclusions thus arising from this study is a historiographical one: exclusive attention to bilateral U.S.-Vietnamese relations during this period almost surely guarantees that the analyst cannot fully grasp the logic that controlled Kennedy's efforts in Vietnam.

A second latent advantage of the long deferral of the present study was the intervening publication between 1988 and 1992 of five volumes of *The Foreign Relations of the United States, 1961–1964, Vietnam*, the official record of our Vietnam diplomacy as edited in the Office of the Historian of the United States Department of State. Before 1992 such studies depended on the partial documentation available from *The Pentagon Papers* and on innumerable other executive and diplomatic records retrieved singly under the provisions of the Freedom of Information Act. *The Foreign Relations of the United States, Vietnam*, now complete from 1961 through 1964, reveals a pattern of decisions that profoundly alters the profile of certain key figures in this drama, and thus of the dynamics of the drama itself.

Also, beginning in February 1994 the General Records of the U.S. State Department for 1963 became available to the public at the National Archives II, College Park, Maryland. Those relevant to the present study are found under the designation "South Vietnam, Political, 1963." My review of all these materials at the Archives has tentatively confirmed the claim of researchers at the Office of the Historian, Department of State, that the record of the deliberations and actions leading to, and immediately following, the coup has now been fully published, with one set of understandable exceptions. Communications between the U.S. government and officials of nations other than Vietnam have been withheld for protection of bilateral communication protocols. In the containers of materials, approximately one hundred documents have been withdrawn for national security reasons. I have requested their release under the provisions of the Freedom of Information Act. If these documents do contain references to U.S. bilateral diplomatic exchanges, they will likely not be released.

The present moment is propitious for a reassessment of the Kennedy administration's Vietnam policy for another reason. All of the American principals in this drama surviving in the late 1980s and early 1990s made themselves available for interviews concerning their recollections of crucial choices, including the deliberate orchestration by President Kennedy of a coup against the government of his ally, Ngo Dinh Diem (a list of individuals whom I interviewed appears in the Sources section).

The focus of this study is the same as its starting point twenty-five years ago: the ethical assessment of U.S. responsibility for the inauguration and outcome of the war in Vietnam. This perspective, reflecting my professional training and native curiosity, is not a fashionable one, especially perhaps in American academic circles. Recognizing the aversion of many contemporary foreign policy specialists to the ethical analysis of diplomacy, I seek in this study to separate the narrative account of what happened in Washington and Saigon in 1963 from the ethical inquiry of why it happened. Thus Part I lays out a narrative of the planning for, and execution of, the coup against Ngo Dinh Diem in detachment from any inquiry into the moral acceptability of the U.S. involvement in such a drastic intervention in the internal affairs of its ally.

This narrative section is followed by a close study of the personal histories and ethical perspectives of five principal actors or institutions who were responsible in complementary ways for the execution of the coup: Dean Rusk, Ngo Dinh Diem, Henry Cabot Lodge Jr., the correspondents and editors of the *New York Times*, and finally President Kennedy himself. These accounts, which constitute Part II, situate the events and choices of 1963 in the context of the characteristic patterns of political conduct of these personalities over the longer time frame required to appreciate their choices made during the Year of the Hare, as 1963 was known in the East Asian lunar calendar.

Finally, an effort is made in Part III to draw some lessons from the somber events of 1963. While a final assessment of the lessons of Vietnam will have to await publication of the official State Department records for the years 1965 to 1975, some significant lessons do appear evident in the events of the Year of the Hare. Unsurprisingly, I emphasize what I consider to be ethical lessons, applicable to the conduct of U.S. policy today and tomorrow. I expect such proposed lessons to generate controversy.

ACKNOWLEDGMENTS

Friendship is both the root and the fruit of kindness. Only such kindness can account for the unwavering readiness of my busy friends, both young and older, to set aside their own important pursuits to review and enrich a manuscript. The end of my labors on *The Year of the Hare* provides the leisure to express somewhat more formally than before my gratitude to such friends.

Robert W. Tucker has steadily encouraged over a decade my inquiry and sought to sharpen its focus. His support and critical questions were responsible for abbreviating and clarifying the text.

Sarah Ann Smith brought to her meticulous review of the work at several stages an understanding of Asian cultures and a mastery of English prose. When a recent illness threatened to delay the final stages of textual revision, her assistance was the steady hand needed to proceed.

Dorothy Brown responded almost instantly to my request for advice by providing enthusiastic support and incisive questions about methodology. Mary McHenry offered useful hints about refining the language and uncovering the implied argument about ethics. Marjorey Boichel Thompson generously drew on her years as Director of Publications for Georgetown's Institute for the Study of Diplomacy to help produce a professional manuscript.

David Oxenstierna prepared me for interviews by thoughtful summaries of the secondary literature and by suggestions for productive lines of inquiry for the interviews. I am equally grateful to all those who readily granted interviews.

Three Georgetown students were patient and enthusiastic collaborators on endless revisions and expansions of the text: Eileen Scully, Tim Hughes, and Peter Cole.

I wish to thank Malcolm Call of the University of Georgia Press, who somehow saw promise in a quite inchoate early draft of this study, and Angela Ray, the freelance editor at the Press, who caught in time for correction numerous areas of imprecision and inconsistency.

At Georgetown's School of Foreign Service, I have received steady support, morally and financially, from Deans Peter Krogh, Charles Pirtle, and Allan Goodman.

Each of these benefactors knows in what ways he or she has made the present work possible.

PROLOGUE: A TALE OF TWO WALLS

T his is a tale of two walls and of the moral logic that linked them. One of the walls was dismantled by the whirlwind of a collapsing empire, beginning with the popping of champagne corks in Berlin at midnight on November 10, 1989. Until that moment, which broke the hold of Soviet hegemony in Europe, no one could finally judge the meaning of that other wall in Washington, whose dark luster had risen on the Mall seven years earlier, as veterans of the Vietnam War took it upon themselves to honor their comrades who had fallen in a doomed struggle in Southeast Asia.[1]

Until the final resolution of the East-West competition in the Cold War in Europe, it was impossible to assess definitively the meaning of that surrogate struggle in Vietnam, which began in earnest just months after the Berlin Wall was raised in 1961. Now that the unstable Soviet domination of European nations has been thrown off, shaking even the internal Soviet empire itself, it is finally time to appraise the justice of the war waged in Vietnam as a substitute for a third twentieth-century European war, which would likely have been Europe's last. Among the many unexpected blessings of life after the Cold War are the leisure and detachment required to inquire gradually and more surely about the wisdom of Washington's policies in Southeast Asia. One can begin with policies of the Kennedy administration. For these officials had fortunately grasped the risks of European military confrontation in the nuclear era and, as a result, expanded the policy of containment to include the apparently more controllable venue of Southeast Asia. Was the new expanse of peace now enjoyed by the United States and its allies in some measure assured by Kennedy's engagement in Vietnam?

It may seem at first myopic to seek an understanding of the lessons of Vietnam in the events of a single year. The choice of the year, 1963, adds to the implausibility of any hope for enlightenment, for the war is popularly associated primarily with Kennedy's successors, Johnson and Nixon. Yet the decisive character of Kennedy's final policies in Vietnam has been underscored recently by leading architects and leaders of the victorious North Vietnamese struggle against the Saigon regime. In November 1995 General Vo Nguyen Giap and his surviving wartime colleagues met with Robert McNamara, who was seeking to establish a joint Vietnamese-American conference on the lessons of the war. The Vietnamese argued that Kennedy's policies in Vietnam were terminally mistaken. Ngo Dinh Diem, they argued, was a nationalist who would never have allowed the Americans to take over Saigon's war effort, leading the Americans and their hapless Saigon allies to costly defeat. Therefore the coup that overthrew Diem in 1963 was the surprisingly early end for the United States in Vietnam.

The coup was itself the denouement, by no means inevitable, of a year in which Washington's Vietnam policies had a remarkably focused concern: how to deal with its autocratic ally, Ngo Dinh Diem. This single policy question engaged the attention of an array of Kennedy's officials, as well as the press. The spectrum of American foreign policy approaches to the common problem thus provides an unusual case study of the foreign policy process during the Cold War period. Senator Mike Mansfield's prescient plea for Kennedy to distance himself from the despotic rule of Diem was shaped by his own reluctant conclusion that Diem, after nine years of growing support and continuous democratic tutelage, would never become a Jeffersonian ruler. The United States could therefore no longer contribute to the increasingly autocratic policies of its ally, whom Kennedy and Mansfield had now been backing for a full decade. It was sadly time now to abandon Diem to his own political instincts and destiny. Mansfield outlined his recommendations to the president in late December 1962. Kennedy reluctantly accepted his friend's suggestion in February, deciding to defer final resolution of the issue until after his expected reelection in 1964.

At the opposite extreme of American diplomatic responses to Diem's problematic alliance behavior was Henry Cabot Lodge Jr., whom Kennedy nominated on June 29 to become ambassador to Saigon. Lodge consistently adopted a forthrightly colonialist approach to South Vietnam, which he judged too important an outpost in the Cold War to be held hostage to its own constitutional government. After allowing Diem ample opportunity to revise his governmental policies in a way calculated to assuage U.S. public opinion, Lodge moved urgently to oversee a coup d'état.

It is the gradual evolution in policy from Mansfield's proposal of American withdrawal from Vietnam to Kennedy's, and Lodge's, supervision of the coup that is the subject of the present study. The coup ended in Diem's assassination and a subsequent reign of chaos lasting eighteen months, until the installation of the Thieu-Ky regime in June 1965. It was the Thieu-Ky government that invited President Johnson to send, in July 1965, fifty-eight thousand American troops to undertake a war that the South Vietnamese government could not wage independently.[2]

The decision of President Kennedy to encourage on August 29, 1963, and personally to direct for two months, the overthrow of Ngo Dinh Diem—when he was well aware that there was little likelihood of his replacement by a more competent chief of state—has long puzzled commentators.[3] This enigma was partially resolved with the revelation that Kennedy had privately communicated to a few friends his intention to remove American troops from Vietnam after his reelection in 1964.[4] For Kennedy, the prospect of instability and/or chaos following a coup in Vietnam was thus less daunting because the United States would, he hoped, no longer be engaged there after 1965. The coup-installed government of South Vietnam would then be on its own.

Most members of the administration, however, including most of the cabinet officials concerned with foreign policy, did not know of Kennedy's intention to abandon Vietnam in 1965.[5] Their collaboration in planning the November 1–2, 1963, coup against Diem, in full knowledge of the likely incompetence of those who would remove and succeed him, remains enigmatic even with the additional evidence in the newly available official records about the coup planning. Only the Kennedy officials' accounts of the decision to remove Diem can make sense of that decision, which otherwise seems whimsical. Indeed, even their own accounts of the pre-coup calculations will fail to persuade some critics that the decision to proceed with the coup was well considered.

After the removal of Ngo Dinh Diem by General ("Big Minh") Duong Van Minh, whose initial rule in Saigon lasted only ninety days before he was in turn overthrown, seven other governments appeared almost with the regularity of miniature moving figures on a Swiss ornamental tower clock, marking the passing hours.[6] When the last, and most lasting, of these regimes resigned at American request on April 21, 1975, Big Minh was once more waiting in the wings, ready to assume the responsibility for surrendering Saigon to North Vietnam.[7]

The retrospective reflections of Kennedy's officials contribute significantly to an understanding of the history of the war by underlining the *conscientious* character of their decision making on the pivotal option to remove Ngo Dinh Diem from power in favor of an unpromising military junta. That decision, which might at first seem a callous act of raison d'état, was, in the minds of many of the officials involved, altogether the opposite of raw realism. The coup was in fact inspired decisively by American republican sensibilities. If the officials had been steering exclusively by an "Old World" ethos of national interest, the option to overthrow Diem would almost certainly have been quickly dismissed. For he was the only hope for maintaining order in the midst of civil war — and a nearly desperate hope at that. Some key American officials nevertheless acted against him because of their repugnance at his formula for maintaining order: repression.

Finally, the Kennedy administration policies were a blend of profound moral indignation against Diem and his family, on the part of Dean Rusk, George Ball, and Averell Harriman, and political opportunism by President Kennedy himself, who finally decided to allow Diem to be sacrificed on the altar of American public opinion despite his own lingering sympathy for Diem. It is only this perhaps uniquely American blend of opportunism and high moral principle that can explain the dynamics of the American decision to remove Diem.

Perhaps in this characteristic synergism of principle and self-interest lie some lessons, as Americans review the dynamics and consequences of their Cold War foreign policy. Still more likely, there may be lessons for other, especially less powerful, nations who are contemplating alliances with the United States. Armed with such sobering historical understanding, potential allies may move more cautiously in the rapids of American alliance politics.

It may seem counterintuitive to claim that organizing, and overseeing, a coup against an allied chief of state would be recalled by its perpetrators as an act of conscience. This apparent paradox is less baffling, however, when one sees it through the eyes of the principals themselves. It was Dean Rusk who articulated most clearly the compulsion in the Kennedy administration to remain committed to South Vietnam, even to the ironic limits of dictating a change in its government. Rusk explained the strategic logic behind this puzzling choice by recounting a seemingly unrelated incident early in the administration, perhaps as early as February 1961.[8] That event was a classified briefing prepared for the most senior officials of the administration, along with the president, on the likely effects of nuclear war. Such a conflict would entail a substantial risk of destroying the Northern Hemisphere and thus the United States itself. After the briefing, President Kennedy, who was stunned by the revelation of the destructive power he had accepted so eagerly, exclaimed to Rusk: "And they call us the human race!"[9] From that moment on, Rusk claims, the administration was determined to avoid any strategy that might eventually entail its unleashing such a catastrophe. The new government thus readily resolved that—until it could persuade its Western European partners to build up their own conventional forces to a level sufficient to resist Soviet aggression without reliance on American first use of nuclear weapons—its own commitment to the policy of containment dictated additional resistance to Communist expansion outside Europe.[10]

Curiously, this resolution led Kennedy and his officials to select South Vietnam as the bastion of Western values. After learning that the European confidence in the nuclear umbrella was a mirage, they scrapped the Eisenhower-Dulles declaratory policy of massive nuclear retaliation and designed a new policy, which they labeled "mutual assured destruction." Even in renaming their nuclear policy for NATO, they signaled their awareness of its inherent risks, thus persuading them to avoid its execution. Since conscience now denied them the option of nuclear warfare, all that was left was local war. And the only local war at hand was the then low-level conflict in Vietnam. Kennedy's commitment to Vietnam, then, was a rational act of desperation, determined by his horror at the prospect of U.S.-Soviet nuclear war.

Kennedy first signaled this implausible option for redrawing the East-West divide at the Seventeenth Parallel in Indochina in an interview with James ("Scotty") Reston of the *New York Times*, as Kennedy emerged from his first alarming confrontation with Nikita Khrushchev in Vienna, in June 1961. Reston recounts the interview:

> Khrushchev had threatened him over Berlin. In his earthy language, the Soviet leader was fond of saying that the way to make capitalist politicians pay attention was to "pull their testicles" on Berlin. He had presented Kennedy with an aide-mémoire, setting December 1961 as the deadline for agreement on a Berlin peace treaty. If the United States did not agree to Communist control over access to that city, the Soviet Union would proceed unilaterally to dominate

the routes from Western Europe to Berlin. The president felt this amounted to an ultimatum, and replied that the United States would fight to maintain access to its garrison in Berlin if necessary. The summit meeting ended on that ominous note.

Kennedy reported this to me quite calmly. He thought he knew, he said, why Khrushchev had taken such a hard line. He felt sure Khrushchev thought that anybody who had made such a mess of the Cuban invasion had no judgment, and any president who had made such a blunder but then didn't see it through had no guts. Now, said the president, we have a problem.

Nothing could be resolved with the Soviets, he added, if they thought we would not insist on our rights and would not fight for them. He had tried to convince Khrushchev of U.S. determination but had failed. It was now essential to demonstrate our firmness, and the place to do it, he remarked to my astonishment, was Vietnam! I don't think I swallowed his hat, but I was speechless. . . .

When Kennedy returned to Washington, he gave orders to send another U.S. division to Europe and to triple the number of U.S. military advisers in Vietnam. . . .

This, I always thought, was a critical mistake. . . . And when Kennedy, alarmed by the inefficiency of the Saigon government under Diem, cooperated in approving Diem's murder, he was all the more convinced that he had to carry on the war.[11]

This irreversible turning point in the Cold War, the shift from the potentially apocalyptic European confrontation over some flash point such as Berlin to the obscure and inscrutable struggle in Vietnam, puzzled Reston.[12] His puzzlement was understandable. The utter incommensurability of interests, armaments, stakes, personalities, cultures, and geography make this substitution formula astonishing even in retrospect.[13]

It has seemed until recently as though this switch was a sort of Athena among strategies, springing fully armed from the mind of her American master. But it is now becoming clearer that Kennedy and his administration may have been deeply influenced—perhaps more decisively than they knew—by Khrushchev's own earlier tortured decision to deflect U.S.-Soviet competition from the tinderbox of Europe to the periphery of global politics, for example, to Vietnam. While studies of the genesis and logic of Khrushchev's volatile foreign policy are still quite inchoate, a recent study of his initial response to his own first briefing on the dynamics of nuclear war reveals the profound shock it presented to his traditional Marxist worldview. Khrushchev later recalled that, in September 1953, when Igor Kurchatov, director of the Soviet nuclear project, briefed the new first secretary of the Communist Party on the dynamics of nuclear war between the superpowers, "I couldn't sleep for several days. Then I became convinced that we could never possibly use these weapons, and when I realized that I was able to sleep again. But all the same we must be prepared. Our understanding is not sufficient answer to the arrogance of the imperialists."[14]

Khrushchev's own shock on first looking into the nuclear cyclone was reinforced in February of the next year by the results of the "Bravo" test of a fifteen-megaton thermonuclear weapon at Enewetak Atoll. Georgi Malenkov, for example, warned as early as March 12, 1954, of "a new world war, which with modern weapons means the end of civilization." Malenkov's statement was echoed by some Soviet nuclear program officials, who warned that the current rate of production of nuclear arms by the superpowers would within a few years risk a conflict that would "create on the whole globe conditions impossible for life. . . . One cannot but acknowledge . . . that over the human race there hangs a threat of an end to all life on earth." This report was forwarded to Khrushchev on April 1, 1954, but was not published. Malenkov, who first had raised the public alarm about the prospective ravages of nuclear war, soon fell victim to his own candor. In January 1955 Khrushchev criticized Malenkov's statement. V. M. Molotov then joined the chorus of condemnation, arguing that the rejection of nuclear war would mean the abandonment of Marxist doctrine about the struggle against imperialism. In February, Malenkov resigned as chairman of the Council of Ministers, opening the way to public attacks on his views. The Party leadership still clung publicly to the role of nuclear war in defeating the forces of capitalism.[15]

With Khrushchev now firmly in charge of foreign policy in the Soviet Union, the leadership was deeply influenced by its participation in the Geneva Conference on July 18–23, 1955, when President Eisenhower argued to Nikolai Bulganin during dinner one night that the development of modern weapons was such that the country that used them "genuinely risked destroying itself. . . . A major war would destroy the

Northern Hemisphere." Eisenhower made the same point with Georgi Zhukov, his old comrade-in-arms against Hitler. "Not even scientists could say what would happen if two hundred H-bombs were exploded in a short period of time, but . . . the fall-out might destroy entire nations and possibly the whole northern hemisphere." Zhukov agreed with Eisenhower. Eisenhower later reported on television his impressions from the Geneva summit: "[T]here seems to be a growing realization by all that nuclear warfare, pursued to the ultimate, could be practically race suicide."[16]

Two months later, Khrushchev definitively rejected the inevitability of war. "Either peaceful coexistence or the most destructive war in history. There is no third way." David Holloway concludes that "a kind of existential deterrence had come into being. The Soviet leaders and the leaders of the United States understood how terrible a nuclear war would be, and each side believed that the other understood this too. On this basis they shared the conviction that neither would start a nuclear war."[17]

Khrushchev's distinctive contribution to Soviet diplomacy and ideology, probably in collaboration with others in the leadership, was in resolving the dilemma of renouncing nuclear war while maintaining the goal of defeating capitalism globally. By June 1960 he had found the solution, namely, the Soviet shift to support wars of colonial liberation.[18] Khrushchev's new tack was articulated, probably not coincidentally, just two weeks before Kennedy's inauguration and was announced to the outside world on January 18, 1961, in a Kremlin press release. Having renounced world war as a suicidal and therefore irrational policy, Khrushchev embraced as "the only way to bring imperialism to heel . . . the 'sacred' struggle of colonial peoples, wars of colonial liberation," including that in Vietnam. Kennedy immediately circulated the forty-page draft of the Kremlin's statement to his top foreign policy officers, with the urgent message: "[R]ead, mark, learn and internally digest it."[19]

Kennedy seems to have followed his own advice, and he drew the appropriate conclusion during the June summit at Vienna about the locus of U.S.-Soviet conflict in the future. Vietnam, as Khrushchev had adumbrated just before Kennedy's inauguration, would be the new if implausible venue. The substitution of Vietnam for Berlin as the arena of containment required an astonishing leap of imagination.

Ellen Hammer, in her elegant study of the Kennedy years in Vietnam, exclaims that Kennedy and his officials "all seemed to regard South
Vietnamese officials as interchangeable."[20] This unmistakable indifference of the U.S. government to the personal makeup of its ally's government in the midst of civil war was itself, however, a function of a far
more crucial indifference, or insensitivity: for the Kennedy foreign policy team, whole nations were interchangeable. Vietnam could serve as a
surrogate for Germany. The awkward consequence of this radical substitution formula was yet to be discovered. Vietnamese officials were dis-
inclined (indeed were culturally and morally unable) to act like European statesmen.

American journalists would soon fathom this paradoxical substitution
of Saigon personalities and customs for those of Bonn. In response, they
would call urgently and anxiously for the removal of the Diem government in favor of a regime more representative of the Western values
of representative government, now oddly enough being put on the line
in Indochina. Hounded by the vivid front-page accounts of oriental
despotism, and the seconding editorials (for example, in the *New York
Times*) that called for a coup against Diem, Kennedy finally and reluctantly went along with the drive by several of his officials to remove
Diem. This advice, to which he finally yielded, was a counsel of despair, made plausible by the Cold War imperative to display—without
the risk of self-extinction—the resolve necessary to deter Communist
expansion.

Kennedy later seemed to regret having given in to the counsel of despair that had urged the coup on him. Days after the assassination of
Diem, Kennedy insisted that Diem and his brother Nhu "were in a
difficult position. They did the best they could for their country."[21]
Kennedy's despair had been reasonable enough. Diem, on whom the
Americans had placed such hopes, was a lost cause for the Anglo-Saxon
and Enlightenment political values for which he had suddenly and dubi-
ously been dubbed the champion. Not only were Washington's values
wholly alien to Vietnam, but the relentless urging of these values on
Diem by American officials and editors smacked of a new cultural colonialism, weakening further his already fragile image as a nationalist
leader in a colonially ravaged land. Quite apart from the debatable relevance of Magna Carta to Saigon in 1963, Diem was utterly unable to

undertake such a westernization of his government precisely because it was being pushed on him publicly by foreigners.[22]

The impasse was final. Diem was the antithesis of the political and moral values being defended through the policy of containment, but Diem was likewise the only non-European besieged ruler willing to accept Washington's intrusive patronage. Kennedy felt pressed to press Diem for reform or, failing that, to remove him. The only remaining alternative was to abandon Vietnam and return the East-West struggle to the more natural setting of the Fulda Gap. But that course was precluded at present by the risks of nuclear war. Unable to live with Diem, Kennedy reluctantly approved the plot to remove him.

Advised by those who knew Vietnam best—William Colby of the CIA and former ambassador Frederick ("Fritz") Nolting—that a coup against Diem would likely bring to power a coterie of ineffectual generals with no capacity to rule in Vietnam, the president nevertheless pressed ahead, taking a desperate gamble to stabilize the situation in Saigon sufficiently to allow him to proceed with his reelection campaign, before finally abandoning Vietnam in 1965.[23] The risky wager on a coup evidently seemed to Kennedy less fraught with danger than continuing to support Diem in the face of almost daily cries of outrage in the press.

For Diem surely had a dearth of democratic credentials. Himself a mandarin, descended from a Catholic mandarin clan, Diem had been anointed as prime minister in 1954 by Bao Dai, the absentee emperor who had already abdicated in favor of Ho Chi Minh in 1946. To Americans, such an appointment soiled, rather than sanctioned, Diem's claim to authority. Bao Dai, the son of a puppet emperor under French colonial rule, had himself twice agreed to serve under French aegis. Diem's slender claim to political legitimacy was thus tainted by an indelible association with colonialism. In George Herring's words, "The French finally granted unqualified independence to the state in Vietnam in June 1954, but the government still nominally presided over by Bao Dai was a fiction. Assuming the premiership in the summer of 1954, the staunchly anti-French Ngo Dinh Diem inherited antiquated institutions patterned on French practices and ill-suited to the needs of an independent nation—'an oriental despotism with a French accent,' one American scornfully labelled it."[24]

During the Second World War, it had seemed likely that President Roosevelt would make a clean break with European colonialism by barring the return of the European powers to their former colonies.[25] With Roosevelt's death, this decision devolved upon Harry Truman, who was less antipathetic to the return of these European powers to their colonial claims. The "fall" of China to communism, and the subsequent war on the Korean peninsula, alerted American leaders to the risks of a political vacuum on the border of China in these strategic former colonies. Truman encouraged a reengagement by France in Indochina.[26] From 1945 to the defeat of the French at Dien Bien Phu in 1954, the French forces received 78 percent of their funding from the United States. Most analysts believe that a second powerful motivation for U.S. support for the French forces in Indochina was the futile hope of persuading France to shoulder a reasonable share of the burden of European security.[27]

Even though Diem himself was bitterly anti-French, his accession to power through delegation by Bao Dai permanently compromised his standing in most American eyes. His subsequent conduct in 1955 of a plebiscite to depose Bao Dai did little to absolve him of the colonialist taint.[28]

Still more damaging to Diem's public image in the United States was his refusal to cooperate in carrying out the nationwide elections called for by the Geneva Accords of 1954. The accords themselves, which did include provisions for such elections, had no legal force in South Vietnam, since neither Diem nor his American allies had signed them. They had merely promised not to overturn them by force, providing that no other powers had violated them in advance.[29] The events leading up to the Geneva meeting made clear that South Vietnam had no obligation to accept provisions agreed to by four hostile powers (China, France, the Soviet Union, and North Vietnam); but Diem's defiance of calls to hold elections in 1956—which he would likely have lost by at least two million votes, the numerical superiority of North Vietnam's portion of the population—continues to diminish Diem's standing in the American memory of the struggle in Vietnam.[30]

To many Americans, fear of elections is a touchstone of political illegitimacy. In Vietnamese eyes, however, the indifference of Diem to such national elections may be less puzzling. For in the two-thousand-year history of Vietnam, no election beyond the village level had ever been held. Thus, the elevation of nationwide elections to the equivalent of a seal of legitimacy of a Vietnamese government might have seemed like another foreign intrusion. Moreover, the Vietnamese were aware that two of the great powers requiring such elections, the Soviet Union and China, were not notably addicted to elections in their own realms.

Equally decisive in Diem's undoing was his repression of Buddhist protests during the spring and summer of 1963. After the slaying of seven religious demonstrators at Hue on the Buddha's birthday, May 8, 1963; the self-immolation of bonzes in Saigon beginning in June; and the mass arrest of almost fifteen hundred bonzes on the night of August 20–21, Diem's fate was sealed. He would no longer serve as a viable partner for the United States in the Cold War struggle between the Marxist threat and the forces of freedom.

When Kennedy had come into office, he had been uneasy about the alliance with Diem inherited from the Eisenhower administration. During his first months in office, he sent Vice President Lyndon Johnson to report on the situation in Saigon. At the same time, he charged the new ambassador, Fritz Nolting, to "find out what kind of man Diem is."[31] Kennedy thus had sought early to review the cards he was holding in Southeast Asia. They were very weak, considering the stakes he might be forced to lay on the table in the Cold War struggle. Shrewdly averse to the risks of nuclear confrontation in Europe, the Kennedy administration had opted to display a resolute stance of nonappeasement by backing Diem in his uphill struggle against Ho Chi Minh. Never, perhaps, had a powerful nation wagered so much on so frail an ally. The game would require nerves of steel and the blessing of good fortune.

After months of vacillation, Kennedy moved in August 1963 to bring down Diem in a military coup that he personally supervised from the White House.[32] At the same moment, Diem was opening his negotiations with Ho, hoping to establish a loose federal government in Vietnam, divided between Ho as ruler of the North and Diem as president in the South.[33] The prospects for such an unforeseen union were auspicious. Both Ho and Diem had begun to sense the risks of Vietnam's becoming the principal battle line of the Cold War. The coup foreclosed prospects for a peaceful reunification of Vietnam.[34]

More than fate, of course, was at work in scripting this tragedy. The character of the two protagonists, Diem and Kennedy, almost mastered their fates. Kennedy himself was almost the last to despair of Diem's reformation. Weeks before the end, on October 5, still hoping for a change of heart by Diem, he ordered a new symbol of U.S. demands to be signaled to Diem: the cutoff of U.S. aid to Diem's personal forces (under Colonel Le Quang Tung) and palace guard.[35] This signal only accelerated Diem's flight and cut the nerve of any possible accommodation by Diem to Kennedy's demands.

Unlike a handful of his senior officials, driven by their instinctive disgust for Diem's repressive policies, the president himself never lost his sympathy for Diem's dilemma. Diem could either show the firmness required for control of an insurrectionary movement in the cities of South Vietnam, or he could make reforms that would please Kennedy but would inevitably undermine his own authority and power.[36] But Kennedy did lose control of events and eventually watched powerlessly as the coup he had authorized in August finally descended on Diem in November, even as Kennedy was urgently signaling Ambassador Lodge to reverse his previous support of the plotters. Only moments, then, separated Kennedy and Diem from the escape that both were desperately seeking from one another.[37] The study that follows recounts the fateful decisions of Kennedy and Diem in their final year, the Year of the Hare.

The newly opened official records of the administration reveal the ongoing volatility of the National Security Council deliberations about the coup. Many historians writing before the full record of these internal debates was made public have too easily assumed that the choice of the coup, like the other cardinal Vietnam policy choices, was inevitable. George Herring, for example, concludes his meticulous study of the entire war with the fatalistic comment: "Vietnam made clear the inherent unworkability of a policy of global containment. . . . By intervening in what was essentially a local struggle, it [the United States] placed itself at the mercy of local forces, a weak client, and a determined adversary. It elevated into a major international conflict what might have remained a localized struggle. By raising the stakes into a test of its own credibility, it perilously narrowed its options. A policy so flawed in its premises cannot help but fail, and in this case the results were disastrous."[38]

A careful review of the daily dynamics of Kennedy's Vietnam deliberations in 1963 fails to support this thesis of inevitability. The fatalism suggested by Herring ignores the palpable reality that Kennedy and Diem came within hours of avoiding this outcome. For Herring's judgment underestimates radically the liveliness and continuity of the debate that raged around Kennedy, and indeed in his own conscience, right up to, and even after, the end of Diem.

To be fair to Kennedy, it is imperative to acknowledge the perspicacity of his choice (and that of Khrushchev) to draw back from the precipice of nuclear confrontation, downgrading containment to the status of local and conventional war. The desperate decision for a coup against Diem, made in late August and scrupulously pursued for two months before its last-minute (and inefficacious) withdrawal on October 29, must be seen in the context of the shock experienced by Kennedy when he learned the realities of nuclear weapons and their effects. The apparent indifference of Kennedy to the fate of his ally, Ngo Dinh Diem, and even of South Vietnam, can be grasped only as an aftershock of his early jolting by a briefing on nuclear war. Alerted to the illusory security of nuclear deterrence, Kennedy plunged heedlessly into the shallows of U.S.–South Vietnamese alliance politics. The road to defeat thus was paved with the most admirable of good intentions.

The present study is animated by the still unanswered question of the link between two epochal defeats in the Cold War era, the political-military defiance of American resolve in Vietnam and the reversal of Soviet expansionism in Europe. Was the American-Vietnamese shared tragedy the price that had to be paid for the containment of communism, or was the American debacle in Vietnam a wholly gratuitous and self-inflicted wound? Could Kennedy have steered a different course in Vietnam and won the two victories at once? Could we now be living in a world unscarred by either wall—that in Berlin or that on the Mall in Washington? Is Herring wrong in proclaiming the U.S.–South Vietnamese defeat an *inevitable* outcome of the strategy of containment?[39]

Suggesting doubts about the claim that the tragic outcome was inevitable, the present study will review almost day by day the decisions and actions that doomed the Kennedy-Diem alliance in that portentous year, 1963. Specifically, the inquiry will examine the governing myths of the alliance and, with equal attention, the disorderly sequence of developments and choices that could have been—and very nearly were—avoided.

When Kennedy's officials moved with full deliberation to overthrow their ally of nine years, Ngo Dinh Diem, two years after quieting his prescient fears about American intervention in South Vietnam's internal affairs, many of them did so in good conscience. The evidence of this paradoxical moral imperative (to overthrow an ally in order to ensure the freedom of that nation) is at hand in the official record of deliberations on the coup. On October 2, after resolving to send the coup plotters their designated signal of bona fides—cutting off U.S. funds for support of Colonel Tung's "palace guard" forces—the National Security Council turned to the delicate question of an official statement that would convey to the public the rationale for this volatile move. The president and most of his advisers were by this time resolved on the need to remove Nhu and, almost inevitably, Diem as well, but they were split on their motivations for this choice. While President Kennedy preferred to stress the military logic of cutting off the funds, Dean Rusk and George Ball argued for a loftier interpretation of their decision. In the official report of the meeting, the note taker observed the divide between those who stressed the military rationale—Kennedy, McNamara, and Maxwell Taylor—and the State Department, which wanted to think beyond mere military expediency. Kennedy, the record indicates, "preferred to base our policy on the harm which Diem's political actions are causing to the effort against the Viet Cong, rather than on our moral opposition to the kind of government Diem is running. Mr. Ball said that he and Secretary Rusk felt that there should be stress on the moral issues because of the beneficial effect which such emphasis produced in world public opinion, especially among U.N. delegates." When Kennedy and McGeorge Bundy then reiterated their focus on the pragmatic agenda of military efficiency, Ball insisted that the State Department was rather concerned with "something more than the objective of merely winning the war."[40]

Such ethical overreach, a perennial feature of twentieth-century American foreign policy (except perhaps for the years of the struggle against nazism, when the alliance with Stalin was supported without scruple), had resonated in Washington throughout the summer of 1963, in harmony with the cadences of the *New York Times* reporting from Saigon and editorializing from New York. It is this apparently irrepressible ethical instinct in American diplomacy that turned what might have been a foreign policy triumph for Kennedy into a tragedy for the American— and Vietnamese—people. In their characteristic quest for "something more than the objective of merely winning the war," the moralists in Kennedy's entourage seem to have been decisively responsible for compromising that war effort. This loss constituted more than a mere military setback: it led to the loss of an American sense of direction in the troubled seas of diplomacy.

THE DRAMA

"SAUVE QUI PEUT":
Signs and Portents

JANUARY 25 TO MAY 7

January 25, 1963. In Saigon it was Tet, the traditional lunar New Year's celebration, and the opening of the Year of the Hare. Saigon was alive with hopes that the fragile government of Ngo Dinh Diem, which was locked in a low-key guerrilla war with the nationalist hero Ho Chi Minh, would survive another year of assault by Ho's Viet Cong. Everyone looked for portents to judge whether 1963 would be as successful as 1962 had been.[1]

The most puzzling and ambivalent portent was evident at President Ngo Dinh Diem's traditional New Year's reception for the diplomatic corps. Brightening the hall was a flowering cherry branch, sent as a Tet greeting by Ho Chi Minh. The diplomats could not conceal their curiosity about this unprecedented gesture of North-South goodwill, sent from Ho by way of the members of the International Control Commission — established to supervise compliance with the provisions of the 1954 Geneva Accords concerning Vietnam — during one of their recent visits to Hanoi. Could this mean that the nine-year struggle between Diem and Ho would soon be resolved?[2]

Across the sea, in Washington, patterns of behavior were equally portentous. January 25 was just another workday at the White House. The report delivered that day by Michael Forrestal to President Kennedy read like any other memo crossing Kennedy's desk in the week that marked the halfway mark in his first term.[3] The president studied the pages carefully, as they reported the first results to reach him from an urgent trip to Vietnam by Forrestal, his close personal friend and now Far East staff specialist with the National Security Council, and Roger Hilsman, director of the State Department's Bureau of Intelligence and

Research, who was soon to be designated as Averell Harriman's successor as assistant secretary of state for the Far East.

Kennedy had hastily dispatched them to Vietnam in late December 1962, the day after he had received Senator Mansfield's report from a prior investigative trip, also undertaken at the president's request. When Mike Mansfield had briefed Kennedy on his pessimistic findings in Vietnam during the president's short family Christmas vacation at Palm Beach, Kennedy had angrily rejected Mansfield's warning about the rapid ascendancy to power of Diem's brother Nhu. Ngo Dinh Nhu was counselor to Diem and director of the strategic hamlet program, and his wife was a delegate to the National Assembly. Evidently their power far transcended their official positions in the government. Mansfield's basic critique of the government in Saigon was authentically American. Diem and Nhu were "failing to institutionalize a diffusion of political power, essentially in a democratic pattern."[4] Mansfield's warning against overcommitment in Vietnam struck at the core of Kennedy's strategy to counter communism at the periphery, rather than in Europe, where confrontation with the USSR might lead to a suicidal nuclear war.[5]

After Mansfield's return to Washington, he prepared another version of his report.[6] Kennedy had decided to send out two low-profile aides, who could verify, or counter, Mansfield's reading of events in Vietnam. The Forrestal-Hilsman report of January 25 was the summary of their findings. The report seemed to challenge Mansfield's pessimism in its opening sentence, which states that "the war in S[outh] V[ietnam] is clearly going better than it was a year ago." A few paragraphs later, however, the negative side of the ledger is called "awesome." While Diem's authoritarian and autocratic ways may not offend "the mute mass of villagers," they have alienated the urban elites and the U.S. reporters. A warning is posted about the risks of such opposition to Diem: "It would be nice if we could say that Diem's image in the foreign press was only his affair, but [it] seriously affects the U.S. and its ability to help South Vietnam. The American press representatives are bitter and will seize on anything that goes wrong and blow it up as much as possible. . . . U.S. interests are so heavily involved in the country that our voice should carry more weight."[7]

Following up on the field trip report, Forrestal wrote to the president on February 4, summarizing conversations he had had with Governor Harriman, now serving as Dean Rusk's assistant secretary of state for the

Far East. Forrestal (who was adopted by Harriman at age seventeen when his father, James, the first secretary of defense, committed suicide while in office) had been placed on McGeorge Bundy's National Security Council staff as "Kennedy's Ambassador to the sovereign state of Averell Harriman." Forrestal was also a campaign worker from JFK's days as a congressman and was a very close friend of Jacqueline Kennedy.[8] Forrestal and Harriman had both decided that Diem would have to be brought to heel, and this would require replacing Ambassador Fritz Nolting, who was far too protective of Diem's oriental autocracy. In the February 4 memo, Forrestal foreshadowed all the key developments of the next nine months, until the unleashing of the coup that overthrew Diem: "The problems remain, however, and I would suggest another technique to solve them. If you approve, Governor Harriman and I will start a quiet campaign in the appropriate departments for the following objectives. . . ." The fourth objective was "to develop gradually a more independent posture for the U.S. in South Vietnam and very carefully to dissociate ourselves from those policies and practices of the GVN [Government of (South) Vietnam] of which we disapprove with good reason."[9]

The relentless drumbeat of U.S. press criticism of Diem had now been addressed by several of Kennedy's closest associates. Both Mansfield and the two junior aides, Forrestal and Hilsman, had urged a radical change of course in Vietnam. Mansfield urged Kennedy to "do less rather than more" there, while Forrestal and Hilsman recommended that he force Diem to do more, rather than less, in the way of attention to public relations. In December 1962 the president had angrily rejected Mansfield's call for gradual disengagement from Diem. But by February 1963 he had come around to the senator's view, differing only on the issue of timing. While Mansfield favored an immediate change of course, the president settled on his second term as the first opportunity to withdraw.[10]

Kennedy's eventual decision to abandon Vietnam and Diem to their own destinies was a wrenching one. His interest in that country was long-standing. His maiden speech in 1957 as the junior senator from Massachusetts was an attack on the French recolonization policies in Vietnam.[11] But by January 1963 Kennedy was convinced that he had to choose between his own destiny (and reelection) and the interests of Vietnam. While maintaining the semblance of being a faithful ally to

Diem, Kennedy would now establish a depoliticized zone between his administration and that of Diem. It was to this end that Forrestal had crafted his February 4 memo, outlining the "quiet program" that he and Harriman were initiating "very carefully to dissociate ourselves from those policies and practices of the GVN of which we disapprove with good reason."

The path to such an independent posture had already been built by the introduction since 1961 of fourteen thousand American political and military advisers at every level of Vietnamese society, with the consequence that, as Forrestal and Hilsman had assured the president in their January 25 memo, "[i]t is therefore becoming possible to accomplish much of what we want at the local level without going through the vastly inefficient national bureaucracy." [12] (When Diem had gathered ample evidence, by early April, that American advisers were bypassing his province chiefs in the distribution of funds, he would make an abrupt about-face, which even Ambassador Nolting was unable to comprehend or counter.)

Forrestal's proposed policy of "dissociation" would involve replacing Nolting, who had become Diem's public apologist, and elevating Kennedy's press relations above his relations with Diem, "to make a rapid and vigorous effort to improve press relations in Saigon, even at some cost to our relationship with the Diem Government." [13]

In their January 25 report, Forrestal and Hilsman had refrained from speculating about the attitudes of the villagers toward the Saigon government, but they reported that Diem had alienated the urban elites, especially those in Saigon. Forrestal therefore proposed on February 8 to Governor Harriman that he urge Kennedy to increase U.S. embassy contacts with Saigon dissidents, even at the risk of offending Diem. This would enhance Kennedy's image of independence and at the same time "increase our alternatives in case of an accident which results in a shift in the Government." [14] Harriman forwarded Forrestal's suggestions to Nolting, who replied on February 27 that he had, with Diem's knowledge, been listening to, and learning from, oppositionists since the time of his arrival in Saigon in May 1961 and would continue to do so. If, however, Harriman's recent instructions meant an effort to build up an alternative government, Kennedy would have to appoint a new ambassador, since Nolting considered acceptance of the constitutional government a matter of personal, professional, and patriotic principle. [15]

Arthur M. Schlesinger Jr. took the occasion of Nolting's reply to suggest to Forrestal that this was the moment to remove Nolting.[16] Late in February, a warning shot from Washington was fired by the release in Saigon of portions of Mansfield's report on his recent visit to Saigon. In the official covering cable from the State Department, Harriman and Rusk drew attention to those sections of the report devoted to the inadequacies of the Diem government.[17]

The Saigon oppositionists, denied a supportive audience at the U.S. embassy, found one with the still small U.S. press corps. In the *New York Times*, Kennedy read the complaints of the educated cadre of Vietnamese intellectuals and would-be bureaucrats who had been systematically excluded from public office. The American press had become their only avenue to power. That avenue intersected Diem's utopian drive to purify Vietnam of every trace of foreign influence. Diem felt that all his rivals for power in Saigon had imbibed from the French a superficial Western mentality antithetical to the restoration of Vietnamese identity and genuine independence. Having himself refused to accept a scholarship to study in Paris in 1918, he distrusted his contemporaries who had made that compromise, including his brother Nhu, who had studied at the Ecole des Chartes in Paris. Diem was determined to bypass this francophile elite while awaiting a new corps of Vietnamese civil servants who would soon be graduating from his own National School of Administration. From this school he hoped to recruit a new group of authentically educated mandarins to contribute to the restoration of the Confucian order.[18]

For the time being, Diem himself, his brother Nhu, and Nhu's party, the Can Lao (a strangely alien hybrid inspired by Leninist and French religious doctrine), would administer the affairs of South Vietnam without the alien influences of French-educated officials. Gradually, Diem had reluctantly admitted more Americans to subordinate administrative roles where his own private cadre of officials was overburdened with administrative responsibilities. Diem's effort to exclude residual French colonial influences had thus opened the door to American influences, no less foreign and no more welcome to xenophobic Vietnamese. Diem's integralist crusade thus recoiled on him as he appeared in the eyes of Vietnamese more and more as "My Diem" (the American Diem).[19]

Diem's effort to restore the earlier Confucian order had already defied the laws of political gravity by deposing in 1955 the flawed emperor,

Bao Dai, leaving only his own unquestioned virtue to serve as the rallying point of Vietnamese nationalism.[20] Now he had dismantled the other characteristic feature of the old Vietnamese order by sidelining the mandarinate, which was "contaminated" by French influence. Only the Ngos and the Can Lao Party (increasingly shadowed by the pervasive American presence) remained as the head (emperor) and hands (mandarinate) of the new Vietnam. Diem's resolve to serve as a sort of Colossus, supporting the burden of Vietnamese rebirth on his own broad shoulders, was perhaps the political posture that Mansfield had recently judged utopian and thus insupportable by the United States.

Diem's nationalist struggle now teetered precariously between political paralysis and Americanization. Given the Cold War resolve of Kennedy and the exigencies of Vietnamese reconstruction, "Americanization" became the order of the day. Americanization in turn provoked the equally purist challenge of some Vietnamese Buddhists. Diem was soon caught in the crossfire of the Saigon aspirants to a rapid "modernization" (westernization) of Vietnam and the activist monks, who resisted foreign influence even at the risk of military defeat by Ho Chi Minh.

Diem's 1961 opening to Kennedy had confounded his critics, who held that he was too much of an idealist to master the complexities of government. He was, they argued, too pure for politics. Even his brother Nhu used to complain to Diem: "You should have been a monk."[21] Diem made perhaps too much of a fetish of cultural integrity. He seemed indeed unable to understand that independence was in the near term incompatible with total political and cultural isolation. But soon, after reviewing the record of initiatives from Ho Chi Minh during the spring, Diem would begin to see that his own dream of integral independence was not too different from Ho's. There might exist a deep resonance between their integralist dreams.[22]

Early in March 1963, twenty-five thousand Buddhists converged at Vung Tau, a South China Sea resort, for the dedication of a new statue of the Buddha. Vietnamese Buddhism was one of the few factors of social cohesion that had survived the French colonial intervention. Not surprisingly, therefore, it reemerged in 1945 as a vehicle of nationalism. In 1950 the First World Congress of Buddhism was held in Colombo, Ceylon (called Sri Lanka since 1972). In 1951 Vietnam formed its own national association under the leadership of the aged and revered Thich

Tinh Khiet. Buddhism constituted a salient feature of Vietnamese nationalism. Somewhat like Hinduism in Gandhi's India a generation earlier, it was the reservoir of widely known cultural symbols in a fragmented society.

Diem himself had sensed this political potential and, despite his own family's three-hundred-year tradition of Catholicism, had meticulously cultivated the Buddhist revival. In the nine years of his rule, Diem had constructed or rebuilt numerous pagodas.[23] Among Buddhists in the countryside, there was a reservoir of goodwill toward Diem in recognition of these services, as Ambassador Nolting was to discover through an outpouring of letters to his office in July, when Diem was under attack from some urban bonzes.[24]

Buddhism was a harbinger of hope for national renewal. Though Buddhists constituted far from a majority of Vietnamese (they represented by a count of the General Association of Buddhists about 30 percent of the population), their four million members were a significant segment of the society. Buddhists outnumbered Catholics almost three to one. (There were 1.5 million Catholics.[25]) The government of South Vietnam could ignore such a constituency only at its own peril. Opposition forces, looking to unseat Diem, had at hand a ready-made vanguard of revolution.[26]

At the same time, Diem was concerned by the continuous complaints from the twenty-one provinces where U.S. advisers had become numerous enough to supplant Diem's authority. For Diem and Nhu, it was clear that the situation was now a matter of survival, of *sauve qui peut* (Every man for himself, and the devil take the hindmost). While the French had taught them this phrase, the Vietnamese had long ago learned the rules of the game from their Chinese masters. Disengagement was a game at which two could play.

Diem and his brother had a big advantage over Kennedy in this rush for the exit. There were just the two of them. They didn't have to drag along with them teams of bureaucrats. By March 5 Nhu was able to signal Kennedy that the release of the Mansfield report had been understood at Gia Long Palace, the presidential residence. "This changes everything," he told a departing embassy official, John Mecklin. Mecklin perceptively warned Washington that the very understatement of the outrage that Diem and Nhu must be feeling was ominous.[27]

Mecklin, no friend of Diem, was back in Washington when the cable arrived later from Ambassador Nolting validating Mecklin's dire prediction. Sure that he understood Diem, Nolting was nevertheless wholly unprepared for Diem's abrupt rejection of his request in April that the United States continue to control the use of all counterinsurgency funds, including the 3 percent of funds coming from Vietnam's own treasury.[28] In the course of a three-hour negotiation with Diem on April 4, Nolting heard him repeat five times that the present Vietnamese status was effectively a "protectorate," as Diem had feared as early as the spring of 1961.[29] That status, which was unacceptable to Diem, would be terminated, beginning with this negotiation. Diem's language was plodding but inflexible. He described the role of the U.S. Agency for International Development (U.S. AID) officials and military advisers—whose pervasive presence had earlier convinced Hilsman that Kennedy could bypass Diem's bureaucracy in his campaign of "nation-building"—as establishing an alternative alien government in the countryside. This was anathema to Diem. When Nolting pointed out that Diem himself had asked for these advisers, the president replied that he had been mistaken in his request. He was now convinced that there were too many Americans, giving too much advice. There would have to be fewer. Everything had indeed changed in the Kennedy-Diem alliance, as Nhu had warned on March 5.

Nolting pointed out that this change would mean a corresponding reduction in U.S. aid. Diem said he would borrow money before he would accept dictation from the United States. To be certain that he had not misunderstood Diem, Nolting pointed out that it was Diem who was demanding a curtailment of the alliance. Diem agreed to this summary.[30] As Nolting concluded: "He gave the impression of one who would rather be right than be President." Diem had tasted the fruit of alliance and spit it out. Now it was a matter of arranging the terms, and the timing, of a divorce.[31]

On April 7 Nolting recommended to Rusk that the United States reduce its allocation to Vietnam by nearly 20 percent, to indicate to Diem the practical price of independence.[32] George Ball replied (for Rusk) that Nolting should avoid hasty reactions and try to arrange for a greater voice for Diem's officials in the distribution of U.S. funds. It seemed for the moment that Diem had called Washington's bluff.[33] A National Security Council meeting on April 10, whose agenda included

Nolting's warning of a critical standoff with Diem on local control of funds, passed over this item. Harriman assured the planning group that a compromise solution was at hand.[34]

Harriman's optimism was short-lived. Two days later Nhu repeated to the CIA chief of station, John Richardson, in their weekly meeting that Diem, after a lifetime of resisting control of Vietnam by foreigners, was culturally incapable of accepting such control by Americans, who were now bypassing province chiefs in their distribution of funds. Thus, the time had come to cut back on U.S. aid programs and to send home 20 percent of U.S. advisers currently in Vietnam.[35] The same week, Madame Ngo Dinh Nhu publicly accused U.S. advisers of treating Vietnamese as lackeys and prostitutes.[36]

In a meeting on April 16, Nolting informed Diem that the State Department had approved his departure for vacation and had asked him to return to his Saigon post afterward (although Nolting had asked to be replaced, for family reasons). He also informed Diem that the United States had no intention of reducing the size of its mission in Vietnam.[37] In response, Diem informed Nolting in writing that he would not accept a U.S. veto over disbursement of South Vietnamese funds, which would violate the sacred principle of South Vietnamese sovereignty.[38] Diem and Nolting, who had earlier reached a remarkable mutual understanding, had now reached an unexpected stalemate.

The stalemate continued and, indeed, intensified through the summer and the fall. Even Ambassador Nolting was unable to recognize in this symbolic defiance Diem's congenital anticolonialism. But Diem had earlier in the spring remarked to the French ambassador, Roger Lalouette, that the Americans had begun to mimic the earlier French control, gradually taking over the direct administration of South Vietnam.[39]

In April, Nolting cabled Rusk that he was perplexed at Diem's stubborn insistence that (unnamed) U.S. provincial aides were usurping his government's authority in the countryside. For the first time, Nolting echoed the *New York Times* in suggesting that Diem was now interested only in the fate of his own regime. Diem responded to Nolting's protests that his only demand was that Vietnam be treated like a sovereign nation, not "a protectorate." Although Nolting warned that this stance would cost Diem dearly in the new U.S. budget for Vietnam, Diem did not budge.[40]

Nolting, who had shielded Diem sedulously from public criticism and bore continual criticisms from some State Department (and White House) officials for coddling Diem, in private was blunt and assertive of U.S. interests and requirements, generated by the substantial investment of personnel and funds. But his diplomatic code was that of the old school, which honored commitments and understood the role of confidentiality in diplomatic relations.

Nolting's only failing in these exacting crises was his insensitivity to the salience of symbolism in Vietnamese politics. What Diem had been demanding ever since the February release of the critical Mansfield report was a symbolic island of independence in a sea of subordination. He needed some symbol of autonomous control of Vietnamese destiny at any price. Even if separate administrative procedures were required to ensure that Vietnam's own financial contribution was under his exclusive control, and even if such dual procedures would prove inefficient, Diem insisted on this symbol of independence. If Nolting had sensed the urgency of this demand, he might have been able to signal Kennedy that the entire alliance relationship had suddenly shifted ground. The concurrent demands from Nhu of a 20 percent reduction in the numbers of U.S. advisers would then have given Washington a chance to rethink on its own terms a possible adjustment to the Ngos' intransigence. Nolting missed the crucial clue of Diem's symbolic demand of absolute control of a minuscule pot of piasters.

"WHO ARE THESE PEOPLE?"

MAY 8 TO JUNE 28

The monk Thich Tri Quang emerged into public life on May 8, at the annual observance of the Buddha's birthday. His pagoda, Tu Dam, was one of the most venerable Buddhist shrines, situated in the ancient imperial capital of Hue, which was closely associated with the eclectic religious heritage of Vietnam. The Catholic element of this mélange had been celebrated just days before by the archbishop, Ngo Dinh Thuc, brother of President Diem, who displayed the white and gold flags of the Holy See at festivities marking his twenty-five years as a bishop. Immediately afterward, Diem reprimanded local officials for this violation of the legal ban on all flags except the national banner. Buddhists, seeking to hoist their own emblem on May 8, were therefore forbidden to do so.[1]

Thich Tri Quang then turned the second day of the festival into a protest against religious persecution, seizing the radio station to broadcast his indictment of Diem. Government security forces, seeking to restore order, entered a melee in which seven people were killed by an explosion. (No one has ever succeeded in identifying those responsible for the explosion.) Impartial observers agreed that the public outpouring had been a genuine expression of frustrated religious fervor.[2]

The disturbance in Hue raised alarm in Washington about the American prospects of successful collaboration with Diem's government. Some State Department officials interpreted a protest by Buddhist monks against a Catholic president as evidence of religious persecution by a minority (Catholic) government against the majority religion (Buddhism).[3] Washington was determined to have Diem discontinue this persecution, so fundamentally alien to the American secular spirit of compromise and religious rights. But Diem made only token adjustments in his policies toward the Buddhists. Unaccountably in Washington's eyes, Diem felt that as a Vietnamese he had a better grasp of the political significance of Buddhism than the two Americans primarily responsible for East Asian affairs, Averell Harriman and Roger Hilsman.

As Diem understood it, Vietnam was a deeply syncretist society. It was not simply "a Buddhist country," as Roger Hilsman, who had been working closely on Vietnam policy with Michael Forrestal and Averell Harriman since early January 1963, insisted.[4] Scholars now agree virtually unanimously that the religious profile of Vietnam is unique. The original animism of Vietnamese society, which antedated the earliest Chinese influence, remains the controlling matrix of Vietnamese religious sensibilities. It has been enriched, and therefore diluted, by successive waves of Buddhist, Confucian, and Taoist influences.[5]

Buddhism originally arrived in Vietnam with the southern march of the Chinese at the end of the first century A.D., while Confucianism was introduced to Vietnam only in the eleventh century. Buddhist leaders at that time even lent a helping hand in establishing the Confucian order, because they were convinced that the Vietnamese people needed the educational and political culture offered by Confucianism. The first teachers in Confucian temples, for example, were Zen Buddhist monks. The dynamism of the emerging Confucian civilization was marked by the competitive educational and professional rigors of triennial literary examinations; the most successful candidates eventually became the principal officials of the Vietnamese state. For centuries, Buddhism and Confucianism were thus complementary facets of Vietnamese life, generating, respectively, the spiritual substance and the political organization of Vietnamese society. Gradually, however, Confucianism was domesticated by ambitious political personalities, who had inevitable suspicions of the monks. Buddhist monks thus increasingly withdrew into lives of seclusion, leaving the political field to Confucian control.[6]

Thich Nhat Hanh, a prominent Vietnamese Buddhist, observes that the cultural interpenetration of Buddhism and Confucianism makes it impossible to estimate accurately the portion of Vietnamese who are Buddhists. Everyone in the countryside has beliefs and habits derived from Buddhism, Confucianism, and animism.[7] William Duiker, too, concludes from this pattern of syncretism that the influence of Buddhism was too shallow to support a political movement of nationalism in Vietnam.[8]

Just as Buddhism gradually declined in public prominence with the ascendancy of Confucianism, so the nineteenth-century period of French colonization saw the rapid decline of Confucianism in favor of Western European and scientific culture. This eclipse of Confucian culture led in turn to a new passive alliance between the long-marginalized Buddhists and the newly disenfranchised Confucians. Western (i.e., French) educational patterns and examinations soon edged out the former process of mandarin examinations, which were discontinued in 1919 (they were revived briefly in 1939 before the Japanese occupation).[9]

The continuing appeal of Buddhism and Confucianism in Vietnam is due in large part to their joint inspiration in the late nineteenth century of the ill-fated royalist struggle for independence for Vietnam, called the monks' war (1885–98). Confucianism took the first steps in this insurrection but was later surpassed by Buddhist monastic leadership. When Vo Tru, the monk who planned the revolution from 1895 to 1898, was betrayed, numerous monks were imprisoned. In North Vietnam, Catholics were likewise prominent in the monks' war. From the 1920s, nevertheless, separate movements of Buddhist and Confucian revival were visible. The Buddhists instilled spirituality and virtue, while the Confucian groups concentrated on secular matters, eschewing religion. The Buddhist activist movement became conspicuous again during the early years of the American military buildup in Vietnam (1961–65). Unfortunately, as Thich Nhat Hanh recounts, the religious movement was penetrated at the very moment of success by outsiders who used the movement for their own political purposes. He explains this infiltration as a product of the monks' lack of trained leaders for political and intellectual programs combined with the opportunism of those who merely wanted to use the "Greater Vehicle" as their own political vehicle.[10]

Washington's response to the emerging Buddhist crisis was delayed by a series of personnel promotions at the State Department. To replace Harriman, who had become undersecretary of state for political affairs on April 4, Rusk was ordered to move Roger Hilsman from his post as director of the Bureau of Intelligence and Research to that of assistant secretary for Far Eastern affairs.[11] Hilsman hit the road running on May 9, the first day after his Senate approval, since he had been working

closely on Vietnam with Forrestal and Harriman since December. Hilsman was the whirling dervish of the State Department. A World War II
guerrilla leader in Burma, he held a doctorate from Yale and had at-
tracted the attention of Robert Kennedy with his policy research writings at the Congressional Research Service. Emerging as the principal
U.S. official responsible for policy in Vietnam on May 9, the same day
that Tri Quang stepped from the recesses of his pagoda to orchestrate
the assault on Diem, Hilsman was the perfect foil for the bonze. This
new personal constellation was an ominous development for Diem. For
Hilsman came to his powerful position confident that he understood the
religious forces at work in Vietnam, which, as he still maintained as late
as 1992, was a country whose population was 98 percent Buddhist.[12] In
such circumstances, the legitimacy of a Roman Catholic ruler with an
inclination to abuse Buddhists was evidently suspect in Washington.

Hilsman's appointment as assistant secretary of state closed the circle
of conspirators against the Diem regime. Hilsman now focused his considerable powers of imagination on a strategy for replacing Diem. What
he searched for at the time was a "Vietnamese Nasser." Asked a quarter
century after the events for the basis of his confidence that the military
coup he began to engineer would lead to a more popular government in
South Vietnam, able to galvanize public support for the war, he answered without pause: "We were looking for another Nasser. Who had
suspected that, in the 1952 Egyptian coup, a future statesman like
Nasser would appear? Why couldn't that happen in Saigon?" Hilsman
wondered.[13] Some of Hilsman's critics refer to these observations as his
"Muslim solution to the Buddhist problem." Even some of his support-
ers have found it difficult to grasp the logic of this solution. At first
glance, the argument seems to be that a chance number (coup number 2)
that paid off handsomely in the Cairo lottery in 1952 might be equally
lucky in Saigon in 1964.

When Michael Forrestal, Hilsman's colleague at the National Security Council, was interviewed shortly before the quarter century anniversary of the coup that he helped to instigate, he outlined equally
convincingly the logic of selecting General Duong Van Minh to replace
Ngo Dinh Diem. Forrestal continued to believe in 1987 that this choice
was compelling, for Big Minh was "tall, a good tennis player, and spoke
English." Forrestal took particular notice of Minh's backhand, which
probably would have stood him in good stead at Hyannisport if the fates

had been kinder.[14] Hilsman and Forrestal were Harriman's lieutenants as he braced to deal with the fallout from the Hue demonstrations and the furor over their repression by local officials. Harriman would need all his analytic powers, in addition to the staff he had selected, for the challenge. As it turned out, this trio was no match for Tri Quang.

Before Harriman, Hilsman, and Forrestal could turn to the "new" Buddhist problem, they had to deal with the problem of the new Nhu, the now openly anti-American counselor to President Diem. Nhu had given an interview to Warren Unna, published on May 12 in the *Washington Post*, calling for a 50 percent reduction in U.S. forces in Vietnam.[15] Hilsman immediately assigned his new staff the task of developing a menu of measures to respond to the Ngos' display of disloyalty. The staff responded on May 15 that all such pressures were risky because they might trigger a coup in Saigon.[16] Doan-Them, a Vietnamese military chronicler, took note in Saigon on May 22 of Kennedy's Washington press conference, where he responded to an inquiry about Nhu's published threats to reduce the U.S. presence. Kennedy had pledged to honor immediately any such request from Diem.[17]

On May 23, Ambassador Nolting was on the eve of his long-delayed family vacation sailing in the Aegean. After receiving assurances from his protégé, friend, and temporary replacement, William Trueheart, that he would be notified of any drastic shifts in U.S.–South Vietnamese relations while on holiday, Nolting left Saigon on May 24.[18] Trueheart, in his first cable to Washington as chargé d'affaires in Saigon, dated May 25, reported a curious conversation with Ngo Dinh Nhu, who mentioned to him a meeting that had been held in Cambodia on May 19, at which both Ho and Nhu were represented.[19] The significance of this apparently oblique comment by Nhu would become gradually clearer as the summer wore on.

Tri Quang, who had organized the May demonstration at Hue, was now a resident of the Xa Loi Pagoda in Saigon. On the morning of June 11, after notifying Malcolm Browne of the Associated Press, several monks drove to a busy downtown intersection in the company of an elderly monk, Quang Duc, assisted him out of the car, and helped him burn himself alive.[20] This self-immolation concentrated the rays of Vietnamese nationalism in the lens of the American media, igniting an answering blaze in Washington. Focused on the liberal sentiments of the White House, the monk's sacrifice captured too the sympathies of those

Americans who were watching out for the "majority" religion of Vietnam, Buddhism, now suffering repression by the Catholic president.
(Later, U.S. official analysis would estimate the size of the activist segment of the Buddhist community, represented by the monks who demonstrated or sacrificed themselves by incineration, at four hundred thousand in a population of fourteen million.[21])

Tri Quang now pressed his case in the court of U.S. public opinion.
Later, summoning a U.S. journalist whose press pass was mistaken for a
White House staff ID, Tri Quang urged her to tell Kennedy to abandon
Diem. "If he does not, he will see ten . . . forty . . . fifty bonzes burning."[22] The monk's incendiary rhetoric found its mark in Washington,
where officials were confident that this was the authentic and authoritative voice of Vietnamese Buddhism. The bonzes' protest was apparently
directed at Diem. The Americans, unable to view themselves as an alien
force and thus as a threat to Vietnamese society, concluded that the protests were triggered by Diem's "foreign" Catholicism and despotism.[23]
Here was a classic case, some Kennedy officials assumed, of religious
persecution that could be cured only by replacing the Catholic despot
with a representative Buddhist leader.

By mid-June, Trueheart, as acting ambassador, became a scourge
against Diem's government. Taking up his campaign on June 11, he
warned Diem's closest assistant, Nguyen Dinh Thuan, that Diem must
be conciliatory to Buddhists: "I told Thuan that I thought if [the] President did not do something of this sort this afternoon he might well be
faced with a public US Government disassociation of itself from [the]
whole affair. . . . (This is, in fact, what I now recommend to Department
unless we have action or the promise of it before the day is out. . . .)."[24]

The same day, Harriman agreed that the Buddhist situation was critical
and, without consulting Dean Rusk, suggested initiatives to Trueheart:

> You [are] further authorized to tell Diem that unless GVN is willing
> to take effective action along the above lines within the next few days
> the US will find it necessary publicly to state that it cannot associate
> itself with the GVN's unwillingness to meet the reasonable demands
> of the Vietnamese Buddhist leaders. . . .
>
> We realize that meeting Buddhist demands . . . runs risk of engen-
> dering further Buddhist demands and that GVN must be prepared
> to . . . accede to such further demands. . . .

FYI—If Diem does not take prompt and effective steps to reestablish Buddhist confidence in him we will have to reexamine our entire relationship with his regime. End FYI.[25]

With Nolting on the high seas and Trueheart riding high in Saigon, the "quiet campaign" that Forrestal and Harriman had conceived on February 4 was finally under way.[26] On June 12 Trueheart cabled a summary of a meeting that he later called "a dramatic démarche":

> I told Diem that I had now received new instructions which went somewhat further than what I have been saying. I then handed him a paper, unsigned and headed "Memorandum," which contained a paraphrase of most of reftel [referenced telegram, Harriman to Trueheart, June 11].
>   . . . Diem then began an exchange with Thuan in Vietnamese, at the end of which Thuan said that the President wanted to point out that any statement by the United States at this juncture would be disastrous for the negotiations with the Buddhists which he expected would begin this evening or tomorrow morning.[27]

Two days later, on June 14, a front-page article in the *New York Times* by Max Frankel reported almost verbatim the contents of Harriman's June 11 cable to Trueheart, authorizing him to threaten to discontinue the alliance between the United States and South Vietnam unless Diem began accommodating Buddhist demands. An embassy official later remembered that Frankel's article "read as though a reporter had been shown the file of classified cables from Saigon."[28] Frankel's article had echoed exactly the "diplomatic" exchanges between Washington and Saigon during the previous seventy-two hours:

> The United States has warned President Ngo Dinh Diem . . . that it will publicly condemn his treatment of the Buddhists unless he takes prompt action to meet their grievances. American diplomats in Saigon have told the Vietnamese in the bluntest terms that Buddhist disaffection could become politically disastrous and that Washington wishes to dissociate itself from President Ngo Dinh Diem's policies. . . .
>   The feeling here [in Washington] has been that a disavowal by the United States . . . could jeopardize cooperation . . . in the long war against the communist guerrillas.

For that reason, Washington has been reluctant to speak out. But it is losing faith in the effectiveness of quiet, backstage pressures.[29]

Hilsman immediately cabled Trueheart: "Unfortunate *New York Times* story stating U.S. has warned Diem it will publicly condemn his treatment [of the] Buddhists . . . will not be carried VOA [Voice of America]. . . . In view *NYT* story fully realize you may wish [to] make no démarches to GVN at this time."[30]

Even though Trueheart was, without Kennedy's knowledge or instruction, threatening Diem with a U.S. decision to abandon him, the acting ambassador had not contemplated any initiative likely to risk stimulating a coup. Indeed, on June 16 he cabled his superiors in Washington, warning that the available alternatives to Diem were unpromising. Only if Diem would not see the error of his ways should Washington act. "I am still not impressed by the competition, nor do I think are any of my colleagues American or foreign. Our best move at this juncture . . . is to press Diem . . . to accept Buddhist crisis as blessing in disguise and to use agreement reached as stepping stone to concessions to other groups (before they demand them). . . . If we find Diem in a mood to freeze up, rather than move forward, then I think his days are indeed numbered."[31] Thus, acting on the June 11 orders from Harriman but without the knowledge of Rusk, Trueheart had told President Diem that future U.S. support was contingent on concessions to Buddhists, even though Washington was aware that such concessions might open a Pandora's box of political demands. Kennedy, who had been kept in the dark about this "dramatic démarche," learned of it on June 14 through a CIA summary of world events. He immediately issued orders that no such threats to Diem should be issued without his personal orders.[32]

On June 17 the *New York Times* announced that Diem was unfit for his responsibilities.[33] Soon American clergymen, including Reinhold Niebuhr, added their "Amen" to the *New York Times* editorial in an advertisement.[34] On June 16 Diem had signed an agreement with the prominent Buddhist leader Thich Tinh Khiet to remove all traces of religious discrimination in Vietnam.[35]

Hilsman continued the barrage of challenges to Diem, recommending on June 19 a hard-hitting demand to rebuild Diem's standing in U.S. opinion. "Diem should avoid identifying the government with his own person and should meet with Buddhist leaders as equals," Hilsman wrote.[36] The following day Diem was requested to approve the appointment of Henry Cabot Lodge Jr. to replace Ambassador Nolting, who had assured Diem on April 16 that he would be returning as ambassador after his vacation.[37] Diem was instantly suspicious, indeed terrified, at this news. He told his assistant, Thuan: "They can send ten Lodges, but I will not permit myself or my country to be humiliated, not if they train their artillery on this palace."[38]

On June 22, at the same meeting where Diem agreed to the appointment of Lodge, Trueheart warned without any authorization that President Kennedy was prepared to blame Diem personally for any further disturbances. Thuan later notified Trueheart that Diem was fully prepared for the battles ahead with Kennedy. Trueheart replied that such confrontations need not take place if Diem would "start acting like an American politician."[39]

President Kennedy, while basking in the nostalgia of his triumphal presidential tour of Ireland, signaled publicly his solution to the Buddhist question in Vietnam. On June 27 he announced the replacement of Ambassador Nolting, who was known to be sympathetic to Diem, by Henry Cabot Lodge Jr., Kennedy's old political rival. Nolting, enjoying a vacation urged upon him by Harriman, learned of his removal over the ship's radio while sailing from Genoa to New York.[40]

Lodge, after his defeat with Nixon in 1960, had sought some final political role for himself and indirectly volunteered to serve in Saigon. Lodge had been mentioned to Kennedy for the post of ambassador by Dean Rusk, to whom Lodge had personally proposed the assignment.[41] A brigadier general in the Army Reserves, Lodge had devoted his active duty tour in 1962 to Vietnam, preparing policy papers on the area. Kennedy, seeking to insulate himself from partisan attack over his evolving policies in Southeast Asia, now chose him despite Forrestal's vigorous objections.[42]

There was a certain plausibility to the appointment, since Lodge had diplomatic experience, having served as Eisenhower's permanent representative to the United Nations. His military rank was likewise an asset in this treacherous war zone. Moreover, as a professional politician, he would be able to handle the members of the press, who were increasingly becoming principal actors in the unfolding drama in Saigon. In addition, he spoke excellent French and had served as liaison officer with the French forces in World War II.[43] Critics of the appointment, however, sought to draw attention to a serious shortcoming, Lodge's modest intellectual endowment.[44] Kennedy decided that the risk was worth taking.

The *New York Times* welcomed the announcement of Nolting's removal in favor of Lodge:

> In selecting his old political opponent Henry Cabot Lodge as the next United States Ambassador to South Vietnam, one of the most difficult posts in the American Foreign Service, President Kennedy has made a shrewd move to emphasize the nonpartisan character of a wearing, hazardous enterprise.
>
> The most serious problem that will face Mr. Lodge in South Vietnam is the nature of the government there. . . . The widespread unpopularity, the narrow political base, the oppressive authoritarian character of the Ngo Dinh Diem government undercuts purely military gains by eroding the will of the South Vietnamese people for the anti-Communist struggle. . . . The future of Southeast Asia largely depends on the success of the anti-Communist struggle there. But can we win with Diem?
>
> It has begun to look as if, in the long run, we cannot. . . . President Diem himself is now facing the alternative of initiating new policies — an unlikely eventuality — or of yielding to others who will, by a sterner exercise of American influence than the United States has yet seen fit to utilize in Saigon.[45]

For the first and last time, the views at Gia Long Palace in Saigon and the editorial offices on West Forty-third Street in New York agreed: Lodge's arrival would be the beginning of the end for Diem.

The precipitate change in Diem's outlook since late May was caused principally by his humiliation at the hands of the American chargé d'affaires, William Trueheart, echoed within hours in the American press. Trueheart was a career Foreign Service officer. He had served with Frederick Nolting on the NATO staff in Paris and had become a close friend of Nolting. Like Nolting, he held a graduate degree in philosophy from the University of Virginia, where he had been elected to Phi Beta Kappa as an undergraduate.[46] In 1961, when Nolting, already in Saigon, noticed that Trueheart had been passed over at a crucial stage of promotion toward the highest rank of Foreign Service officers, he asked to have Trueheart sent to Saigon to boost his career.

Now Kennedy had fired Nolting and appointed Lodge, who was not due to arrive until late August. Thus one of the most critical U.S. embassies in the world was left, during the Diem regime's final crisis, in the hands of an untried chargé d'affaires. If Kennedy was hoping merely for a holding action until Lodge's arrival, he was disappointed. Without authorization from Kennedy or Rusk but on the orders of Averell Harriman, Trueheart had already threatened that Kennedy would terminate the alliance unless Diem changed his behavior.[47]

Michael Forrestal had, sometime in the spring, persuaded Harriman to offer Trueheart a promotion in Washington. As Trueheart recalled a quarter century later: "It was quite a promotion for me!"[48] As promised, Trueheart was promoted to be director of the State Department's Southeast Asian Affairs Bureau. By the time of his promotion early in 1964, however, Roger Hilsman, whose deputy Trueheart had been slated to become, had been sidelined by President Lyndon Johnson because of Hilsman's role in the coup.

"SLEEPING IN THE SAME BED, DREAMING DIFFERENT DREAMS"

JUNE 29 TO AUGUST 23

On June 29 the Ngo family met in a planning conclave at Hue.[1] There the die was apparently cast for a new strategy of all-Vietnam reunification and the dismissal of the Americans. The same day Trueheart informed Washington that Tri Quang's activist sect of bonzes had openly expanded its agenda to call for Diem's overthrow. "Others in activist group without doubt have 'tasted blood' of politics and either see religious issue as way for political changes or have discarded religious issue for outright political objective—change in regime. This latter group appeared [to] seek to discredit GVN to extent possible and is willing to receive overtures from political opposition groups. Thus, this group (which may include bonze Tri Quang) has aims going beyond legitimate end originally sought by Buddhists."[2]

Early July was the time set aside for remembering independence in the United States and in South Vietnam. In the same week Americans celebrated July Fourth as the anniversary of the adoption of the Declaration of Independence at Philadelphia, while South Vietnamese honored the "double seven," the seventh of July, as the date of their independence. A certain irony characterized the White House Fourth of July observance in 1963. John Kennedy was just back in Washington from an exhilarating, untroubled, and triumphant tour of Europe that included a nostalgic visit to Ireland and concluded with the first visit of an American Catholic president to a pope, the newly elected Paul VI. Stopping over at the White House before a well-deserved July Fourth celebration at Hyannisport, the president met hurriedly with his staff to review critical developments in foreign policy that had occurred during his tour. At the top of the list was Southeast Asia.[3]

Surely Kennedy, with his relish for irony, must have smiled at the timing of his staff in broaching with him for the first time on the Fourth of July the possibility of a U.S.-sponsored coup against Diem.[4] John Adams, Kennedy's fellow Bostonian, had first proposed the rituals for observance of the adoption of the Declaration of Independence: "With solemn acts of devotion to God we ought to commemorate it. With pomp and parade, with shows and games, sports, guns, bells, bonfires, and illuminations from one end of the continent to the other from this time forward forever more."[5] Now the president was extemporizing a Fourth of July observance that included a military coup against a friend, client, and ally, Ngo Dinh Diem. These were probably not the sorts of "guns" Adams had had in mind in his anniversary formula.

Present at the meeting, interrupting their own holiday plans, were George Ball, Averell Harriman, McGeorge Bundy, Roger Hilsman, and Michael Forrestal. After exploring the possibility of "getting rid of the Nhus"—that is, Diem's brother Nhu and his wife, Madame Nhu—and finally judging it impossible, Hilsman cautioned that the Buddhist activists, who had been on the streets again on July 2, might be contemplating an escalation of their demands in order to topple Diem from power.[6] He went on to inform the president that Ambassador Nolting—whom Kennedy had fired during his stopover in Dublin the week before and who was now back in Washington—had warned that a coup might usher in civil war.[7] The president, asking to see Nolting on Monday, July 8, left for the holiday.

On the morning of July 5, Undersecretary of State Ball discussed with Nolting the prospects for a coup. Nolting pointed out the risks of *public* pressure from Washington: the likely hardening of Diem's resistance and, simultaneously, the encouragement of a coup, with its risks of chaos or civil war.[8] In the *New York Times* on July 3, a front-page article from Saigon by David Halberstam had stated: "Some American officials are reported to favor a new Vietnamese government. . . . It is widely believed here that any statement from Washington critical of Ngo Dinh Diem for his handling of the Buddhist crisis would touch off an internal military strike at the government."[9]

The American officials who favored such a change of government included Trueheart in Saigon and Harriman, Hilsman, and Forrestal in Washington. While such a disposition toward a coup was only then being leaked to the press, the idea itself was more than a year old by this time. It had first been conceived by John Kenneth Galbraith in November 1961, after his brief visit to Saigon to size up Diem at the request of President Kennedy.[10] Galbraith, who had then been back in Washington from his post as ambassador to New Delhi, had "purloined" a copy of the "top secret" Maxwell Taylor report to Kennedy, recommending that the president send eight thousand advisers to Vietnam. Aghast at this proposal, Galbraith had secured Kennedy's approval to visit Vietnam to evaluate personally the adequacy of Diem's government.[11] After three "intensive" days in Saigon, Galbraith judged the government to be illegitimate, urging Kennedy to "drop Diem" in favor of a military regime.[12]

Galbraith's argument in favor of the coup was recognizably in his style:

> [A]dministratively Diem is exceedingly bad. He holds far too much power in his own hands. . . . He has also effectively resisted improvement for a long time. . . . Whether his political posture is nepotic, despotic, out of touch with the villagers and hence damaging or whether this damage is the figment of Saigon intellectuals, does not bear on our immediate policy and may be bypassed. . . .
>
> The key and inescapable point, then, is the ineffectuality (abetted debatably by the unpopularity) of the Diem government. . . . Nor can one accept the statement . . . that this is the inevitable posture of the Asian mandarin. . . . There is no future for mandarins. The Communists don't favor them.
>
> It is a cliche that there is no alternative to Diem's regime. This is politically naive. . . . No one considered Truman an alternative to Roosevelt. . . . It is a better rule that nothing succeeds like successors.
>
> We should not be alarmed by the army as an alternative.[13]

Galbraith later admitted that he may have been influenced while composing the cable by the resonance of the phrase "nothing succeeds like successors." Quite likely the phrase amused Galbraith's former student, who was its obviously expected reader. No one, however, has been more trenchant in critiquing the cable than Galbraith himself. A quarter century later, Galbraith admitted that the original coup cable misrepresented his own private counsel. For Galbraith's genuine judgment was that Kennedy should simply abandon Diem and "return that section of the world to the obscurity for which God had so manifestly destined it."[14] Asked why he had lied to the president on such a decisive matter, Galbraith admitted that his motivation was to hold on to his slender and informal power with Kennedy. "If I had told him to abandon Vietnam before his reelection, I would have been cut out of the inner circle."[15]

Kennedy in 1961 had dismissed the counsel urging a military coup. Now, in 1963, he was reassessing its wisdom as he measured the distance between the Fourth of July and his imminent reelection campaign. During the holiday weekend at Hyannisport, Kennedy may have been dreaming of independence—his own independence from Diem. In Saigon, too, there were dreams of independence. But the dream was of independence from the Americans, who had begun to browbeat Diem as the French used to do. Since Fritz Nolting's departure and abrupt dismissal as ambassador, Diem had been beleaguered by Trueheart to reach an accommodation with Tri Quang and the Buddhist activists, even though Trueheart now understood their political aims.[16]

The day after the July 7 independence observance, the South Vietnamese government opened the long-delayed conspiracy trial against fourteen coup plotters who had attempted to topple Diem's government in 1960 (with the active participation, as the government claimed in court, of George Carver, who was still in 1963 an official of the CIA).[17] One of those indicted for conspiracy, Nguyen Tuong Tam, committed suicide before the opening of the trial.[18] Perhaps the timing of the trial was meant to warn another band of conspirators of the risks of such intrigue.

In his Independence Day address, Diem had announced the formation of a Committee of Reconciliation to adjudicate the grievances of Buddhists concerning religious persecution.[19] The prospects for a successful reconciliation would depend, of course, on the aims of the Buddhist activists. If it was Diem's head that Tri Quang was demanding, Diem would understandably be reluctant to accommodate the demand.

At the same time, Diem was reluctantly coming to terms with the inevitability of reconciliation with another erstwhile adversary, Ho Chi Minh. Relying on the good offices of the French ambassador, Roger Lalouette, and of Mieczyslaw Maneli, the Polish representative to the International Control Commission, Diem and Ho were exchanging initiatives for forging a federation of North and South Vietnam, a risk-filled and desperate strategy to allow each of them to escape the entangling alliances that they had entered in their earlier, perhaps immature, dreams of independence.[20] Having now learned the ancient lesson that military alliances are rarely exercises in altruism, each had separately concluded that the cost being exacted by China from Ho and by the United States from Diem was too high a price to pay for independence. Now was the dangerous hour of emancipation — for both Diem and Ho — from the colonial controls of Washington and Peking. Now Diem had decided it would be "sink or swim with Ho Chi Minh." Independence would be an all-Vietnamese dream, not a Cold War mirage.

Diem was about to ask Kennedy to remove his advisers and to discontinue his $1.5 million-a-day support for the South Vietnamese government. These were the exacting conditions set by Ho Chi Minh for negotiating a cease-fire.[21] Presumably Diem was exacting a reciprocal renunciation of Chinese support for North Vietnam. The goal of the July negotiations was an even playing field, cleared of great power obstacles, Chinese or American. This was not, of course, the independence Diem had once dreamed of; it was, however, as the events of the previous month had conclusively demonstrated, the only independence that was not a mere illusion.

As Diem and Ho dreamed their new dreams, Diem's old ally Fritz Nolting was expected back in Saigon from Washington, having won Kennedy's approval to make one last effort to get the U.S.–South Vietnamese alliance back on track. Diem had tried several times to get Nolting to return from his June vacation while Trueheart was issuing imperial edicts on the conduct of South Vietnamese internal policies. Trueheart somehow always mislaid Diem's messages, which could only be routed through the embassy that Trueheart now controlled.[22] Now, in July, it was too late for reconciliation between Saigon and Washington. The new avenue to independence led straight from Saigon to Hanoi. With the pressure tactics applied by the United States in June and with the removal of his protector, Ambassador Nolting, Diem had been drawn into the arms of Ho Chi Minh in a precarious strategy for survival. Nine years of American investment to build a secure barrier between Diem and Ho had been swept away in a wave of abusive language by the ranking American representative, Trueheart, abetted by Averell Harriman, apparently without presidential authorization. At the same time, Ho too was changing course. Chafing under Chinese meddling in Vietnamese affairs and straitened by the ravages of a sustained drought, he signaled a willingness to compromise with Diem on Vietnam's future.

Through Mieczyslaw Maneli, Ho sent a message that Diem would not be challenged as head of a southern government in a federated Vietnam. Speaking to an Australian journalist, Wilfred Burchett, Ho added a personal greeting: "Shake his hand for me. Diem is a patriot in his own way."[23]

The July 7 Saigon independence observance had been marred by a clash between U.S. reporters and Diem's police. Several journalists were briefly detained, and some cameras were destroyed after an altercation during a Buddhist demonstration at Chantareansey Pagoda. After interviewing Diem's minister of information, Trueheart relayed to Washington a temperate and cautious analysis: "According to Tao, police claim that correspondents provoked them by protesting police hold-up of procession and that one correspondent struck police first. Tao says he does not wish to pursue this, not feeling sure of police story. Given extreme emotional involvement of correspondents these days—amounting regrettably to intense hatred of all things GVN, in certain cases—I would not feel sure about refuting police."[24] After Trueheart declined to intervene on their behalf, the reporters telegraphed Kennedy directly, complaining of the "swift unprovoked and violent attack."[25] Trueheart countered this view with his own belief that these correspondents had been openly calling for a coup. Such a posture, Trueheart suggested, might dampen Diem's confidence that the journalists' work in Saigon was in his nation's interest.[26]

At the same time that Trueheart was identifying the overtly political goals of the U.S. press corps in Saigon, the CIA was reporting its assessment of the undisguised political program of the Buddhists:

> Buddhist strategy is polarizing around the views of Thich Tri Quang . . . who has openly stated his intention not to cease agitation until the Diem government falls. Thich Tri Quang also has indicated his intention, if necessary, to call for suicide volunteers. . . .
>
> Thus, the Buddhists, at least those under the influence of Thich Tri Quang, appear to be consciously transferring their struggle to the political realm. . . .
>
> . . . [S]ome of the Buddhists leaders appear completely set on the elimination of the Diem regime by one means or another. . . .
>
> However, if he [Diem] makes the gestures of further conciliation toward the Buddhists currently being pressed upon him, he has no

assurance that these will satisfy them and no guarantee that such gestures, which could be interpreted as additional signs of weakness, would not merely whet the appetite of his antagonists for further unsustainable concessions.[27]

Reviewing this report from the CIA at the White House, Forrestal thought it unworthy of the president's personal attention but wrote to McGeorge Bundy that it echoed the views of an odd grouping of officials: Harriman, Hilsman, and Nolting.[28] While Forrestal was unblinkingly urging Harriman to press ahead with pressures on Diem to accommodate the Buddhists, although acknowledging that this would amount to an exercise in self-destruction for Diem, Ambassador Nolting had been urging the opposite course of action on Capitol Hill. Just before taking his return flight to Saigon, Nolting had testified at a hastily convened session of the Senate Foreign Relations Committee. In response to sharply honed questions, mostly based on the recent flurry of critical news reports from Saigon, Nolting was more candid about the weaknesses of the Diem government than he had been in the White House meeting on July 5.

Chairman William Fulbright opened the meeting with a warm welcome and the observation that Nolting's successor in Saigon, Henry Cabot Lodge Jr., was a former member of the Foreign Relations Committee. Senator Mansfield, whose knowledge of the situation was the most profound of all the members and whose February 1963 Foreign Relations Committee report had probably been the decisive element in driving Diem and Nhu to seek accommodation with Ho Chi Minh, remained silent. Nolting's opening statement echoed the State Department's satisfaction at the increased leverage it now enjoyed in South Vietnam through the expanded adviser program, which allowed the fourteen thousand U.S. personnel to work directly with province chiefs, bypassing the sluggish bureaucracy of Saigon. Nolting did not mention Diem's April complaint about these administrative end runs.

In response to several senators, Nolting was refreshingly forthright about the obstacles that the Saigon government placed in the way of the U.S. mission. Describing the regime's inefficiency, Nolting lamented: "They make more booboos than one could imagine." Recounting his patient efforts to urge Diem to take more care about repressive measures that cost him support at home and abroad, Nolting attributed the regime's bad press partially to Diem's own ineptness. "One of our constant problems is to get them to put their best foot forward and, by golly, they put the wrong one forward nine times out of ten." Discussing the onset of the Buddhist crisis of May and June, the ambassador called the May 7 decree, forbidding the flying of Buddhist banners, the beginning of "a series of bonehead plays."[29]

Seeking to grasp the significance of the Buddhist religious factor in the volatile mix of Vietnamese politics, Chairman Fulbright asked what percentage of Vietnamese were Buddhists. Nolting's answer reflected Diem's own estimation, namely, that it was impossible to tell because the only available census was prepared by the French, who had concluded that 10 percent (1.4 million) were Catholic, lumping together all the rest as "Buddhist" and thus failing to differentiate further among animists, Confucianists, and adherents of other sects such as Hoa Hao's. Despite this quantitative ambiguity, Nolting himself observed that, emotionally or culturally, "Vietnam is a Buddhist country." Systematic discrimination in favor of Catholics would therefore be an obvious source of contention and instability. Nolting contended, however, that during his two years in Saigon he had been aware of no such persecution or hostilities.[30]

On the more general question of Diem's viability, Nolting insisted that despite his authoritarian and inefficient ways, Diem seemed more dependable than any alternative leader yet to surface. Diem was committed to the gradual cultivation of self-government at the village level while maintaining a tight grip on central governmental actions. American-style political institutions were as yet nowhere on the horizon in Vietnam.[31]

Frank Lausche, senator from Ohio and chairman of the Foreign Relations Subcommittee on Far Eastern Affairs, then came strikingly close to warning of the gathering storm surrounding Kennedy's policy in Vietnam:

Senator Lausche: One more thought. Has any negation been issued by the State Department to these charges that we are throwing Diem overboard?

Mr. Nolting: Ben [Chalmers B. Wood, director of the Working Group on Vietnam], can you help me on that? Not that I know of. No direct, not directly.

> *Senator Lausche:* Is that sound to allow a statement of this type to go
> unchallenged if the statements are false? You don't have to answer
> that question. I had grave doubts about it.
>
> *Mr. Nolting:* If I might just express a view on that without answering
> your question directly, Senator. . . . I am sure that the reassurance
> on this point will be given, has been given, and certainly I will give
> it again when I get back to Vietnam.[32]

For the moment, Nolting's denial of the accuracy of the coup reports was technically accurate: Kennedy had not yet given his approval to a coup.

After stopping at Dean Rusk's office for final instructions, Nolting flew to Saigon. With Kennedy's anxious approval and at Diem's repeated request, Nolting had returned to make one final desperate effort to save the U.S. investment in Vietnam. Nolting was quizzed by Diem on the rationale for his abrupt transfer from Saigon: "Does this represent a change in policy in Washington?" At Diem's insistence, Nolting cabled the question to Rusk, who responded on July 10 in the name of the "Highest Authority" that no change of policy was contemplated. Diem's response, difficult for both the old friends, was candid: "I believe you, but I don't believe the message you have received."[33] Diem's blunt rejection of the reassurances that Nolting passed on from Rusk marked the chasm now dividing Kennedy and Diem.

When Nolting then confronted his protégé William Trueheart about failing to communicate news of the crisis that had erupted during his holiday, as Trueheart had promised, the junior diplomat responded only that "things were moving too fast."[34] One of the rapid changes that may have inspired Trueheart's "dramatic démarche" of threatening Diem during Nolting's absence was the carrot of rapid promotion in the department that Harriman had held out to him.[35]

Nolting captured the new mood in his cable to Washington on July 15. Diem, he wired, "is, in brief, in a martyr's mood himself. . . . He is visibly tired. Our main problem at [the] moment is to get him relaxed enough to take the helm and steer the ship on a true and sensible course."[36]

The *New York Times* had defined the crisis in Saigon as one of religious discrimination: a Catholic government engaged in repressing an overwhelmingly Buddhist population. To counter this dangerous misrepresentation of the problem, Nolting in early August invited another correspondent to interview Diem.[37] Diem welcomed Marguerite Higgins of the *New York Herald Tribune* for an interview on August 7, startling her by recounting the dressing-down he had received from Trueheart, who had twice threatened to abandon Diem if he did not measure up to American standards of pluralism by encouraging the Buddhist protest. Then Diem wondered aloud:

> What am I to think of the American government . . . ? Am I merely a puppet on Washington's string? . . . If you order Vietnam around like a puppet on a string, how will you be different . . . from the French? I hope . . . that your government will take a realistic look at these young generals plotting to take my place. . . . I am afraid there are no George Washingtons among our military. . . . The West must give us a little time. . . . The spiritual basis of democracy is to be found everywhere in Vietnam, and especially in our villages, and we are building democracy there. . . . Gradually, when the war ends, we can move to greater democracy on a national level. . . . But it is impossible — a delusion — to think that a solution for Asia consists in blindly copying Western methods.[38]

"The West must give us a little time," Diem pleaded. But Diem failed to grasp that Kennedy too was short on time. He had only fifteen months until his race for reelection would be judged by the American electorate, which had awarded him his first term by a hair's breadth three years before.[39] Diem would have to be a more presentable ally during the long campaign trials if JFK was to win again.[40]

Diem knew by heart the story of Vietnam's long march to independence from China. Over the centuries, Chinese governors in Viet had dutifully taken up the yellow man's burden of educating the Viet people to behave as much like the Chinese as possible. As Frances FitzGerald noted: "Ten centuries later, the Viets had adopted Chinese technology and the Chinese religions; their aristocracy sent its sons to compete for the mandarinate. Then in the 10th century, to the Chinese surprise, this same aristocracy raised troops to expel the armies of the declining T'ang dynasty from the Red River Delta. . . . Writing in Chinese, the great Vietnamese military leader, Ly Thuong Kiet, rebuked the Chinese for claiming sovereignty over a state whose identity depended on her relationship to the Empire of the Center." Ly had argued that the duties of the father (China) to its son (Vietnam) now required the acknowledgment of the maturity that Chinese culture had created in Southeast Asia. The original gift of culture now demanded the gift of independence.[41]

The same eternal demand for independence now echoed in Diem's complaints about the Americans. Speaking to Higgins, he insisted:

> The key to good relations between the United States and Vietnam . . . is respect for the substance of sovereignty. The newer independence is, the more passionate is the people's attachment to it.
>
> We want to tap these deep roots of our Confucian traditions. . . . Vietnam's priority is stability, central control, respect for authority and order. The Americans are breaking Vietnamese psychology and they don't even know what they are doing.[42]

Now, on August 12, Nolting withdrew from his two-year savings of trust with Diem all his personal authority to alert Diem bluntly to the mortal danger posed by his defiance of Washington. He reminded Diem that the United States had resolved to make its continued alliance with Diem conditional on his submission to a specific demand: immediate fulfillment of his public pledges of reconciliation with the Buddhists. Nolting summarized the difficult meeting in a cable:

> I gave President Diem my own observations and convictions regarding the attitude, not only of high officials of his own government, but of many lower Vietnamese; stressed absolute necessity for him to take account personally of the crisis resulting from Buddhist problem.
>
> . . . He reverted again and again to the bad faith of the bonzes, to their sabotage of the war effort, etc. He complained that nobody in the outside world recognized the falsity of the religious issue or the fact that it was being used for subversive action. I told him . . . that . . . so far as the US was concerned he had to stick to and implement fully the policy of conciliation. . . . Otherwise, we could not support him.[43]

The warning was futile. The next evening Nolting received a message from Hilsman concerning his failure in this last mission: "Appears here that [Vice President] Tho press conference projects essentially unbending and non-conciliatory policy which is in flat contradiction to Diem promise to take our advice and make an announcement of GVN determination to follow policy of conciliation."[44] On August 14 a seventeen-year-old monk immolated himself in Huong Tra province.[45]

Nolting's final cable from Saigon, on August 14, was somber:

I saw him early this morning and he had slipped back into post-
ponement and vacillation. . . . I told him bluntly that for our part
we could not accept this. . . . We were absolutely frank with one another. . . . I stuck to the position it would be impossible for the US
Government to continue our present relationship to him and to his
government if he did not promptly make a declaration which would
show clearly who was running the country . . . and would restore faith
in GVN's intention to carry out its announced policy of conciliation. . . . He asked me to thank President Kennedy for all he has done
for Viet-Nam.[46]

Nolting had warned Diem that his failure to seek accommodation
with the Buddhists would provoke the end of American support for his
government. This was a sobering threat coming from Nolting, who had
been removed from his post in June precisely because he appeared too
conciliatory to Diem.[47] Nolting's call for accommodation by Diem to
the demands of Buddhist activists was an ultimatum to yield power to
the bonzes in the foreseeable future.[48] The reforms demanded by Washington were understood in Washington to invite abdication. Understandably, Diem drew the line at abdication, as Nolting had warned
Washington officials in July before he returned to Saigon.[49] In his determination to reform Diem, Kennedy was playing with fire — the fire
of freedom, burning quite as brightly, and equally self-destructively, in
the eyes of Ngo Dinh Diem as in those of the bonzes poised for self-
immolation.

In early August, Trueheart sent through Hilsman to Ambassador-
designate Lodge a suggested message concerning Buddhist demonstrations that Lodge might release to journalists upon his arrival in Saigon.
Trueheart proposed that the new ambassador recall to the press that,
while religious tolerance remains a cardinal American principle, the recent religious demonstrations are "an internal Vietnamese affair." When
this text reached the desk of Averell Harriman on August 10, Harriman
ordered Hilsman to change the wording, because Diem's repression of
Buddhist demonstrators "is not [an internal affair]. It has repercussions
all over the world."[50]

Trueheart's caution about injecting the United States into this apparently religious controversy was the fruit of his own month-long wrest-
ling with this problem from May 23 to June 29. He finally concluded

that the monks following Tri Quang had "gone beyond legitimate ends originally sought by Buddhists."[51] Kennedy's personal envoy, Robert Manning, had registered the same warning, namely that the Buddhist demonstrators had now clearly abandoned religious motivations for palpably insurrectionary ones: the overthrow of the Diem government.[52]

Tri Quang had said as much to Marguerite Higgins soon after her arrival in Saigon, linking the urgency to overthrow Diem to the imperative of opening negotiations with Ho Chi Minh. Diem, Tri Quang believed, was the sole obstacle to such negotiations.[53] (Diem was himself, of course, already engaged in such negotiations with Ho Chi Minh.) Tri Quang had since 1958 been determined on a policy of removing Vietnam from the ravages of a cold war by adopting a neutralist foreign policy, aligned with none of the great powers.[54]

After his 1963 relocation to Saigon, Tri Quang joined forces with the author Mai-Tho-Truyen, a former member of Diem's cabinet who was now the architect of the movement to overthrow him. Conceding that the resort to sacrificial suicide by monks was done in defiance of the highest-ranking Vietnamese Buddhist official, Thich Tinh Khiet, Mai nevertheless boasted of the auspicious progress evident to date.[55] As Lodge would later demonstrate by granting to Tri Quang asylum in the U.S. embassy, the ambassador probably had not been sufficiently warned in advance of the double game being played by the neutralist monks of Xa Loi.[56]

On August 15 Kennedy met in the Oval Office with Henry Cabot Lodge Jr. The usually comprehensive official record of meetings on Vietnam is interrupted here. This archival lacuna was partially, if inadvertently, filled by McGeorge Bundy's later remark, at his staff conference on November 22, that it might eventually be necessary to replace Lodge since he "seems inept at conducting diplomatic relations with the new [Big Minh] government in Saigon." In this context, Bundy remarked that Lodge "was just the type needed during his first months in Saigon when he was supposed to create a posture which would indicate to any would-be revolutionist that the US would not automatically side with Diem."[57]

Two more self-immolations occurred in mid-August: on the fifteenth a twenty-year-old monk burned himself in sacrifice; the next day, at Hue's Tu Dam Pagoda, an elderly monk, Thich Tieu-Dieu, also took his own life.[58] In Washington, in a meeting with the ambassador of New

Zealand, Roger Hilsman indicated that the United States no longer regarded these dramatic self-immolations as acts of religious protest but as political tactics to overthrow the government, which had been condemned by the Buddhist hierarchy.[59]

Lodge himself later claimed that he received no particular mandate from Kennedy on August 15 except to solve the acute crisis in U.S. public support for the war caused by press images of burning bonzes. He stopped at Honolulu on August 20 to be briefed by Nolting, who assured his successor that Diem had promised to seek accommodation with the Buddhist leaders. While Nolting was trying to reassure Lodge on this prospect, Nhu unleashed on August 20–21 a midnight attack on the Saigon pagodas, arresting 1,462 monks.[60] Gordon Cox, the Canadian representative in Saigon of the International Control Commission, informed the U.S. government later that the crackdown on August 21 was fully warranted by the warlike preparations being made in the pagodas and the evident intention of Tri Quang and his followers to overthrow the government.[61]

Kennedy ordered Lodge to proceed immediately to Saigon, not stopping in Hong Kong as planned.[62] While Lodge was in transit to Saigon, George Ball, now acting secretary of state, sent a memo to Harriman in response to a message to be cabled from Harriman to Lodge:

> I think the first telegram which our new ambassador to Saigon receives should not display the pomposity and verbosity of the Department of State at its worst.
>
> Moreover, I think we ought to go slow on advising Cabot to "eliminate the Nhus" as one of his first acts. After all, we ought to offer him a chance to look the situation over and give us a fresh reading. I think that Cabot will resent being told the obvious.[63]

Blocked from using a diplomatic cable to urge Lodge to move immediately against Nhu, unnamed senior officials of the State Department sent the same message through the *New York Times* of August 24. On the front page, Tad Szulc wrote of a possible reversal of U.S. policy in Vietnam: "As one official [in the State Department] put it tonight [August 23], 'a lot of thought is being given' to the outlook for internal changes in Vietnam."

4

"DOING BUSINESS ON THE WEEKEND"

AUGUST 24 TO AUGUST 27

It was an odd fivesome on the course at the Chevy Chase Country Club near Washington just after noon on Saturday, August 24. Averell Harriman arrived on the ninth tee, followed by Michael Forrestal and Roger Hilsman. George Ball was enjoying a rare golf outing with U. Alexis Johnson, his deputy. Ball was undersecretary of state and, during this leaderless weekend in Washington, acting secretary of state. Ball and Johnson's game was abruptly interrupted by the unannounced arrival of Harriman and his two deputies. Harriman's star was now rising in the Kennedy administration, after he had brought news to Kennedy at Hyannisport in July of his successful negotiation from July 15 to 22 of a ban on atmospheric nuclear testing. Making the August 3 cover of *Time* for this diplomatic coup, Harriman had provided Kennedy with some much-needed support for his next presidential campaign.[1]

"The Governor" stalked onto the tee, asked Johnson to step out of earshot, and addressed Ball. Harriman insisted that Ball leave Johnson at the club and meet privately with Harriman and his two young assistants.[2] Ball agreed, convinced that the urgent business proposed by Harriman could not be shared with Johnson, the third-ranking officer of the State Department. Harriman sensed that Johnson would sound the alarm if he were privy to the conversation at Ball's home that afternoon. For Harriman, urged on by Forrestal and Hilsman, now proposed sending a cable to Lodge, then in his second day in Saigon, telling him to begin plotting the overthrow of Ngo Dinh Diem.[3] Johnson, who had long experience in Asia and was a close ally of Dean Rusk, could be counted on to cause trouble.

In Saigon, Tri Quang had slipped through Nhu's net around Xa Loi
54 Pagoda and had gained asylum in the U.S. embassy, where Lodge visited

him.[4] Other Vietnamese visitors, too, were calling on their contacts in the embassy. In his first round of discussions with the staff on August 24, Lodge learned of numerous pleas by high-ranking officials of South Vietnam for Kennedy to move decisively against Nhu. During a twelve-hour period on his first day in office, Lodge dispatched three cables reporting on the Saigon bureaucratic pincer-movement to remove Nhu.

At 11:00 A.M., August 24 (11:00 P.M., August 23, Washington time), Lodge summarized a conversation between Nguyen Dinh Thuan, Diem's closest nonfamily collaborator, and Rufus Phillips, a CIA and AID (Rural Affairs) veteran in Vietnam. Thuan had urged the United States to demand that Nhu relinquish power. U.S. tolerance of Nhu's tactics against Buddhists would otherwise provoke chaos. The South Vietnamese Army would readily turn against Nhu if it knew that the United States "would under no circumstances support a government with the Nhus in control."[5] Thuan himself had no intention of abandoning Diem and doubted that Diem would abandon his brother, as Thuan himself was now urging.

Phillips had been very busy during the previous two days. Lodge's next cable, sent seven hours after the first one, summarized another conversation Phillips had reported to the ambassador, involving General Le Van Kim. Kim's message was identical to Thuan's: the army was loyal to Diem but would move against Nhu. If the United States called for dislodging the Nhus, there would be a unified military response.[6]

Forty-five minutes after Lodge cabled his summary of the Kim-Phillips conversation, CIA chief John Richardson cabled CIA headquarters, where Richard Helms was acting director in the absence of John McCone. General Tran Van Don, Diem's army chief of staff, had summoned CIA officer Lucien Conein to his headquarters on August 23 to explain that martial law had been declared by Diem earlier in August at the request of ten army generals. The army sought to force the bonzes who had arrived in Saigon from pagodas outside the capital to return to their own cities or villages. In agreeing to this army demand, Diem had insisted on safe conduct for the bonzes. He had also resisted closing schools, because young people needed an opportunity to express themselves. But Don insisted that separating the Nhus from Diem was impossible and that Diem could not reliably be replaced by generals, or other civilians, as the chief of state.[7]

Before retiring at the end of his first eye-opening day as ambassador, Lodge offered Kennedy his advice, which fell on deaf ears in Washington:

> Suggestion has been made that U.S. has only to indicate to "Generals" that it would be happy to see Diem and/or Nhus go, and deed would be done. Situation is not so simple, in our view. Specifically, as indicated . . . above, we have no information that officers with troops in Saigon are disposed to act in this way. Moreover, there is no showing that military have agreed among themselves on a leadership.

> Action on our part in these circumstances would seem to be a shot in the dark. Situation at this time does not call for that, in my judgment, and I believe we should bide our time, continuing to watch situation closely.[8]

Lodge's midnight counsel to Kennedy's associates was to sit tight. No improvement was likely in Diem's behavior; Nhu was universally disliked, but indispensable to Diem; Diem was irreplaceable. U.S. initiatives to replace Diem and Nhu would be "a shot in the dark."

Yet despite advice from top officials in Saigon, Forrestal, Hilsman, and Harriman cast their—and Kennedy's—lot with "the shot in the dark" option. Hilsman drafted a reply to Lodge's cables, which was now put before George Ball for approval. Ball refused to authorize the cable without Kennedy's approval but agreed to interrupt Kennedy's holiday at Hyannisport to request clearance for the cable, which would unmistakably, if only contingently, authorize a military coup.[9] Kennedy wondered why the matter could not wait until his return on Monday. The president was already familiar with the imminent move to remove Nhu, and possibly Diem, on the basis of a memorandum that Forrestal had enclosed in his weekend reading file.[10] Ball encouraged Kennedy to authorize the cable: "It has to be done."[11] Finally, Forrestal put Harriman on the line to Kennedy, who consented to the cable if it was cleared by the State and Defense Departments.

Rusk, who was at Yankee Stadium without a secure telephone, approved the cable on the supposition that Kennedy had agreed already.[12] Robert McNamara, climbing mountains in Wyoming, was thought to be unavailable and had left Roswell Gilpatric as acting secretary of defense. Gilpatric, thinking that the matter was a State Department responsibility, consented but did alert Maxwell Taylor, chairman of the Joint Chiefs of Staff and the president's most trusted military adviser on

Vietnam. Both Gilpatric and Taylor feared that this weekend cable might be an end run around the constitutional officers of the government.[13] In obtaining Gilpatric's clearance for the cable, Forrestal neglected to mention one detail of his prior telephone conversation with the president: Kennedy had explicitly made his approval conditional on the concurrence of the Defense Department. Omitting this detail, Forrestal left Gilpatric with the impression that he was being informed of a decision already approved unilaterally by Kennedy.[14] Richard Helms, acting director of the CIA that weekend, likewise received the impression that Forrestal's call was merely to notify the Central Intelligence Agency that a decision had finally been taken on a problem Kennedy had seemed unable to resolve.[15]

The cable was dispatched to Lodge at 9:36 P.M.

> 243. Eyes only Ambassador Lodge.
>
> US Government cannot tolerate situation in which power lies in Nhu's hands. Diem must be given chance to rid himself of Nhu and his coterie and replace them with best military and political personalities available. . . .
>
> . . . We wish [to] give Diem reasonable opportunity to remove Nhus, but if he remains obdurate, then we are prepared to accept the obvious implication that we can no longer support Diem. You may also tell appropriate military commanders we will give them direct support in any interim period of breakdown [of] central government mechanism. . . .
>
> Concurrently with above, Ambassador and country team should urgently examine all possible alternative leadership and make detailed plans as to how we might bring about Diem's replacement if this should become necessary.[16]

Ball, who revised cable 243 for stylistic improvements, had no doubts about the wisdom of its dispatch, then or later. He was appalled at Diem's repression of the Buddhists, whom Harriman, but apparently not Ball, understood to be launching an insurrection. To Ball, "Diem was an offense to America." He therefore dispatched the cable, which eventually ushered in a new government, without considering the abilities of the generals or civilians who would succeed Diem: "I didn't know any of the [Vietnamese] personalities." Ball explained that he and Rusk had an informal division of labor, with Ball monitoring European problems and

Rusk keeping an eye on Asia, which he knew well. Ball also felt that he could rely on Lodge to pick out promising Saigon leaders (after forty-eight hours in his new post). Curiously, despite this confidence, Ball agreed with many of his colleagues that Lodge "wasn't too bright."[17]

Over the weekend, William Colby, former CIA chief of station in Saigon and a close student of Vietnamese leadership, flew to California to brief John McCone, director of the CIA, on the cable, approved in his absence by Helms. Colby returned to Washington with McCone on Sunday.[18]

John McCone was the Horatio Alger of the young administration. An immigrant multimillionaire, McCone had gotten his start in the shipping industry, then founded and sold the Bechtel Corporation. After the Bay of Pigs debacle, Kennedy had sought control and bipartisan support of CIA initiatives by persuading McCone, a close ally of Eisenhower, to take on this volatile "company." Under Eisenhower, McCone had headed the Atomic Energy Commission. McCone soon enhanced his stature with Kennedy by effecting the timely discovery of the installation of Soviet missiles in Cuba in 1962. Because he had made his mark in the shipping industry, McCone, who maintained a close personal scrutiny over CIA assessments of worldwide shipping activities, noticed in September 1962 increased Soviet shipping to Cuba. He then ordered increased aerial surveillance of Cuba, which revealed new roads and military installations on the island. Inquiring of the CIA analysts whether these construction sites portended any threat to the United States, McCone was reassured that Soviet policy was too cautious for such a bold initiative. Unsatisfied with the response, he persisted in monitoring other maritime movements until photographs revealed missile installations. The extra moments provided by McCone's skepticism gave Kennedy more time to manage the emerging crisis, assuring McCone's personal clout with Kennedy.[19]

McCone returned to Washington on Monday, August 26, determined to reverse the orders that had authorized a coup in Saigon. On the long flight from California, Colby had been able to fill McCone in on some of the personalities and forces at work in Vietnam, on which Colby (after two years as chief of station in Saigon) was Washington's leading authority. Colby's interpretation of the enigmatic Ngo brothers, Diem and Nhu, made interesting and illuminating listening on the trip.[20] Ngo Dinh Diem's record of constructing some semblance of order in Saigon, after his unheralded arrival in 1954, provided the indispensable histori-cal context for his recent crackdown on Buddhist demonstrators. In 1954, with the blessing of absentee emperor Bao Dai, Diem had taken power as prime minister, only to discover that Saigon was a cauldron of plots, rival sects, and pitched battles among private armies. It was a Southeast Asian version of the nightmare painted in an earlier era by Hobbes, that of an anarchic situation that demanded the imposition of absolute rule by Leviathan. Religious sects, opium dealers, prostitution rings, generals fronting for mandarin families, lazy bureaucrats, Com-munists, and francophile bourgeoisie everywhere competed for power. Gradually, with advice and money from the CIA, Diem had mastered this postcolonial chaos by cunning and coercion.

When the Buddhist crisis had then erupted during the spring and summer of 1963, Diem had mistaken the disturbances as a reprise of the earlier political and personal challenges to his authority, failing to sense that the Buddhists were not merely another in a long string of rivals for control. For this was the first challenge that had arisen from ideology. Tri Quang and his intimate group of comrades at the urban pagodas had staked out a new political arena, above the petty quest for power: the re-moval of the Americans and of any Vietnamese leaders cooperating with the United States.[21] Tri Quang's goal was the reunification of Vietnam, which Diem and Kennedy were blocking.[22]

Diem's own agenda was equally nationalistic but had until very re-cently been less isolationist than Tri Quang's. His priority, now that he had apparently imposed some tenuous order, was to plunge forward with his program of social and educational services to bring Vietnam into the mainstream of Asian patterns of development. From this imper-ative of expanding modern state services to the population came his and Nhu's dream of *agrovilles*, newly constructed clusters of family dwellings that could benefit from security and services provided by Saigon.

In this effort at an epochal leap forward for his people, Diem was hampered by a bureaucracy inherited from the French, whom he had chosen to retain until he could establish an authentically Vietnamese civil service.[23] Diem's instrument of reform was his prized School of Ad-ministration, modeled on the French Ecole Nationale d'Administration. Diem's only fully trusted ally was his wily and Machiavellian brother Nhu, whom Colby compared to Lenin, the political genius who trans-ferred all political power in Russia to a secret, tightly controlled party that he hoped would succeed in manipulating the bureaucracy. For this purpose, Nhu had formed the Can Lao Party, a clique that could run the country behind the decorous facade of a government. Acutely aware of the incompatibility of their visions of government, the Ngo brothers were nonetheless inseparably yoked together, because Diem held power and Nhu understood power.

After painting this portrait of these problematic allies of the United States, Colby reminded McCone of the risks inherent in removing the Ngos: if this ruling team was a fragile reed, still Kennedy had no choice but to lean on it or leave Vietnam. Colby had been able to identify no reliable alternatives in his two years of close analysis.[24] Arriving at his office that Monday, McCone found he was not alone in his dissent over the coup. McNamara was on the telephone rounding up officials for a meeting of the National Security Council to review the cable.[25]

In Saigon, Truong Con Cuu, South Vietnam's newly appointed acting foreign minister, had presided at his first diplomatic reception the night before. In other circumstances, the distinguished guest list might have represented an auspicious inaugural: Henry Cabot Lodge Jr. chose the occasion for his own diplomatic debut, as did Mieczyslaw Maneli, the Polish diplomat who was serving as the Communist-bloc representative to the International Control Commission. Maneli, whose authority did not bestow diplomatic status, had been a conspicuous new name on the guest list for Truong's official inaugural: no Communist diplomat had ever been invited to such an official function of Diem's government.

Maneli was introduced to Ngo Dinh Nhu by Monsignor d'Asta, the papal delegate to South Vietnam, one of eighty diplomats accredited to South Vietnam as a result of Diem's widening international stature. Nhu's words might have been enlightening to the new American ambassador if he had chosen to join that small circle around Nhu, Asta, and Maneli: "Vietnamese people mistrust not only the Chinese, but all colonizers. Now we are interested in peace, and only peace. I believe the ICC can play an important role in restoring peace in Vietnam." Later, Maneli was invited to Gia Long Palace, another diplomatic first.[26]

On receipt of Ball's cable, Lodge had instinctively sought to escape control by Kennedy in this crisis. He cabled a request to bypass "step one" in the phased coup strategy of the previous day's cable, the requirement first to offer Diem a chance to remove his brother Nhu.[27] Ball approved the modification, allowing Lodge to go directly to the generals, effectively encouraging a coup. Ball was careful to approve this radical acceleration of the coup schedule by the "back channel" transmission network of the CIA. As a result, no record of Ball's new authorization came to Rusk's attention in the troubled months ahead.[28]

Lodge then held an embassy "country team" meeting with the innovative agenda of orchestrating a coup against the government to which he was soon to be accredited. This item on the agenda naturally took precedence over the more pedestrian discussion of plans for his visit, later that morning, to Gia Long Palace to present his credentials to Diem. While awaiting this diplomatic formality, Lodge ordered CIA chief Richardson to proceed directly to "step two" of the plan, alerting the generals of Washington's green light for a coup. After the staff meeting, Richardson methodically went about contacting dissident generals to unleash an attack on Ngo Dinh Diem.[29] Despite his personal misgivings, Richardson took his orders from the new ambassador.

The day before, General Nguyen Khanh had informed Richardson that he and other generals believed Diem's brother Nhu was contacting officials in Hanoi to inquire about the meaning of Ho Chi Minh's private and public statements about a new federation of North and South Vietnam. Khanh warned the CIA that the Nhu-Diem pact with Ho would spark a military coup d'état.[30] Ho's earlier rejection in Geneva of Kennedy's July 1962 proposal for neutralization of Vietnam had now been reversed.[31] Now Diem was unconsciously mimicking Kennedy's gesture of accommodation with the North, of which Diem had never learned.[32]

Lodge was beginning a very busy week. Accredited by Kennedy to the government of South Vietnam and by George Ball (with Kennedy's tacit consent) to the military junta now preparing to take power, Lodge had to divide his attention between ambassadorial and conspiratorial responsibilities. Reporting to Washington the substance of his first discussion with Diem, on August 26, on the occasion of presenting his credentials, Lodge recalled his effort to shock Diem into realizing how poor an image he was projecting in the Boston-Washington corridor: "I realized I knew very little about Vietnam, but I felt I knew something about the U.S. . . . It was interesting to me that people whom I had known all my life in politics thought that Madame Nhu was the Chief of State of Viet-Nam and that I had met several people in Massachusetts who had seen her picture on the covers of magazines and had read some of her statements about barbecuing the priests and total destruction of the Buddhists and that this had shocked public opinion."[33]

This version of Lodge's opening encounter with Diem was apparently significantly sanitized for the record. Anne Blair, in her study of Lodge's stewardship in Saigon, reports his own prepared text for the meeting, which she says he used fully when speaking to Diem: "I want you to be successful. I want to be useful to you. . . . I don't expect you to be a 'yes man.' I realize that you must never appear — let alone be — a puppet of the United States. . . . The American President, unlike some Chiefs of State, does not have unrestricted power. While his word is absolutely good and can never be questioned, the American President, nevertheless, cannot undertake future commitments which would not be supported by public opinion, as this public opinion is influenced by the press and is expressed in the Congress, notably in the Senate."[34]

While assuring Diem that he should not imagine his role in the U.S. alliance as that of "a puppet," Lodge pointed out that Congress constitutionally holds "the power of the purse" over foreign policy expenditures, such as the $1.5 million-a-day then being expended in South Vietnam. Lodge implied that Congress was insisting on reform in Saigon as a condition for continued aid to Diem. In fact, no such pressure existed within Congress, so Lodge himself would be required to stir it up. He therefore soon inquired of Rusk whether the House Foreign Affairs Committee might be encouraged to issue such a threat. Bundy and Hilsman preferred the Senate as the fulcrum to move Diem. Knowing Senator Frank Church's dim view of Diem, they worked with him in preparing a September 12 resolution, condemning Diem's "religious persecution."[35]

In Washington at that moment, Kennedy held a full-dress review of the weekend cable saga. Refreshed after the secluded weekend with his family at Hyannisport, Kennedy opened the noon meeting with a blunt challenge to Hilsman and Forrestal, who had spearheaded the weekend drive to improve the president's fortunes by eliminating the threat hovering over him from Diem's erratic behavior in Saigon. Kennedy put Hilsman on notice that he, Forrestal, Harriman, and Ball may have been overreacting to Diem's bad press in the United States. The record of the meeting notes that Kennedy "stated that it was essential that we not permit [David] Halberstam unduly to influence our actions. Hilsman assured the President that this was not the case." After crediting Diem and

Nhu for their efforts to improve their image but conceding that they remained "repugnant," Kennedy cautioned: "When we move to eliminate this Government, it should not be as a result of *New York Times* pressure."[36]

Tension then rose when Kennedy asked Maxwell Taylor for his prognosis of the coup that Ball's cables had authorized. Seizing on an infelicitous formulation of the question by Kennedy, Taylor aimed another shot at Hilsman:

> The President asked General Taylor, in light of his experience in the Pentagon, what chance a plan such as outlined in State cable 243 would have of succeeding. General Taylor replied that in Washington we would not turn over the problem of choosing a head of state to the military. . . .
>
> Mr. McNamara then raised the question of who Ambassador Lodge believes could replace Diem, stating that if we stand by and let a weak man get in the Presidency we will ultimately suffer. In this regard the President asked if the Foreign Minister who recently resigned [Vu Van Mau] might be a good candidate, to which Hilsman replied in the negative — stating that it is his view that the Generals would probably support Big Minh. . . .
>
> The President stated that there should be another meeting tomorrow to discuss the matter further. Mr. McNamara stated that, as a matter of first priority, we should procure biographical sketches of the key personalities involved, following which General Taylor suggested that we should talk to Ambassador Nolting. The President agreed and stated that Nolting should be brought to the meeting tomorrow, following which Mr. Hilsman commented that Nolting's view are [*sic*] colored, in that he is emotionally involved in the situation. Upon hearing this, the President observed, "Maybe properly."[37]

The next day Ambassador Lodge reported a sequence of meetings with those plotting to overthrow the government (Tran Thien Khiem and Big Minh).[38] After reviewing Lodge's schedule, Rusk observed that Lodge had not yet urged Diem to remove Nhu, perhaps because of Lodge's full calendar of meetings with possible coup leaders. "He may be waiting to see what the Vietnamese Generals are going to do." Rusk was, of course, unaware that Ball had authorized Lodge to ignore the appeal to Diem.[39] While awaiting the outcome of Lodge's soundings,

Kennedy met again with his principal foreign policy advisers, including the former ambassador Frederick Nolting. Kennedy listened to all sides of the debate and concluded the session by repeating Nolting's view that the generals offering their services for a coup probably could not pull it off.[40]

SELMA AND SAIGON

AUGUST 28 TO AUGUST 31

On August 28 Kennedy faced the fork in the road of the U.S.–South Vietnamese alliance that had deflected the East-West struggle from the European nuclear tinderbox to the steaming jungles of Indochina.

Unfortunately, Kennedy's mind was elsewhere as he faced the day. There was his personal preoccupation with his wife's health, as she recovered from the premature birth and sudden death of their third child, Patrick, earlier in the month. Moreover, looming on the Ellipse, just across the Rose Garden and adjacent public playing fields, was the gathering of civil rights demonstrators for the long-delayed March on Washington. That assembly would bring to the capital demonstrators who had been crisscrossing the South throughout the spring after the Birmingham and Selma showdowns of early May. In a June 22 White House meeting, the president had finally prevailed upon the planners to shift the site away from the Capitol itself to avoid any risk of alienating southern congressmen who were then taking up Kennedy's civil rights legislation. With his keen sense of risk and possibility, Kennedy was hoping the march would be large enough to impress Congress and moderate enough to assuage fears of civil unrest.[1]

At the core of Kennedy's concern about the march was his constant preoccupation with reelection. In June, Kennedy had seen a poll indicating that his approval rating had slipped dramatically, from 60 to 47 percent. His cautious support of civil rights in the South, which included dispatching federal marshals to the University of Alabama to enforce a federal court order and subsequently mobilizing the Alabama National Guard, had already cost him the support of almost five million Democratic voters. "He's cramming the nigger down our throats," one Birmingham voter told a pollster.[2] Today's march might be a catalyst for

Congress or a catastrophe for Kennedy. These would be fateful hours. Meanwhile, he had to focus on Vietnam.

Kennedy's August 28 noon meeting with all his principal advisers on Vietnam, along with Lyndon Johnson and Frederick Nolting, opened with William Colby's summation of a cable just received from John Richardson. Surely Colby, a close friend of Richardson, must have been shocked by the content of the cable, an urgent call for swift follow-through on support for the coup authorized on August 24. Colby's shock resulted from his certainty that Richardson, who had been his top assistant in Saigon from 1960 to 1962, was as thoroughly skeptical of the abilities of the coup plotters as was Colby. They both knew Big Minh — soon to emerge as the successor to Diem — to have "a head of solid ivory," as Colby later remarked.[3]

Richardson's warning cable to speed up the transfer of power did not "compute" for Colby. Richardson had summarized:

> Situation here has reached point of no return. Saigon is armed camp. Current indications are that Ngo family have dug in for last ditch battle. It is our considered estimate that General officers . . . understand that they have no alternative but to go forward. . . .
>
> Situation has changed drastically since 21 August. If the Ngo family wins now, they and Vietnam will stagger on to final defeat at the hands of their own people and the VC [Viet Cong]. Should a generals' revolt occur and be put down, GVN [Government of (South) Vietnam] will sharply reduce American presence in SVN [South Vietnam]. . . .
>
> It is obviously preferable that the generals conduct this effort without apparent American assistance. Otherwise, for a long time in the future, they will be vulnerable to charges of being American puppets, which they are not in any sense.[4]

Richardson had cabled his wholly unequivocal support of the U.S.-sponsored coup after several days of around-the-clock meetings with the generals who were about to dispatch Diem and Nhu. In Washington, Richardson's words had the authority of on-the-scene reality, to which Kennedy and Rusk continually and explicitly deferred throughout the sustained crisis. Because of Richardson's well-known respect for Diem and his closeness to Nhu, his sudden apparent shift into opposition and open collaboration with the plotters were still more persuasive to the

Washington officials who had only impersonal knowledge of the Saigon actors.[5]

When Kennedy added that General Paul Harkins agreed with Lodge and Richardson that the coup should go ahead, Nolting expressed surprise about Harkins's support, since he had been with Harkins in Saigon less than two weeks earlier. He then went on to make his lonely argument against the American government's involvement in overthrowing an allied head of state: it was a dishonorable act. As the minutes of the meeting record, Nolting argued: "Further encouragement to the generals opposing Diem runs counter to our agreement on continuing economic assistance which we reached with Diem some time ago. Diem foresaw at that time a disagreement with the U.S. about how they were running the internal affairs of Vietnam. Nolting said he had grave reservations about proceeding against Diem. The good faith of the U.S. is involved. In addition, he had given personal commitments to Diem which were based on instructions sent to him from Washington when he was Ambassador."[6]

Kennedy needed little prodding to recall the near collapse of the American-Vietnamese joint venture in November 1961. Diem had resisted an offer of U.S. troops, presented by Vice President Johnson earlier that year, fearing that they would evoke destructive memories of the French era in Vietnam. He then reversed his course in October, writing to Kennedy with a request for U.S. advisers. The deteriorating military situation in Laos, which opened up a path for Ho Chi Minh's forces to reach South Vietnam, had provoked this change of heart. Maxwell Taylor, then on a visit to Saigon, had welcomed Diem's request, seeing an opportunity to employ the New Frontier strategy of "flexible response." Diem's unexpected request was the first opportunity that presented itself to test this new strategy.[7]

The request for American advisers had cost Diem far more than it had cost Kennedy. For Diem, it was the first compromise of his dream of independence. Chastened earlier by the spurious promises of independence Bao Dai offered him, when he accepted the responsibility of the prime ministership briefly in 1933, Diem had pledged to shield South Vietnam from any further taint of foreign influence. Now, with explicit assurances from Kennedy that no political strings were attached to the service of these seven hundred military advisers, Diem had warily welcomed this gift horse.[8] He had finally reconsidered his lifelong conviction that independence for Vietnam would require absolute isolation from outside influence. Alliance, he had hoped in 1961, was not necessarily the enemy of independence; it might indeed be its progenitor.

In opening his fragile society to these foreign ways, Diem had made the first serious compromise of his principles. For his lifelong dream had been one of purity — total integrity for Vietnamese culture, free from all foreign contamination. After more than a century of interference in that culture by the French and Japanese, Diem had set his face toward a restoration of the Nguyen dynasty, which had been reestablished by Gia Long in 1802. Gia Long's achievement had rested, however, on his acceptance of foreign financing and advisers. The short-lived restoration was overwhelmed by the French invasion of 1861. Diem had determined to avoid the same miscalculation.[9]

Once he accepted the burden of ruling, however, Diem found that his dream had to be adjusted to the realities of alliance politics. Nevertheless, when the Kennedy administration in 1961 added to the authorization of seven hundred troops certain codicils requiring U.S. involvement in Saigon decision making, Diem had balked. "Vietnam," he informed Ambassador Nolting, "does not wish to become a protectorate of the U.S." After reconsideration, the condition attached to dispatch of the troops was merely one of "mutual consultation."[10]

With his insistence on the weight of Kennedy's earlier commitment ("the good faith of the U.S. is involved"), Nolting now on August 28, 1963, reminded the president of the formal promise of noninterference that Rusk had sent in Kennedy's name in November 1961, at the insistence of Diem. George Ball then turned the tables on Nolting by accusing Diem of bad faith in having gone back on his word to resolve the Buddhist issue peacefully. Harriman agreed with Ball. "We put Diem in power and he has double-crossed us. Diem and his followers have betrayed us."[11]

The president focused the debate on logistics: How could Lodge and Harkins build up the coup forces? Hilsman answered that Lodge now wanted to aid the generals with U.S. military equipment and his own public statement of support for the rebels. The meeting adjourned until 6:00 P.M., so that Kennedy could observe the historic civil rights march.

The marchers had arrived on a steaming August noon. Kennedy had decided not to follow Harry Truman's courageous lead on June 26, 1946, in joining the civil rights assembly at the Lincoln Memorial and giving the first civil rights speech by a twentieth-century president.[12] Kennedy watched Martin Luther King Jr.'s "I Have a Dream" speech on television. When the leaders of the march met with Kennedy at 5:00 P.M., the president echoed King's magic "I have a dream" anthem admiringly. In response to the leaders' demand that Kennedy broaden his civil rights bill, submitted to the Congress on June 19, the president tallied the present congressional headcount on his own bill with little confidence of passage. At 6:12 the president excused himself to return to the Vietnam meeting.[13]

The rally at the Lincoln Memorial was the climax of months of agitation in the South that had tested several barriers between the races: separate school and university systems for Negroes and whites, and the segregation of eating places. (The term *black*, used on the afternoon of August 28 by John Lewis, was an innovation in American language.[14])

Since April of that year, a storm had been gathering in response to lunch counter sit-ins in Birmingham, Alabama. Police commissioner Eugene ("Bull") Connor attacked protesters with police dogs on Good Friday, April 12, and arrested King. On May 2 five hundred Negro marchers were arrested. The next day police turned fire hoses on demonstrators while white residents tossed bricks. Newspapers on May 4 carried photographs of a Negro woman being attacked by a police dog. King's brother's house was bombed. The mayor of Birmingham lamented: "This nigger has got the blessing of the Attorney General and the White House." The president responded by sending in federal troops.[15]

The spring upsurge in American racial unrest and protest mobilization was the object of intense interest in Vietnam, where an analogous outbreak of religious protest was hobbling the Diem administration. On May 12 the Vietnamese military chronicler Doan-Them took note of the Birmingham disturbances and Kennedy's response of dispatching the National Guard. The chronicler would later note that a surprisingly large number, one hundred thousand, assembled for the Washington civil rights march of August 28, 1963.[16]

On May 18 at Vanderbilt University, Kennedy had pledged to defend the Negro. Three days later a U.S. District Court ordered the integration of the University of Alabama. But Governor George Wallace moved to bar the Negro students.[17] June 11 had been a moment of showdown in integration. (It happened to be a showdown as well in Saigon. It was the morning of the first of the dramatic self-immolations by the bonzes.) That evening Kennedy addressed the nation: "We preach freedom around the world. . . . But are we to say to the world . . . that this is a land of the free except for the Negroes?" Kennedy addressed the crisis in constitutional and moral terms, decrying discrimination. At a press conference he conceded that his action in favor of integration was costing him votes but insisted that integration was a nonpartisan issue.[18]

Earlier that same month, Diem's government had cracked down on bonzes demanding their rights and had arrested students demonstrating in protest. Kennedy could not ignore the parallels between Selma and Saigon.[19] An apparently random historical parallel thus made it difficult for the president to ignore repression in Vietnam while challenging it in Alabama. The president would have to be forceful in the face of Diem's brutality in repressing public protest. But the similarity of the situations was deceptive, perhaps leading Kennedy to overestimate his own responsibilities and authority in Saigon. Kennedy focused on the relevance of the twin crises of August 28 to his narrowing chances for reelection. While his leadership in racial integration was costing him dearly in conservative constituencies, his continued refusal to take a strong position on the Buddhist crisis in Saigon was equally damaging to his thin base of liberal (and especially editorial) opinion.

What had been planned for 6:00 P.M. as a full-dress National Security Council meeting on Vietnam began late (6:12), after the civil rights leaders departed. The president abbreviated the session, perhaps overwhelmed by the majesty of the civil rights march.

Anticipating a showdown at the evening meeting, Bundy had telephoned Rusk at 5:46 P.M. to insist that Rusk attend the meeting himself to defend Harriman and Ball against the challenge planned by McNamara and Taylor. Rusk agreed.[20] Kennedy had already approved new instructions to Lodge, insisting that he should feel under no pressure because of the August 24 cable to stick with a coup but should use his own judgment. Rusk requested once more that evening that Lodge follow his original orders (canceled on August 25 by George Ball) to tell Diem bluntly that Kennedy wanted Nhu out of Saigon.[21]

Lodge immediately replied in the negative, refusing to relay to Diem Kennedy's requirement to rid himself of Nhu or face the consequences. Thus, disagreeing with General Harkins, who still insisted on a final showdown with Diem before the coup, Lodge cabled his views to Washington:

> We are launched on a course from which there is no respectable turning back: The overthrow of the Diem government. There is no turning back in part because U.S. prestige is already publicly committed to this end in large measure and will become more so as facts leak out. In a more fundamental sense, there is no turning back because there is no possibility, in my view, that the war can be won under a Diem administration, still less that Diem or any member of the family can govern the country in a way to gain the support of the people who count, i.e. the educated class in and out of government service, civil and military—not to mention the American people. In the last few months (and especially days), they have in fact positively alienated these people to an incalculable degree. So that I am personally in full agreement with the policy which I was instructed to carry out by last Sunday's telegram.[22]

At noon on the following day, August 29, Kennedy brought together several advisers (but not Ball, Taylor, and McCone) to consider the contradictory recommendations received overnight from Lodge and Harkins. Predictably, McNamara and Nolting continued to insist on warning Diem of his impending sentence before its execution. Nolting modified his earlier insistence on the binding character of Kennedy's 1961 assurances to Diem, conceding now that Lodge should notify Diem that the United States wanted a new deal—including a veto over religious repression of Buddhists—as a condition of continued support. Rusk and Bundy insisted that Lodge be allowed to proceed to overthrow Diem. Cables were prepared in a meeting by "a smaller group."[23]

Rusk's cable to Lodge appeared to keep the option of allowing Diem to dismiss Nhu and save himself. But the text, which was cleared by Kennedy himself, shifted the ground subtly by recalling that Washington had already indicated to the Saigon Generals that after the Nhus were removed the fate of Diem would be in their own hands.[24]

In a separate (and unnumbered) cable, Kennedy personally assumed responsibility for proceeding with the coup:

> I have approved all the messages you are receiving from others today, and I emphasize that everything in these messages has my full support. . . . Until the very moment of the go signal for the operation by the Generals, I must reserve a contingent right to change course and reverse previous instructions. While fully aware of your assessment of the consequences of such a reversal, I know from experience that failure is more destructive than an appearance of indecision. I would, of course, accept full responsibility for any such change as I must bear also the full responsibility for this operation and its consequences. . . . When we go, we must go to win, but it will be better to change our minds than fail. And if our national interest should require a change of mind, we must not be afraid of it.[25]

Kennedy had placed his personal seal on the coup plans. Still smarting from his vacillation about the Bay of Pigs invasion, Kennedy with this cable took personal responsibility for the policy.

With the receipt of this cable from Kennedy, Lodge now held all the cards he needed to remove Diem. While the August 24 cable was sent in Kennedy's absence from the White House, a fact that would have allowed Kennedy himself to deny any personal responsibility for such a precipitate action, Lodge now held his old rival's personal approval.

The secret cable of August 24, now explicitly approved by Kennedy, was broadcast to the world (and presumably to any would-be coup leaders) via the *New York Times*, in Halberstam's August 30 front-page dispatch from Saigon:

> Highly informed diplomatic sources say Americans have decided that no government that includes Ngo Dinh Nhu and his wife can win the war against Communism and that the Nhus cannot be separated from the government.
>
> Therefore, these sources say, the United States is ready to initiate action that might lead to the overthrow of the government. . . . The most likely form of American action . . . will be a demand to President Ngo Dinh [Diem] to get rid of the Nhus immediately. The Americans do not believe that there is a chance this will happen. One high source said that the Americans were past the point of negotiating and that they had decided on action. . . .

Most observers here believe that Americans will give a signal to key elements of the military and say in essence that they want a new government. . . .

Americans see President Diem as . . . better-intentioned than the Nhus, but . . . he is no longer a serious political figure.

On August 31 Lodge would conclude — as McCone, Colby, and Nolting had been maintaining all along — that there were neither George Washingtons nor Benedict Arnolds among the Saigon generals. Lodge then turned in desperation to the colonels. This change of rank involved an indefinite delay in the change of government.[26]

The next morning Lodge's embassy added to its staff a resident "minister-counselor for Buddhist affairs," Tri Quang himself, who took up residence in the embassy until the successful overthrow of Diem two months later.[27] During this lengthy stay, an embassy official, Robert Miller, reported that Tri Quang unabashedly undertook to influence U.S. policy against the government of Diem. Despite their generous interpretation of Tri Quang's fundamentally pro-U.S. sentiments and malleability to U.S. influence, embassy officials reported that Tri Quang displayed remarkable indifference to the "facts" he reported to them. When he saw that his response to some question from U.S. officials did not sit well with them, he would easily reverse himself completely in twenty-four hours. The questions concerned his own views of the Buddhist use of violence for political purposes, as well as his authorship of a public letter denouncing Ambassador Nolting.[28] Among Tri Quang's other efforts to influence U.S. policy was his denigration of his primary Buddhist critic, Buu Hoi. Tri Quang informed the embassy staff that Buu Hoi was a lackey of Diem, whose financial support enabled Buu Hoi to support several mistresses. Tri Quang attributed this information to Buu Hoi's mother, a Buddhist nun.[29] Tri Quang's attack on Buu Hoi was designed to discredit a dangerous Buddhist critic, who would make his case against Tri Quang in Washington in early October.

Embassy officials did include in their generally supportive study of Tri Quang the undisputed fact that, as he admitted, he had previously been associated with the Viet Minh.[30]

6

....

THE PRESIDENTIAL SEAL

SEPTEMBER 1 TO OCTOBER 4

When Lodge cabled that the first coup initiative had collapsed, Kennedy's government breathed a sigh of relief and sought to regroup. While Lodge searched for coup-minded colonels, Rusk searched for a consensus in the administration. On August 30 Lodge had cabled to Rusk:

> 1. I agree that getting the Nhus out is the prime objective and that they are "the greater part of the problem in Vietnam, internally, internationally and for American public opinion."
>
> 2. This surely cannot be done by working through Diem. In fact Diem will oppose it. He wishes he had more Nhus, not less.
>
> 3. The best chance of doing it is by the Generals taking over the government lock, stock and barrel.
>
> 4. After this has been done, it can then be decided whether to put Diem back in again or go on without him. I am rather inclined to put him back, but I would not favor putting heavy pressure on the Generals if they don't want him. . . .
>
> 10. If the Generals' operation does get rolling, I would not want to stop it until they were in full control. They could then get rid of the Nhus and decide whether they wanted to keep Diem.
>
> 11. It is better for them and for us to throw out the Nhus than for us to get involved in it.
>
> 12. I am sure that the best way to handle this matter is by a truly Vietnamese movement even if it puts me rather in the position of pushing a piece of spaghetti.
>
> 13. I am contemplating no further talks with Diem at this time.[1]

In puzzling polyphony with the "top secret" cables between Lodge and Washington, the *New York Times* editors commented in their editorial "Vietnam's Complexities Grow," which appeared on August 31:

> The United States seems to hope an anti-Communist junta of military leaders will replace the Ngos. . . .
>
> From the standpoint of the free world and the internal progress of South Vietnam, the *best thing that could happen* would be a *military ousting of the Ngos* and the subsequent formation of a government of the most dedicated, capable anti-Communists available. Ideally, such a government should be composed of civilians, except for the military men who would head the defense and security organizations. *It should submit itself to the test of an election promptly.* [emphasis added]

The U.S. embassy's efforts to destabilize the Diem government were now so notorious that the French ambassador, Roger Lalouette, personally made a formal request that Lodge abandon his conspiracy with the coup plotters. Calling on his Asian experience and familiarity with the risks of colonial rule, he made a last effort to stay Lodge's hand. Dutifully, Lodge promptly relayed to Washington Lalouette's own words:

> "Diem has a steadfastness and determination which is rare in Asia and is valuable. In many ways he is the best Chief of State in Southeast Asia. His weakness is that he is not a political leader, cannot make speeches, cultivate the press, etc.
>
> "He is much better off with Nhu than without him. Nhu is efficient and intelligent. The war against the Viet Cong can be won with Diem administration in office.
>
> "The present situation is largely the work of the press, helped greatly by Vietnamese ineptness. In the days of French administration, suicides of Buddhists were very common and had no effect whatever on the population. They create much more excitement abroad than they do in Vietnam."
>
> When I left, he said: "Let me say two things — first, try to calm American opinion and, second, no coups."[2]

Within a week Lalouette was recalled to Paris. In a meeting with the foreign minister, Maurice Couve de Murville, Lalouette predicted the outcome of the crisis he had vainly sought to defuse: "Diem is finished."[3]

The same day, Rusk called in the French ambassador to Washington, Hervé Alphand, to discuss rumored French initiatives toward Vietnamese unification and the consequent neutralization of South Vietnam. The ambassador suggested that neutralization might now be inevitable, for there was a split between Ho Chi Minh and Mao Tse-tung [Mao Zedong]. Whereas Mao had once wanted continued military struggle in the South, he had now changed course and was seeking a political solution. Ho's stance was anti-Chinese and neutralist.[4]

At the end of a week's plotting against Diem, John Richardson cabled on August 31 a message of defeat: "This particular coup is finished." Lodge, several hours later, echoed this resignation, referring to an identical report from Harkins. He agreed that the coup cable (243) had been well advised but was now a dead letter. "A U.S. coup against this criminal government is, of course, out of the question."[5]

After receipt of these discouraging cables, and in the absence of Kennedy, who was back at Hyannisport for the Labor Day weekend (and his tenth wedding anniversary celebration), Dean Rusk convened a Saturday meeting in the department, having decided, against Bundy's advice, to invite Lyndon Johnson. Harriman remained at his estate in Middleburg, Virginia, for the weekend.

Chairing the session in the absence of the president, the secretary was assertive: "We will not run a coup in Saigon and we will not leave South Vietnam." McNamara, McCone, and Vice President Johnson agreed.[6] Rusk opened by turning the clock back to before Ball's August 24 cable. (Ball, too, was absent.) Rusk asked if anyone doubted the coup was finished. Hilsman tried, in the absence of Ball and Harriman, to keep the prospect of a coup alive by insisting that Diem had alienated mid-level Vietnamese bureaucrats and military officers. Asked by McNamara for evidence of such disaffection, Hilsman turned to Paul Kattenburg, who had personally talked to *three* disaffected officials and who volunteered that some U.S. reporters knew of still others.

Hilsman then switched to blaming Nhu for the recent French suggestions that Saigon seek unification with the North, which constituted "treason" by Nhu. Rusk countered humorously that Washington should be cautious about charges of treason since its own week-long efforts to drum up a coup in Saigon might also look like treason in some suspicious Vietnamese eyes.

McNamara urged the group to order Lodge once more to reopen communications with Diem. Rusk added: "We must start with the situation we are now facing. . . . We were making steady progress during the first six months of this year and what we should do is go down the middle of the track and hope to recover that."[7]

Of Secretary Rusk's two policy premises articulated in this meeting — "We will not run a coup in Saigon and we will not leave South Vietnam" — only one survived the two-month tug-of-war with Diem and Lodge in Saigon. That principle — "We will not leave South Vietnam" — had been forged in the crucible of World War II. Failure to assist Czechoslovakia in 1938 had opened the floodgates of aggression. Rusk would not be another Neville Chamberlain. As a Rhodes scholar in 1932–34, Rusk had witnessed the Oxford Union debates that repudiated the defensive resort to war. He felt that World War II could have been avoided if the British and French had stood by their pledge to defend Czechoslovakia from Hitler's rapacious grasp. Feeling, therefore, that World War II was "an unnecessary war, a great burden on the conscience of the West," Rusk had been taught by history the awful price of appeasement.[8]

Now, to his distress, he had found that, despite his own counsel in 1949, the United States was legally committed to the defense of remote nations in Southeast Asia. If the Southeast Asia Treaty Organization (SEATO) should choose to extend its mantle to Laos and Vietnam, the United States would have to agree. He could only pray, when the new administration had been warned about war in that theater by Eisenhower, that nothing would come of the rumblings in Laos. Yet if there really was Communist aggression in Southeast Asia, Rusk would be unable to dismiss cavalierly the analogy of Munich. For despite the utter incommensurability of Laos and Czechoslovakia in almost every relevant respect, the salient similarity was the indelible SEATO commitment made by the United States "absentmindedly," as Rusk later argued, "with virtually no discussion either in Congress or in the press."[9]

This fit of absentmindedness was a burden inherited by the new administration. Its own enlightened agenda had focused on the reform of NATO strategy, which nevertheless was inextricably linked, at least in the minds of Kennedy and his secretary of state, with Vietnam. For Rusk's resolve to remember Munich committed him to resist any significant change in the boundaries existing between East and West. Control of all of Vietnam by Ho Chi Minh would represent such an alteration. Despite the remoteness, the global insignificance, and the unfamiliarity of Southeast Asia to most Americans, Vietnam risked evoking a U.S. investment because of the current intractability of war in Europe.[10]

Rusk's skepticism of the coup strategy won Johnson's vigorous second: "We must . . . stop playing cops and robbers." Conceding that it was hard to deal with Diem, Johnson compared this difficulty to his Capitol Hill battles with Congressman Otto Passman: "We never ran a coup on Passman."[11]

Late that evening Rusk's instructions went out to Lodge: "Start talking to Diem." He then urged Lodge to inform Diem in advance that Kennedy would express concerns about Diem publicly on television on Labor Day.[12] The next day, Sunday, September 1, Bundy telegraphed to Kennedy at Hyannisport some suggested wording for his planned television interview with Walter Cronkite on Labor Day:

> 1. We agree with the Government of South Vietnam on many central issues. . . .
>
> 2. Yet now there are serious differences . . . over certain acts of arbitrary power, some of them strongly repressive, which that government has allowed. . . . As a democratic people, we cannot approve of this kind of repression in a situation in which we are closely engaged and where our resources provide much of the government's strength.[13]

It was auspicious for CBS's inaugural half-hour news broadcast (doubling the time devoted to the evening news) that Kennedy had accepted Cronkite's invitation for an interview on Labor Day. Responding to Cronkite's question about prospects for victory in Vietnam, Kennedy opened with an expression of admiration for Diem's early struggle against daunting odds to establish some semblance of security and order as a foundation for resistance against the Communist assault. Then, responding to an inquiry about his own intentions in Southeast Asia, Kennedy insisted that it was "their war, to win or lose," observing that the United States favored "whatever helps the war effort."[14] The interview continued:

Cronkite: Do you think this government [Diem's] has time to regain the support of the people?

Kennedy: I do. With changes of policy and perhaps of personnel, I
    think it can win. If it doesn't make those changes, I would think
    that the chances of winning it would not be very good.[15]

Ten days into the coup planning, this ultimatum further bolstered the
spirits of those generals still hedging their bets.[16]

In Saigon, on the same day as Kennedy's interview, Mieczyslaw Maneli, the Polish ICC delegate, kept his appointment with Nhu at Gia
Long Palace. During the spring Maneli had carried to Foreign Minister
Pham Van Dong in Hanoi the assurance that Diem, anxious by that time
to counter the increasing pressures on him by Kennedy, was now open
to overtures from North Vietnam. The North Vietnamese economy was
in ruins. Hanoi was struggling against the ravages of a drought that drew
saltwater into the riverbeds along the coast and decimated the rice crop.
Ho Chi Minh now hoped for relief by trading coal to the South for rice
during the crisis. But Nhu deflected Maneli's inquiries about the present
state of such negotiations. Later in the day, when Nhu met Lodge, he
was more forthcoming about his contacts with the Viet Cong.[17]

The next day Harriman agreed with Kennedy that Lodge should negotiate directly with Diem.[18] Forwarding the president's orders that
evening to Lodge, Rusk insisted that Lodge move immediately to negotiate with Diem.[19] Lodge wasted no time informing Rusk that he had no
such intentions.[20] On September 5 Lodge cabled his reasons: Diem was
beyond the pale of rational political discourse. "As to 'political support
at home and abroad' in your paragraph 4, I do not believe the GVN really understands this at all. They are essentially a medieval, Oriental despotism of the classic family type, who understand few, if any, of the arts
of popular government. They cannot talk to the people; they cannot cul-
tivate the press; they cannot delegate authority or inspire trust; they cannot comprehend the idea of government as the servant of the people."[21]
Kennedy already knew the Boston legend that the Cabots speak only to
the Lodges, and the Lodges speak only to God. Now he was painfully
learning the Saigon corollary that the Cabot Lodges never speak to the
Ngos, much less to the Nhus.

September 5 was a busy day for Roger Hilsman, who had become
preoccupied by reports of open negotiations between Nhu and representatives of Ho Chi Minh. Nhu had bluntly informed Lodge three days
earlier that he was in contact with Maneli, whose ties to Hanoi were no

secret. Hilsman sought the views of some principal U.S. ambassadors about the possible significance of such initiatives.[22] On the same day he cabled Vice President Johnson and George Ball, who were traveling in Sweden and Portugal respectively.[23]

Undeterred by Lodge's adamant silence, the White House review session on September 6 outlined the purpose of Lodge's next session with Diem, which "should not be a showdown."[24] That evening Rusk once more cabled Lodge: "You should initiate dialogue with Diem soonest."[25] Lodge yielded and met Diem on September 9. At three junctures in their talk Lodge demanded a "change of personnel and a change of policies," specifically requiring that Ngo Dinh Nhu leave Vietnam for three months until after the U.S. Congress passed the bill of appropriations for Vietnam. Lodge attributed Diem's lack of receptivity to the idea of dismissing his brother to his "medieval view of life," which "makes it hard to get a new idea across to him."[26]

With the collapse of the coup strategy in Saigon, Washington shifted to a more subtle and symbolic policy. On September 10 twenty officials gathered to receive the hurried reports from the seventy-two-hour field trip by General Victor ("Brute") Krulak, a Diem supporter, and Joseph Mendenhall, a Foreign Service officer who bitterly opposed the regime. They offered mutually contradictory interpretations of the local situation. Kennedy provided the only light moment of the meeting when he quipped, "You two did visit the same country, didn't you?"[27]

More decisive than these polar presentations were the views of Saigon embassy personnel hostile to Diem who had returned on the Mendenhall-Krulak flight. During the flight Krulak had discovered that one of the two, John Mecklin, the United States Information Agency (USIA) director in Saigon, had smuggled onto the plane some television footage of Diem's repressive acts, censored by the South Vietnamese government. Krulak, in charge of the military plane transporting the group, ordered Mecklin to off-load the film in Alaska and encouraged him to accompany the film during its Alaska sojourn.[28] Mecklin left the film behind. The other member of the country team, Rufus Phillips, was an eight-year veteran of the AID program in Vietnam and was on close terms with most of the Saigon officials.[29] His views bore the authority of experience dwarfing that of everyone else at the meeting with Kennedy.

He was convinced that the U.S. effort was doomed if Nhu remained in office, which he would do unless Kennedy could manage to demonstrate his own independence.

"How?" Kennedy asked. Phillips proposed a symbolic gesture, perhaps inspired by his years of immersion in Vietnamese culture. "Cut all aid to Colonel [Le Quang] Tung." (Tung had conducted the August 20–21 pagoda raids on orders from Nhu.) The challenge to Nhu through rejection of Tung's forces would steel possible rebels to attack Nhu.[30]

Kennedy then listened to the views of Mecklin, who urged him to send in U.S. troops to remove Diem and Nhu. Kennedy, after asking what the U.S. troops would do then, showed increasing interest in Phillips's relatively low-risk proposal of a merely symbolic intervention.[31] This symbol — cutting off financial support for Tung — became the U.S. government's answer to bonze-burning. Taking his cue from Kennedy, McGeorge Bundy then asked Hilsman to draft a set of policy options that would place the Phillips proposals in the middle of the spectrum of potential effectiveness and risk.[32] Hilsman sent to the White House two draft cables addressed to Lodge, one of which would authorize him, without notifying Diem, to cut off funds to Colonel Tung's forces.

The next day Rusk opened a meeting with a repetition of his earlier observation that "Lodge hasn't gotten through to Diem. We cannot assume that Diem will not move in our direction." Secretary of the Treasury Douglas Dillon agreed that an effort to "get in real touch with Diem" was imperative. McCone concurred, pointing to Lodge's inexperience in Vietnam; he had been there for a total of three weeks. Kennedy asked for the draft letter to Diem that he had requested. Bundy said it had not been prepared. Closing the meeting, the president repeated the request for Lodge to sound out Diem on U.S. concerns.[33] The following day, September 12, Rusk cabled these instructions, requiring frequent talks with Diem and reassuring Diem of continued support by Kennedy, which might be needed to counteract evidence of recent U.S. coup efforts.[34]

Lodge squandered no time considering these orders. By return cable, he declined once more to see Diem:

Do not see advantage of frequent conversations with Diem if I have nothing new to bring up. Believe mere repetition of points already made would look weak. Visiting Diem is an extremely time-consuming procedure, and it seems to me there are many better ways in which I can use my waking hours. One is by going ahead with my diplomatic calls on the members of the Cabinet who are numerous and who give me interesting information and, of course, another is to spend some time thinking. Not enough hours in the day to do everything I want to do.[35]

The mystery of Lodge's intransigent resistance to Kennedy's explicit orders was resolved only later, when Lodge voiced his triumph at having finally forced Diem to seek an interview looking toward reconciliation and accommodation with American interests. By mid-September Lodge's cables to Rusk had become more translucent. His diplomatic strategy was to demand that Diem kowtow before the American ambassador. Then they could get on with the war. On September 16 Lodge cabled: "But it seems to me a healthy thing for people to feel that they must see the personal representative of the President of the US to get some of the largesse which they hope to get out of the US Government. If they got into the habit of coming to me with requests for favors, it ought to be possible, in the not too distant future, to get them to do at least a few of the things we want them to do."[36]

Suddenly Kennedy's frustration with his ambassador's defiance of orders to negotiate immediately with Diem boiled over in a decision to send a top-level delegation of aides to Saigon. The mission, to be headed by McNamara and Taylor, was announced to Lodge, who protested this presidential interruption of his strategy of seeking obeisance from Diem in return for largesse. On September 18 he urgently cabled Rusk, seeking to cancel the McNamara mission: "I have been observing a policy of silence which we have reason to believe is causing a certain amount of apprehension and may just be getting the family into the mood to make a few concessions. The effect of this will obviously be lost if we make such a dramatic demonstration as that of having the Secretary of Defense and General Taylor come out here."[37]

The goal of Vietnamese concessions to Washington was in sight, visible now in the desperate face of Nhu, who seemed to Lodge to be "a lost soul, haunted and pitiable. . . . The Furies are after him."[38] (Nhu knew enough to realize that the source of the present threat was no mere ancient Western myth but Kennedy's ambassador.) Breaking Lodge's month-long silence now would make the United States look weak in Asian eyes. Concessions could only be extracted by silence and disapproval.

Harriman, like Lodge, had been appalled at the prospect of a cabinet-level visit to Saigon, which Harriman described to Michael Forrestal as "a disaster." He lamented that Kennedy was sending McNamara and Taylor, who were "opposed to our policy" of removing Diem.[39] Harriman next telephoned McGeorge Bundy to have U. Alexis Johnson removed from the group selected for the visit because he had been "a bit brainwashed by Nolting." In Johnson's place, Harriman persuaded Bundy to send Forrestal himself.[40] (The only State Department representative on this delicate mission now would be William Sullivan, who had been selected by Harriman more than a year earlier as his own special assistant and interpreter.)

Once Forrestal was appointed to replace Alex Johnson, Hilsman gave him a private letter to deliver personally to Lodge, in which Hilsman assured Lodge that the bureaucracy was rapidly aligning itself with the Lodge-Harriman agenda of ousting Diem: "[A] determined group here will back you all the way." Since Diem will not yield to persuasion, "what we must work for is a change in government" in Saigon. And since generals will act only in response to pressure from below, that is, from the colonels, the United States must signal these colonels "by [budgetary] cuts directed at what we disapprove." Such cuts would serve to stiffen the spines of the colonels who would have to spearhead any coup.[41] Later, on October 5, Kennedy ordered precisely such a cutoff of funds for Tung, on the ostensible grounds that Tung's troops were not subject to the general staff and thus useless to the war effort. Since Tung answered only to Nhu, this change in U.S. policy would symbolize the direction of American planning.[42]

Phillips had captured Kennedy's attention with his symbolic strategy to encourage a rebellion against Nhu, which might spare Diem and yet save face for Kennedy. It had been especially attractive when presented alongside Mecklin's alternative of a U.S. invasion. The scheme had only one drawback: it was based on the illusion that Diem could be separated from Nhu. To his credit, Lodge immediately derided the suggestion for its unreality. The text of Lodge's reply captures the gap between Kennedy's thinking and the political context of developments in Saigon:

2. Language in paragraphs 17 and 19-h on "restriction on role of Nhus" seems unrealistic for these reasons: . . . .

b. In an interview with the Italian journalist Gambino . . . Nhu says in effect that he can and would like to get along without the Americans. He only wants some helicopter units and some money. But he definitely does not want American military personnel who, he says, are absolutely incapable of fighting a guerrilla war. . . . He wants Viet Nam to be treated as U.S. treats Yugoslavia — giving them money but not seeking to influence their system of government. . . . The war cannot be won with the Americans because they are an obstacle to the revolutionary transformation of society which is the prerequisite of victory. Then come these words. "If the Americans were to interrupt their help, it may not be a bad thing after all."[43]

Lodge continued:

3. The above leads me to the conclusion that we cannot remove the Nhus by non-violent means against their will.

4. I also conclude that we cannot assume that Diem and Nhus have the same aims as we. Clearly Nhu wants our help without our presence which, in his view, we use as an excuse for interfering in their internal system of government. Get us out, he argues, and he can be as free to do as he wants as Tito is now. And Nhu is a strong influence on Diem.

5. . . . . [T]he only thing which the US really wants — the removal of or restriction on the Nhus — is out of the question.[44]

There were gaps of communication in Washington as well, between Diem's defenders and those who had decided to "drop Diem." Fritz Nolting and Averell Harriman, for example, were symbols of this struggle. Nolting one day was awaiting a staff car at the State Department to take him to the White House, to participate (at the request of President Kennedy) in a National Security Council meeting. As Averell Harriman and Dean Rusk were about to enter the secretary's limousine, Harriman barked: "What are you doing here, Nolting?" Nolting, responding that the president had personally requested his presence at the meeting, inquired if he might ride along with them in order to save the trouble of a second car for the same destination. Harriman agreed, directing

Nolting to sit up front with the chauffeur. Harriman then rolled up the window separating the two compartments of the car.[45]

In the back seat rode Harriman and Rusk, whose association symbolized the novel profile of power in America. Harriman, whose wealth was the reward for his father's effort to span the sparsely settled continent with its first railroad, was for the moment one step removed from the seat of power that had been eluding him: secretary of state.[46] At his side was the present secretary, a classic American success story. The son of an impoverished family in Georgia, Rusk had risen through the ranks of public service to one of America's highest nonelective offices. His hold on that position was limited only by his inherited poverty: Rusk had agreed to Kennedy's offer of the position on the condition that he would serve for only the first term of Kennedy's presidency. Rusk's reason for this self-imposed limit was his determination to leave government after four years in order to earn a large enough salary in the private sector to permit him to meet the financial burdens of his children's college educations.[47] After his reelection, Kennedy would then be appointing a new secretary of state, perhaps Harriman himself, as now seemed increasingly likely.

Vietnam, Ambassador Lodge liked to repeat, was a backward and medieval society. Vietnamese still employed soothsayers, for example, to offer advice on omens or auspices that might foretell the destiny fate had marked out for individuals and policies. If such a seer had been able to watch the arrival of Rusk's car at the White House, with the secretary and undersecretary chatting happily in the back and the cashiered ambassador riding shotgun in the front, the diviner would have been able to warn Diem infallibly that his fate was sealed. In the isolated front seat sat Diem's defender. Behind him were the two officials now steering Vietnam policy. Both, for complementary reasons of domestic politics and international commitments, were determined to reform, or remove, the government in Saigon before time ran out on them. This synergism of expediency and moral passion was a potent mix.

McNamara's visit to Vietnam from September 23 to October 1 was an eye-opener. The end of the regime—through a coup or assassination—was in sight, but the situation was not very reassuring: the chances of an improvement resulting from a change of regime was no better than fifty-fifty and thus fraught with unknown risks. Moreover, it seemed to be only a matter of time until Nhu would agree to the formation of a federation with Ho, as Nhu had recently warned Joseph Alsop, a *Washington Post* columnist.[48] In the event of such North-South negotiations, the regime might be overthrown by the South Vietnamese Army. If the United States did not publicly support Diem, McNamara was told, he would be overthrown in a month, with no reasonable hope for a better regime following the coup. But if the United States moved to overthrow Diem itself, the successor regime would be tarred as a puppet government. Any hope that democracy would emerge in the wake of a coup was an illusion.[49]

John Richardson, still the chief of station in Saigon despite Lodge's effort on September 13 to remove him, gave McNamara an equally bleak interpretation of the options available to the United States.[50] Diem was still widely respected, but even his trusted ally Nguyen Dinh Thuan, the secretary of the presidency, had reported to Diem an atmosphere of suspicion and fear, which he warned might trigger a coup. After a coup, Thuan had told Richardson, there would be no one to take Diem's place who would enjoy the authority to rule.[51]

In the midst of this civil uproar being reported to McNamara, the Diem government on September 27 presided over an election for the National Assembly in which there was a massive voter turnout (even if not the 92 percent claimed by the Diem government).[52] The U.S. embassy report on the election conceded that this turnout represented an impressive achievement of control and bureaucratic organization, coupled with a surprising ability to prevent Viet Cong disruption of the proceedings.

In Washington on September 28, George Ball, acting secretary of state in the absence of Secretary Rusk, who was in New York for the General Assembly of the United Nations, cabled Lodge. Recommending that Lodge plan for eventualities that might include a coup, Ball urged a quick analysis of personalities among the abundance of talented potential leaders who might succeed Diem. Ball suggested that Vice President Nguyen Ngoc Tho would be a logical choice for chief of state.[53]

Only two days later, Tho himself punctured this balloon by dismissing the possibility of U.S. support of a coup as "idiotic," even though there was no available remedy for Vietnam's ills with Diem in power.[54]

Finally, it was General ("Big Minh") Duong Van Minh who completed the circle of despair in Saigon. Meeting with General Taylor on October 1, Minh lamented the sorry state of his country but was unable to identify any rival leader who would be more successful as a ruler than Diem. Taylor concluded helplessly that "General Minh sees his country in chains with no way to shake them off." [55]

But Lodge's instinctive optimism was invincible in urging, during the McNamara-Taylor visit, more aggressive American broadcasts in Vietnamese extolling the Anglo-Saxon tradition of democracy. Lodge anticipated an acceleration of protests against Diem's autocracy to arise naturally among the large Voice of America audience. "Would it not be a splendid thing for our world-wide reputation for us to get hard things done in Viet Nam through the power of American ideals?" [56]

Lodge's own presentation to the visiting team was a remarkable demonstration of neocolonialism. "The current government is probably beginning its terminal phase. . . . Our interest in the land and our interest in the people is such that it transcends the question of who happens to be in control of the government at any particular time." [57]

From their intensive series of conversations with leading personalities in Saigon, including the eventual coup leader General Big Minh and the civilian figurehead of Minh's ephemeral government, Vice President Tho, McNamara and Taylor were fully aware of the consensus among Diem's enemies (as well as the conviction of his principal assistant, Thuan) that there were no viable options for the Americans in Vietnam. Only three options were available, it seemed. First, the United States could continue to support Diem, whose desperate government had created an environment of fear and hostility in Saigon. If Kennedy continued to support Diem, Diem's regime might survive the present crisis, although such support had become morally and politically offensive to many influential Americans, both in government and in the press. Second, the United States could withdraw support from Diem with a new policy of official silence. If Kennedy chose this option, an indigenous coup would ensue within a month. Finally, the U.S. government could immerse itself in promoting a coup. Kennedy now knew that Vice President Tho, mentioned as a possible successor to Diem, had branded this an "idiotic policy."

While this ominous prognosis might have been expected to suggest to McNamara and Taylor the urgency of a rapid withdrawal from Vietnam,

they surprisingly reached a consensus on the wisdom of yet a fourth op-
tion, which had been the preference of Roger Hilsman since at least
September 23, when he wrote to Lodge endorsing the cutoff of funds to
Colonel Tung as a signal of Kennedy's bona fides in support of a coup.[58]

The subversive purpose of this cutoff of funds to Colonel Tung was
put bluntly in a memo from William Sullivan. Writing the day after returning to Washington, Sullivan summarized his findings on the trip
and the dynamics of the new Kennedy démarche in Vietnam. His memo
to Roger Hilsman is the most authoritative text yet declassified that indicates the impact on Washington's thinking of Diem's reported negotiations with Ho Chi Minh. Sullivan in this memorandum gives equal
weight to Diem's unwavering refusal to undertake political reform and
his more recent initiative to abandon the United States in favor of Ho
Chi Minh.

> The ultimate objectives of the United States in Viet Nam do not
> coincide with Diem-Nhu objectives. We wish to defeat Viet Cong
> subversion so that South Viet Nam may develop as a free state. They
> wish to defeat Viet Cong subversion so that Viet Nam can develop as
> a totalitarian state. . . .
>
> The fact is that Nhu is exploiting two principal elements of power
> to produce his totalitarian state. The first is the Vietnamese Estab-
> lishment . . . the second is the military power of the United States.
>
> He will eject the second [U.S. military power] by a deal with North
> Vietnam when he feels he has adequate means to continue in power
> without its assistance.
>
> I conclude therefore that it is in our interest to make common
> cause with them [the discontented Saigon establishment] to over-
> throw the current regime.[59]

The fourth option, cutting off financial support for the forces of
Colonel Tung as a signal to potential coup leaders, may have been the
worst of all the available options. Abandoning Diem by a formal renun-
ciation of the alliance would have caused an uproar in Congress, but
nothing like the eventual consequences to which the coup predictably
led. Failing to support Diem visibly would likely have generated a local
coup, for which the United States could not have been blamed (or, perhaps even worse, blamed itself). Directly organizing a coup would at
least have given Kennedy direct control over the coup leaders and the

subsequent formation of a successor government. The option Kennedy chose, on the basis of McNamara and Taylor's consensus report, elicited a coup that inevitably escaped Kennedy's control and ushered in a paralytic government for which the United States nevertheless felt responsible.

Near the close of their tour of Vietnam, McNamara and Taylor had met Diem, who was calm and—according to Taylor—undaunted by the dangers that surrounded him. In fact, his calm and detached air reflected a new—if hazardous—resolve of Diem to spring a trap on Kennedy. First, he signaled his awareness of the coup planning, now in its fifth week.[60] On instructions of Kennedy, McNamara and Taylor took no notice of Diem's objections to being ousted from government. Instead, they urged him to reform while he still had time. Diem, however, was preoccupied with Ho Chi Minh's offer of alliance and was now ready to dismiss the American meddlers.

Before leaving Saigon, Taylor had tipped his hand to President Diem himself in a letter on October 1.

> It was not until the recent political disturbances beginning in May and continuing through August and beyond that I personally had any doubt as to the ultimate success of our campaign against the Viet Cong.
>
> Now, as Secretary McNamara has told you, a serious doubt hangs over our hopes for the future. Can we win together in the face of the reaction to the measures taken by your Government against the Buddhists and the students? As a military man I would say that we can win providing there are no further political setbacks.[61]

In response to the symbolic self-immolation of bonzes in Saigon, Washington had now chosen its own symbol of protest: abandoning Colonel Tung. But there was still a difference of opinion about how to present these stern measures to the American public. Rusk and Ball wished to make the actions a moral protest against Diem and Nhu's dictatorship, while Kennedy preferred to stress the pragmatic need for reform to improve the war effort.[62]

Rusk missed the crucial White House meetings of October 3–4 because of the U.N. General Assembly session and associated bilateral meetings. Among the important conferences was a meeting with Diem's representative, Buu Hoi. A scientist of world renown, a prominent Buddhist, and an early political rival of Diem, Buu Hoi had intermittently represented South Vietnam on diplomatic missions. He was now in the midst of his most momentous one: serving as Diem's delegate to the U.N. General Assembly, which was about to take up the charge of religious repression of Buddhism in Vietnam. He had brought letters from two of the most authoritative religious leaders condemning Tri Quang's activist sect, which was perverting the Buddhist movements by utilizing it for purely political purposes. In a Washington meeting with Harriman and Hilsman, Buu Hoi's presentation had been greeted with Harriman's gesture of removing his hearing aid and closing his eyes.[63] (It was a nervous gesture he often displayed in the presence of Asians.) Hilsman had listened longer, but with equal openness. Hilsman later notified Rusk that Buu would claim that the Buddhist crisis was over and would further claim that Nhu was indispensable to the war effort.

Speaking to Rusk himself, Buu said that Nhu's judgment was better than that of Diem, who often made serious miscalculations, such as preventing the flying of Buddhist flags in Hue. Diem ought to be pressed to hand over more power to Thuan and to appoint Nhu to handle on his own the strategic hamlet program, which undertook the relocation of groups of the rural population, in order to provide government services more efficiently and to ensure security from assault.[64] But Washington felt no need of Buddhist enlightenment on the impasse between Diem and the Buddhists.

WHO WILL KOWTOW?

OCTOBER 5 TO OCTOBER 28

On October 5 both Dean Rusk and McGeorge Bundy cabled Lodge, reporting the policies adopted that week. Rusk's cable was unambiguous:

> Actions are designed to indicate to Diem Government our displeasure at its political policies and activities and to create significant uncertainty in that government *and in key Vietnamese groups* as to future intentions of United States. . . .
>
> 12. If, as we hope, Diem seeks clarification of U.S. policies and actions, you should present an exposition of how our actions are related to our fundamental objective of victory. . . . Heart of problem is form of government that has been evolving in Viet-Nam. Diem's regime has trappings of democracy, but in reality it has been evolving into authoritarian government maintained by police terrorist methods. . . .
>
> 19.h *Changes in Personnel* . . . can only be achieved by some feasible reduction in influence of Nhus, who are — justifiably or not — a symbol of authoritarianism. Future role of Nhus in government is therefore of paramount importance.[1]

In his separate cable, Bundy insisted that Washington was not seeking to stimulate a coup, but he urged close (and deniable) attention to this possible eventuality.[2]

Also on October 5, John Richardson was forced to abandon his crucial post as chief of station in Saigon. Lodge had written on September 13 to Rusk requesting Richardson's transfer because Vietnamese junior officers, possible key figures in a coup, suspected the station chief of betraying their plans to Diem and Nhu.[3] When CIA director John McCone shrewdly refused to make the requested transfer, Lodge had cabled Rusk on September 24: "It is really a pity. Had my request been granted, I believe the coup might have been pulled off."[4] Lodge yielded for the moment, but finally David Halberstam effected the transfer by reporting in the *New York Times* on October 4 that Lodge wanted Richardson replaced.[5] The strategy worked because of a well-known CIA policy to remove agents whose identity has been uncovered.[6] When Richardson left Saigon on October 5, the last obstacle on the American side to the execution of a coup had been cleared.[7]

On Tuesday, October 8, after a weekend break to recover from their grueling travel and negotiations on the choice of policies to be executed in Saigon, Robert McNamara and Maxwell Taylor met in another hastily scheduled executive session of Fulbright's U.S. Senate Foreign Relations Committee. As Nolting had done in the same room in July, McNamara briefed the members with unflinching candor about the fragility of the Saigon government, on which the United States had already wagered such enormous stakes. Once more, Senator Mansfield, a member of the committee, abstained from the long exchange of views.

McNamara, conceding the inscrutability and consequent unpredictability of Vietnamese behavior, rallied to the defense of Kennedy's partnership with Diem. In response to Senator Wayne Morse's doubts about association with a tyrannical regime, the secretary sought to explain the historical situation in which Diem found himself:

I do draw attention to the fact that for 10 years that government [of Diem] has held a country together when . . . it has been under intense attack from the Communists, adjacent to it on all sides. . . . [South Vietnam] is a country made up of political, social and economic institutions out of the feudal ages, and the problem . . . the Diem government or any other government [faces], is how to transition that country from a set of feudal institutions to a set of 20th Century institutions in literally a matter of months. . . .

Now, I don't wish to overemphasize this or lead you to feel there is a sophisticated form of democracy in the countryside. There isn't. But there is at least the beginning of the elements of democracy, something they have never had before.

Now, these are accomplishments. They should be offset against the brutal repression that that government has applied during the period May to August, and as a matter of fact, I personally believe had been applying theretofore but doing it in a somewhat more sophisticated fashion, at least to the point of keeping it out of the newspapers.[8]

Conceding to the committee that the Buddhist crisis had been a catastrophic setback to the U.S. program to support Diem, General Maxwell Taylor then argued that the alienation of many senior Vietnamese military officials from the Ngo brothers was almost inevitable in the precarious situation of civil war in a nation that was surrounded by hostile neighbors. "We need a dictator in time of war and we have one." Taylor compared Diem's repressive measures to Lincoln's controversial abrogations of constitutional rights during America's civil war.[9]

Either the exasperated concession from Taylor that the United States was supporting a dictator or his incendiary evocation of Lincoln's least admirable war policies goaded Senator Albert Gore Sr., a Democrat from Tennessee, to a level of ferocity rare in the records of the committee's deliberations. "How many of these coolies down in the rice paddies have made an ideological commitment to Communism?" After a baffling exchange, in which Gore asked McNamara how many of the Viet Cong were under the command of Ngo Dinh Nhu, Gore admitted that he was no expert on Vietnam but still felt that there were no natural resources there "except ignorant population and rice."[10] (Gore had made visits to Vietnam as a member of the committee.) Gore then lamented that Kennedy had not taken advantage of the Buddhist crisis as a perfect excuse to bail out.

In a long exchange with Senator Frank Church, McNamara demonstrated stunning intellectual mastery of the fragile rationale for the sanctions that he and Taylor had successfully recommended to Kennedy the previous Friday.

> *Senator Church:* Do you think that we, as a government, . . . can and should attempt to exert influence and direction on this government to avoid further deterioration in the political situation?
>
> *Secretary McNamara:* I do, and I believe we are.
>
> *Senator Church:* Isn't it within our capacity in view of the fact that the government totally depends upon the aid that we supply it, isn't it within our capacity to exert definite pressures?
>
> *Secretary McNamara:* Yes, it is within our capacity to exert pressures, but it's not within our capacity to assure action in accordance with

our recommendations. This is an independent government and I think it is quite inappropriate for us to think of it as a colony or to expect it to act as a colony.[11]

The McNamara-Taylor session represented the acme of the U.S. debate about relations with the Diem government. No one in the administration ever equaled this incisive analysis of the drama then under way.

The meeting of the committee with Secretary Rusk the following day held equally high promise. Rusk had just met with Buu Hoi, Diem's ambassador to the U.N. for the Special Session planned on the widely condemned policies of religious repression, and with Andrei Gromyko, the Soviet minister of foreign affairs, to whom Rusk had presented a bold new Vietnam proposal on September 28. In his on-the-record comments, Rusk said only that the reduction of aid to South Vietnam was designed to put Diem in the position of a supplicant ("demandeur") for Lodge's generosity, which would be tied to internal reforms. Rusk, like McNamara and Taylor, reached with the senators a level of candor not recorded in the White House sessions.[12]

In the off-the-record portion of the session, Rusk announced the secret initiative Kennedy had made to Khrushchev, presented by Rusk to Gromyko on September 28, to arrange a joint U.S.–North Vietnamese withdrawal from South Vietnam. Gromyko had replied, as expected, "nyet." The committee members who had showed up by the time the secretary went off the record now knew that Kennedy had explored all the possibilities for maneuver except two: withdrawing from Vietnam or forcing Diem to "reform," that is, to conform to U.S. expectations. Neither option seemed promising.[13]

That evening, October 9, at 6:00 P.M., Kennedy held one of his frequent and entertaining news conferences at the State Department. The president's friend, *Time* White House correspondent Hugh Sidey, wrote later that Kennedy's conferences were considered by many "the best matinee in town."[14] Just four days after authorizing Lodge to cut off funds for Colonel Tung's forces (the signal previously demanded by the coup plotters), Kennedy was asked, apropos of recent coups in Latin America, his own attitude toward military coups. In his best matinee style, Kennedy glibly answered the theoretical question about U.S. coup policy, fortuitously prompted by pressing issues far from Saigon.

Q: Could you say, sir, how our policy is progressing in Viet-Nam in meeting what you have established as desirable last month, a "change of personnel and a change of policy" that would help the government there better get on with the war?

The President: I don't think that there have been significant changes of the kind that —

Q: For better or worse?

The President: I say I don't think there have been changes in the situation in the last month. I think we are still dealing with the same problems we were dealing with a month ago.[15]

The next question, concerning the very recent military coups in Honduras and the Dominican Republic, was uncomfortably close to the mark of the last week's coup-signaling to Saigon:

Q: Mr. President, was Assistant Secretary [for Latin America] Edwin Martin's statement [on U.S. response to military coups] cleared with you . . . ?

The President: No, I was informed generally of what Mr. Martin was saying. . . . In the first place, our policy is not reversed. If attention could be drawn to Secretary Rusk's statement of Friday evening in regard to the coups in the Dominican Republic and Honduras, we made it very clear that we are opposed to an interruption of the constitutional system by a military coup.[16]

The following morning, October 10, it was John McCone's turn to face Senator Fulbright's committee. The committee's questioning concentrated on the charges that Ngo Dinh Nhu was a totalitarian ruler, using police-state methods. McCone turned to William Colby, one of the most knowledgeable men in Washington regarding the regime. Colby, who remained supportive of Diem to the end, nevertheless gave an unvarnished and wholly disconcerting account of the history, current situation, and behavior of the Diem regime:

The country itself was divided [in 1954] into a series of warlord areas. . . . He [Diem] spent quite a few years acquiring authority over his country and putting this into one nation and in the course of this he crushed each one of these opposition elements in turn.

This, I believe, explains his concept of the only way to hold this country in one piece would be by the strong hand at the top. . . . There would be elections, there would be judicial systems, there would be police services and all of these would have a facade which would meet our western concepts of democracy. But underneath it, it would be clear that the actual control, namely, the actual authority came from the top. The election would be more in our terms a plebiscite. It wouldn't be an election. The police would be able to arrest people without trial, without notice, and they could descend and pick them up and hold them for an indefinite period. There was a certain degree of police brutality. The arrest of prisoners and the interrogation of prisoners would be handled by methods that we would not approve of.[17]

Despite their familiarity with the seamy side of Saigon power struggles, both McCone and Colby insisted that Diem remained the sole promising candidate to lead Vietnam through this dirty war. For nobody had yet identified a viable alternative leader around whom the country could unite.[18]

On October 5 Kennedy had agreed to withhold the $250,000 monthly CIA subsidy to the security forces of Colonel Le Quang Tung, who had been in charge of the August 20–21 crackdown on the pagodas. This decision to suspend funds had been taken in response to a demand by potential coup leaders for an earnest of American resolve to remove Diem. Two weeks later there was still no sign of a coup in the making. Then on October 22 the *New York Times* spelled out on its front page the specific significance of the suspension of funds. Halberstam reported from Saigon:

> Col. Le Quang Tung's troops are seen here as being used primarily as the political-military force of Ngo Dinh Nhu. . . . Today's action [the suspension of payments] was believed to be a direct move against Ngo Dinh Nhu. . . .
>
> This cutback in aid appeared to be chosen as a way to get at Ngo Dinh Nhu and to show United States displeasure over the pagoda raids. . . .
>
> The United States is extremely unhappy with the role of Ngo Dinh Nhu . . . [and] has suggested to President Ngo Dinh Diem that the war effort might be improved if Ngo Dinh Nhu left the government.

On October 25 the South Vietnamese State Information Service denied rumors circulating in Saigon concerning secret negotiations between the government and Ho Chi Minh.[19]

In Saigon the standoff continued. Neither Diem nor Lodge would kowtow. Finally, Diem set a date for the showdown, to be held at his summer retreat at Da Lat: October 27. On learning of Diem's belated invitation, George Ball immediately congratulated Lodge. "He has finally decided to come to you. . . . This meeting looks like one of the best chances we have had."[20] A month before, Lodge had expressed hopes for just such an opening to present his demands: "I will, of course, go— which will be *the first time I will have been asked to do him a favor.* . . . I think that we should press on and that my job will be to . . . advise them [Diem and Nhu], and when expedient, *to do favors for them.*"[21] It had been a taxing month, but now Lodge's strategy of silence seemed vindicated. The meeting would turn out to be a superficially cordial one. But reconciliation was not on the agenda.

Before departing for "the summit," Lodge had cabled Bundy on October 25:

> We should not thwart a coup for two reasons. First, it seems at least an even bet that the next government would not bungle and stumble as much as the present one has. Secondly, it is extremely unwise in the long range for us to pour cold water on attempts at a coup. . . . We should remember that this is the only way in which the people in Vietnam can possibly get a change of government. *Whenever we thwart attempts at a coup,* as we have done in the past, we are incurring very long lasting resentments, we are assuming an undue responsibility for keeping the incumbents in office, *and in general are setting ourselves in judgment over the affairs of Vietnam.*[22]

Lodge then alerted Bundy to the down side of a coup: "Certainly a succession of fights for control of the government of Vietnam would interfere with the war effort." But Lodge added some cautions against undue optimism in Kennedy's ranks on the prospects for political reform in the wake of a coup. Recalling his view of the plotters, Lodge wrote: "I do not think his [General Tran Van Don's] promise of a democratic election is realistic. This country is simply not ready for that procedure." A final suggestion on the makeup of a post-coup cabinet was imaginative, suggesting a post for Tri Quang, the monk then residing in Lodge's embassy.[23]

As Lodge was waiting at the Saigon airport on Sunday, October 27, for his flight to Da Lat, he renewed his reassurances to General Don that he had U.S. backing for the coup.[24] Lodge's report to Rusk, cabled from Saigon the next evening, was full of foreboding: Diem's expected capitulation to American pressure was not offered. On the contrary, Diem took the opportunity to throw down the gauntlet to the ambassador, informing Lodge that he was certain that the CIA's Lucien Conein had been meeting with rebel generals and that John Mecklin, Lodge's USIA officer, was allowing Buddhist leaders to print their antigovernment propaganda in the embassy. Lodge, feigning disbelief, demanded proof, promising to dismiss any U.S. official guilty of subversion.[25]

After a lavish feast, Diem got down to business, asking as Lodge had hoped about the meaning of the commodity import suspension: "How long would it last?" he inquired. (Thuan later told Lodge that careful studies had now convinced Diem that the South Vietnamese economy would collapse if the U.S. support payments were discontinued.[26]) Lodge replied that the matter was in Diem's power. All he had to do was select one policy change he was willing to undertake to placate American public opinion, that is, press, editorial, and congressional opinion.

Lodge's overall view of Diem seemed somewhat softened by their Da Lat meeting.

> He is very likeable. One feels that he is a nice, good man living a good life by his own lights, but also feels that he is a man who is cut off from [the] present, who is living in the past, who is truly indifferent to people as such and who is simply unbelievably stubborn. . . .
>
> I said I agreed [that we must get on with the war against the Communists] but we must consider US opinion; we wanted to be treated as equal partners; we do not want Vietnam to be a satellite of ours; nor do we want to be a satellite of Vietnam's. We do not wish to be put in the extremely embarrassing position of condoning totalitarian acts which are against our traditions and ideals. *Repeatedly I asked him: What do you propose to do for us?* His reply several times was either a blank stare or change of subject or the statement: *"je ne vais pas servir," which makes no sense. He must have meant to say "ceder" rather than "servir," meaning: "I will not give in."* He warned that the Vietnamese people were strange people and could do odd things if they were resentful.[27]

Lodge's gracious correction of Diem's French had uncovered the root of the Kennedy-Diem impasse. No words spoken in Washington during the same six weeks came nearly so close to the heart of the tragedy unfolding: What Lodge saw merely as client accommodation to force majeure, Diem saw as neocolonialism.

At lunch on October 28, on the occasion of the dedication of the Da Lat Atomic Energy Center, the morning after the showdown, Lodge and Diem were both silent, but Secretary Thuan tried to reassure Lodge that Diem was still considering some concessions to the Americans but that Lodge should realize that "the President must save face." Lodge countered that Kennedy had precisely the same problem: "Nobody, not even Americans, likes to be put in the position of supporting totalitarian acts, which are totally contrary to our way of thinking." [28]

While Lodge was cabling this pessimistic assessment to Washington, Diem was drawing up his final plans to accept Ho's offer of negotiations to establish a federation between North and South Vietnam. On October 29 he appointed a trusted ally and war veteran, Tran Van Dinh, as ambassador to New Delhi, where he would also hold the portfolio as Diem's representative to Ho. Negotiations between Ho's delegate, Le Duc Tho, and Tran Van Dinh were scheduled to begin on November 15. [29]

8

LAST RITES AND FINAL JUDGMENTS

OCTOBER 29 TO NOVEMBER 22

Clouds were gathering over Camelot. McGeorge Bundy was wavering. On a memo he had prepared in advance of an October 29 meeting of the president and the responsible constitutional officers, including Lyndon Johnson, Bundy revealed his misgivings in a handwritten question: "Should we cool off the whole [coup] enterprise?"[1] By the end of the meeting, everyone but Rusk and Harriman had caught the contagion of caution.

In their first systematic analysis of the military balance of rebel and loyal military units, Colby pointed out that the two factions were nearly evenly matched, with about ninety-eight hundred troops on each side. In an uncharacteristic moment of wishful thinking, the president observed that "it always looks that way before the opening shot of a coup, but immediately," he recalled, "some loyalists desert the head of state, as they did in Korea." Maxwell Taylor called Kennedy up short on this speculation, pointing out that coups succeed or fail because of the personalities and authority of a few key officers. Chastened, Kennedy wondered aloud: "Who are these key people?"[2]

The debate pivoted on the personal intervention of Robert Kennedy, who tried to pour cold water on the plot. Conceding that he had been out of the cable loop (unsurprisingly, given his cabinet post as attorney general), he blurted out: "This makes no sense on the face of it. . . . To support a coup would be putting the future of Vietnam and in fact all of Southeast Asia in the hands of one man not now known to the U.S. . . . We have a right to know what the Generals are planning. If we send out the draft cable as it stands, it will appear that we are in favor of a coup."[3]

Rusk rushed to protect Lodge's efforts to remove Diem. He prefaced his remarks with the observation that most military leaders had given up hope on Diem, a premise that the attorney general immediately challenged. Rusk countered: "If we say we are not for a coup, the Generals will turn against us and the war effort will drop off." Taylor countered with a warning that even a successful coup would upset the military campaign, since all the provincial government officials would have to be replaced at once.[4] When McCone agreed with Taylor, the president inquired why a coup would entail a wholesale exchange of top officials throughout the country. Taylor explained that the rebels would be unable to trust Diem's top appointees.

After another dismissal of Diem by Rusk and Harriman, the president himself moved closer to his brother's skepticism: "If the military forces are really evenly matched [which seems to have been news to him], any attempt to engineer a coup would be silly. If Lodge agrees, we should instruct him to discourage a coup." McNamara pointed out that this would constitute an about-face in Lodge's current instructions. Kennedy then asked what Lodge had been instructed to do. The answer was that his formal instructions, frequently ignored, were to avoid imputable support for the coup but to keep close to the plotters.[5] After a follow-on meeting at 6:00 P.M., Bundy cabled Lodge to shift gears: "We reiterate burden of proof must be on coup group to show a substantial possibility of quick success; otherwise, we should discourage them from proceedings."[6]

As Bundy's cable was being prepared for transmission to Saigon, Lodge was proposing that Washington consider resuming full payments to Diem *even if* he refused to make any symbolic concessions to American demands.[7] In a subsequent cable, Lodge hinted at a change of heart, concluding that his October 27 meeting with Diem at Da Lat had been "another step in the dialogue . . . Diem had begun. . . . If U.S. wants to make a package deal, I would think we were in a position to do it. The conditions of my return [to Washington] could be propitious for it. In effect he said: Tell us what you want and we'll do it. . . . See also Nhu's statement on release of all Buddhists and students now in jail." In his cable Lodge passed on some tender words for Kennedy, spoken by Diem at the same meeting, in what was later known to be a valedictory testament. "When I got up to go, he said: Please tell President Kennedy that I am a good and frank ally, that I would rather be frank and settle questions now than talk about them after we have lost everything. (This looked like a reference to a possible coup.) Tell President Kennedy that

I take all his suggestions very seriously and wish to carry them out but it is a question of timing."[8]

Meanwhile, General Harkins cabled that Lodge seemed to be ignoring his standing orders, cabled on October 5, not to encourage a coup. Lodge had in fact openly encouraged General Don two days earlier. Harkins's urgent protest was a plea for common sense:

> I'm not opposed to a change in government, no indeed, but I'm inclined to feel that at this time the change should be in methods of governing rather than complete change of personnel. I have seen no batting order proposed by any of the coup groups. I think we should take a hard look at any proposed list before we make any decisions. In my contacts here I have seen no one with the strength of character of Diem, at least in fighting communists. Certainly there are no Generals qualified to take over in my opinion. I am not a Diem man per se. I certainly see the faults in his character. I am here to back 14 million SVN people in their fight against communism and it just happens that Diem is their leader at this time. Most of the Generals I have talked to agree they can go along with Diem, all say it's the Nhu family they are opposed to.
>
> After all, rightly or wrongly, we have backed Diem for eight long hard years. To me it seems incongruous now to get him down, kick him around, and get rid of him.[9]

Lodge, responding to Bundy's demand sent from Washington at 7:22 P.M. on October 29, that Lodge discourage any but surefire coup plans, recast the order to mean that he should discourage only coups that were patently doomed.[10] Finally, in a burst of unconscious irony, he then rejected Rusk's recent order to turn over the embassy to General Harkins if a coup occurred in Lodge's imminent absence: "It does not seem sensible to have the military in charge of a matter which is so profoundly political as a change of government." (This axiom was apparently not applicable to Vietnamese generals, but only to Americans like Harkins, whom Lodge described as "a splendid General and an old friend of mine, to whom I would gladly entrust anything I have."[11])

Bundy wasted little time in transmitting his last effort to stop any coup involving a risk of failure.

> 1. Our reading your thoughtful 2063 leads us to believe a significant difference of shading may exist on one crucial point. . . .

2. We do not accept as a basis for U.S. policy that we have no power to delay or discourage a coup. In your paragraph 12 you say that if you were convinced that the coup was going to fail you would of course do everything you could to stop it. We believe that on this same basis you should take action to persuade coup leaders to stop or delay any operation which, in your best judgment, *does not clearly give high prospect of success.* We have never considered any betrayal of Generals to Diem, and our [document number not declassified] explicitly rejected that course. We recognize the danger of appearing hostile to Generals, but we believe that our own position should be on as firm ground as possible, hence we cannot limit ourselves to proposition implied in your message that only conviction of certain failure justifies intervention. We believe that your standard for intervention should be that stated above.

3. Therefore, if you should conclude that there is not clearly a high prospect of success, you should communicate this doubt to Generals in a way calculated to persuade them to desist at least until chances are better.[12]

When Kennedy next met with his principal advisers at 10:00 A.M. on November 1, reports of the coup were already flowing in from Saigon. Most poignant was Lodge's summary of his final telephone conversation with Ngo Dinh Diem:

At 4:30 a telephone call [came] from President Diem and the following conversation occurred:

Diem: Some units have made a rebellion and I want to know: What is the attitude of [the] U.S.?

Lodge: I do not feel well enough informed to be able to tell you. I have heard the shooting, but am not acquainted with all the facts. Also it is 4:30 A.M. in Washington and [the] U.S. Government cannot possibly have a view.

Diem: But you must have some general ideas. After all, I am a Chief of State. I have tried to do my duty. I want to do now what duty and good sense require. I believe in duty above all.

Lodge: You have certainly done your duty. As I told you only this morning, I admire your courage and your great contributions to your country. No one can take away from you the credit for all you have done. Now I am worried about your physical safety. I have a report that those in charge of the current activity offer you and your brother safe conduct out of the country if you resign. Had you heard this?

Diem: No. (And then after a pause) You have my telephone number.

Lodge: Yes. If I can do anything for your physical safety, please call me.

Diem: I am trying to re-establish order.[13]

In her study of Lodge, Anne Blair records a much less tranquil dialogue: "Mr. Ambassador, do you realize who you are talking to? I would like you to know that you are talking to a president of an independent and sovereign nation. I will only leave this country if it is the wish of my people. I will never leave according to the request of a group of rebellious generals or of an American Ambassador. The U.S. government must take full responsibility before the world in this miserable matter."[14]

About 7:00 P.M., Saigon time, Diem and Nhu finally decided to abandon Gia Long Palace. They were driven in a small Citroën 2CV belonging to Nhu's aide Cao Xuan Uy to the home of their friend Ma Tuyen, in Cholon. After many telephone calls, Diem and Nhu agreed early the next morning to surrender. Diem called Minh to offer his surrender and to ask for safe passage to asylum. The deciding factor for Diem was the risk of bloodshed in the struggle.

In 1985, shortly after Lodge's death, Mike Dunn, Lodge's personal assistant and close friend, revealed in an interview that Diem called Lodge once more, at 7:00 A.M. on November 2, just minutes before his arrest and assassination. Asking for Lodge's help in his last hour, Diem was literally "put on hold" by the ambassador. Returning after a few moments to the telephone, Lodge offered the brothers asylum, but with no promise of transportation until the following day. Dunn then volunteered to go personally to save the brothers from the coup leaders. Lodge adamantly refused: "We just can't get that involved." Dunn suggested in the same interview that when Lodge had put Diem on hold, he immediately notified Lucien Conein, the CIA officer at the coup headquarters, of Diem's (previously unknown) whereabouts. Conein later vigorously denied this account of Diem's discovery at the Chinese church.[15]

Big Minh, fearing an attempt by Diem to recover power, then unilaterally ordered an aide, General Mai Huu Xuan, to murder the brothers. The Ngos, handcuffed prisoners, were killed in an M-113 armored personnel carrier by Major Duong-Huu-Nghia at a spot just in front of the Cinéma Olympique. The mutilated bodies were then displayed to the plotters at the military headquarters near the airport.[16]

Before submitting to their fate, Diem and Nhu had privately entered Saint Francis Xavier Church in Cholon to receive communion. In Saigon it was the Feast of All Souls or, in Vietnamese liturgical terms, "the Feast of the Dead." The dominant motif of the day's liturgy is judgment. Worshipers recall their sins, plead for forgiveness, and look forward to justification through God's mercy at the final judgment. This expectation of merciful judgment is heard in the Dies Irae:

> Dies, irae, dies illa
> Solvet saeclum in favilla:
> Cuncta stricte discussurus!
> Iudex ergo cum sedebit,
> Quidquid latet, apparebit;
> Nil inultum remanebit.
> Rex tremendae maiestatis,
> Salva me, fons pietatis. . . .
> Lacrimosa dies illa,
> Huic ergo parce, Deus.

> Day of wrath!
> O day of mourning

> When from heaven the Judge descendeth,
> On whose sentence all dependeth!

> When the Judge His seat attaineth,
> And each hidden deed arraigneth,
> Nothing unavenged remaineth.
> King of majesty tremendous
> Fount of pity, then befriend us.
> Ah! That day of tears and mourning!
> Spare, oh God, in mercy spare him![17]

At the daily White House staff meeting four hours into Diem's overthrow, Forrestal expressed satisfaction at its excellent execution. His boss, McGeorge Bundy, taking note of the "representative" character of the junta, commented that this military takeover was the sort acceptable to the United States.[18] At 10:00 A.M. the principal foreign policy officers of the government, with the exception of Lyndon Johnson, met. Fifty minutes into the morning meeting (of which no record survives) Kennedy left to attend mass for the Feast of All Saints at Trinity Church, Georgetown. It was to be his last mass in Washington.[19]

As he entered the church hurriedly, Kennedy heard the liturgical readings for the feast. The liturgy is an ironic interplay between rejoicing and lamenting at the experience of persecution. "Let us rejoice" (*Gaudeamus*) were the opening words of the mass, celebrating the salvation of persecuted peoples "from every nation, race, tribe and language." The gospel read in the mass, too, was a meditation on the happiness of those who suffer, echoing the theme of suffering joy. The Beatitudes were quoted from the Gospel of Saint Matthew:

> Happy those who mourn;
> they shall be comforted.
> Happy those who hunger and thirst for what is right;
> they shall be satisfied.
> Happy the peacemakers;
> they shall be called sons of God.
> Happy those who are persecuted in the cause of right;
> theirs is the kingdom of heaven.[20]

The president left church at 11:29 to return to the meeting in progress.[21]

While Kennedy was at mass, Rusk cabled Lodge, urging him to avoid holding a reception for the rebel leaders, who might be compromised if they acted as though they were "reporting to headquarters." Rusk then took a call from Senator Fulbright, assuring him that U.S. involvement in the coup was minimal.[22]

After learning of Diem's offer to surrender in return for guarantee of safe passage to the airport, Rusk sent a long cable of warm congratulations to Lodge, urging him to reveal that Diem had been engaged in neutrality negotiations with Ho Chi Minh. The secretary added that the evening press briefing by Robert Manning would emphasize the constitutional character of this coup, virtually the result of a national referendum rather than a sinister trick by foreigners.[23]

During the night of November 1–2, word arrived of Diem's and Nhu's deaths by "suicide." Rusk cabled Lodge to establish the truth, if any, of the suicide story. Lodge responded that suicide was possible because the arresting officers had inadvertently left a loaded pistol in the personnel carrier.[24]

Twice on November 2 Kennedy held off-the-record meetings. At the first meeting, when Kennedy received word of Diem's assassination, he leaped to his feet in shock and rushed out of the room.[25] After the evening meeting, Bundy urged Lodge to notify the generals that "they should not be under the illusion that political assassination is easily accepted here." Bundy added that the "American people and Government remember great services to freedom rendered by Diem."[26] That evening, Washington learned that authentic photographs were being offered for sale to the international press of the bullet-riddled bodies of Diem and Nhu, lying face down in the carrier, hands bound behind them.[27]

The *New York Times* heaved a sigh of relief. Its two-year campaign to replace Diem with a popular South Vietnamese leader, who could galvanize support for the war effort, had finally prevailed. In their commentary on Sunday, November 3, the editors pointed to the visible relief of the dancing, cheering masses in Saigon as evidence that Diem and Nhu had indeed been an obstacle to military victory because of their despotic rule. The coup then was "inevitable," even though Kennedy's public protests against the government "helped to prepare the psychological atmosphere for the coup." It was then a "desirable" denouement to the summer-long standoff between Diem and the Buddhists, who would welcome the new president, Nguyen Ngoc Tho, a Buddhist. But the *Times* recalled that the 1960 U.S.-led coup in Laos had proved abortive. Hence, to seize this opportunity, the generals should proceed swiftly to hold an election.

In the same issue of the *Times*, the unsigned "News of the Week in Review" account recalled Diem's dictatorial manner and total disregard for democratic freedoms, as well as the obvious unsuitability of a Catholic ruler in a nation 70 percent (*sic*) Buddhist. The editors were optimistic about the popular rapport that President Tho would enjoy with the masses. General Minh, too, was popular both in Saigon and in Washington. Recalling the role of Kennedy's Labor Day broadcast in encouraging the generals to oust Diem, the *Times* underlined the enormity of the global stakes of this frontier clash between East and West.

James ("Scotty") Reston, one of the few Washington journalists not mesmerized by the Kennedy charisma, asked in his column the same day, "Where do we go from here?" He broke with Washington euphoria by reporting on squabbles among the leaders in the forty-eight-hour-old government, predicting that stability in Saigon was months away. He observed, however, that administration officials were more comfortable with instability there than with repression.

Immediately after the coup, even before the ensuing chaos had begun to engulf Saigon, editors and columnists were second-guessing Kennedy on this change of course. While the *New York Times* coverage of the coup was cautiously optimistic, others saw the coup as an act of presidential folly. In Washington, the *Evening Star* stated the obvious public reaction to State Department denials of U.S. involvement in the coup: "The people who believe this can be comfortably housed in a telephone booth." The *Washington Post* editors grasped the cardinal nature of the event: "We have now been plunged from the utterly untenable to the utterly unknown." Equally skeptical was the reaction at the *Chicago Tribune:* "There seems . . . to have been a division of opinion within . . . the American government about the advisability of throwing the internal affairs of South Vietnam up for grabs at a time when the United States was heavily involved in that country's war for survival. . . . Whether the chances of winning that struggle have been enhanced or weakened cannot now be answered with any certainty."[28] In the *Wall Street Journal*, Philip Geyelin warned: "Coup confronts U.S. with big risks. . . . a power struggle could hurt war against reds."[29]

With another day's reflection, and perhaps some prompting from the White House, editors at the *Washington Post* adopted a more optimistic tone, pointing to the rejoicing in the streets of Saigon as proof that Diem was "unpopular, arbitrary, and inefficient." Since Diem had made the mistake of delaying elections, leaving no alternative to a coup, the editors urged on Big Minh the scheduling of free elections, in order to demonstrate the new government's popularity. The *Christian Science Monitor*, also on November 4, echoed State Department views in observing that "the Ngo family eliminated itself." Since the tide of democracy is very deep in Vietnam, the editors argued, power should be turned over promptly to civilians.

Columnists completed the spectrum of opinion on U.S. support of the midwar coup. Warren Unna, who had signaled as early as May 12 that Diem and Nhu were looking for an exit from the U.S. alliance, was exhilarated at this courageous choice by Kennedy. "The Kennedy administration's policy toward South Viet Nam . . . seems to emerge smelling like a rose." Without any CIA involvement—the coup "worked too well," and the CIA itself could not have accomplished the task so effectively—Kennedy had pushed the regime overboard by his "extraordinary Labor Day TV interview." Now Kennedy had a clean slate to deal with "a sovereign government more representative of its people."[30] Joseph Alsop urged Kennedy to avoid the pious charade of pulling out of the coup a civilian government that would be merely an illusion. Alsop, who had championed Diem even though he considered Nhu "half-mad . . . plunging from folly to folly," foresaw what a farce a civilian government would inevitably entail.[31]

Alsop's dire prophecy was fulfilled within weeks of the coup. Joseph Buttinger later observed that, before the following coup on January 30, 1964, "South Vietnam had no less than sixty-three political parties, few of which counted more than several dozen followers."[32] Premier Phan Huy Quat, who headed the longest-lasting post-coup civilian government—which held power for four months, from February to June 1965—explained to U. Alexis Johnson that in Vietnam "twenty persons is the numerical limit of a political party."[33]

Alsop's courage in ridiculing Kennedy's anticipation of a new day for democracy in Vietnam stemmed from his diagnosis of the moral passion that had induced Kennedy's government to encourage the coup: guilt over association with an autocratic regime. Alsop's term for the journalists and pundits who had demanded Diem's ouster was "the breast-beaters." These people had earlier made a hero of Diem because he had ousted the repressive French colonialists. Just as the breast-beaters had become disenchanted in turn with Diem, they were bound later to turn their guilt on the new junta, thus spinning once more the wheel of misfortune for South Vietnam.[34]

Bundy learned that the generals would issue a statement deploring the assassinations and insisting on their own innocence of this crime. In response to Lodge's urging, they had also agreed that dance halls could be reopened. Finally, they voiced their gratitude to Lodge.[35]

Later, on November 6, Lodge drew some conclusions on the coup in his summary cable to Kennedy:

There is no doubt that the coup was a Vietnamese and a popular affair, which we could neither manage nor stop after it got started and which we could only have influenced with great difficulty. But it is equally certain that the ground in which the coup seed grew into a robust plant was prepared by us and that the coup would not have happened with [when] it did without our preparation. General Don as much as said this to me on November 3. Our actions made the people who could do something about it start thinking hard about how to get a change of government.[36]

Pointing to the coup as a new paradigm for American diplomacy, Lodge added, "[A]ll this may be a useful lesson in the use of US power for those who face similar situations in other places in the future." Without united action by the U.S. government, the coup would not have been possible. "Nothing could put the cause of freedom into a stronger position than for those on the side of freedom to be able to clean their own house and not to be so often in a situation where we have to put up with autocrats . . . or . . . Colonel Blimps."[37]

Kennedy responded immediately to Lodge's cable: "As you say, while this was a Vietnamese effort, our own actions made it clear that we wanted improvements, and when these were not forthcoming from the Diem Government, we necessarily faced and accepted the possibility that our position might encourage a change of government. We thus have a responsibility to help this new government to be effective in every way that we can, and in these first weeks we may have more influence and more chance to be helpful than at any time in recent years."[38]

Meanwhile, Washington was busy coping with the fallout from the action of overthrowing an allied government. The burden fell on Bundy and Forrestal. Bundy's wit shines through the record of several staff meetings. On November 4 he steered a discussion that addressed the fears of Latin American governments. These governments worried about the precedent of Kennedy's immediate recognition of a military junta in Saigon that had executed a coup against a constitutional chief of state. Rejecting Arthur M. Schlesinger Jr.'s tortured effort to erect a Manichaean theory of Eastern and Western (good versus bad) coups, Bundy put the reality more candidly: "If we like people, we would say what they did was constitutional and if we didn't we would not." Commenting on the enthusiasm of Saigon crowds for the generals, Bundy half-jokingly suggested that Latin American juntas might learn to include such demonstrations in their coup planning. He went on to warn the White House staff of the imminent release of the assassination photographs, commenting on the indelible detail of the tied hands of the victims: "This is not the preferred way to commit suicide."[39]

In Saigon, Lodge, after his inaugural meeting with the new government, regretted the leaders' insensitivity to the need to deny assassinating Diem. He was learning that Asians are slow to place public relations ahead of other considerations, such as the facts. He had also pointed out that "it would obviously be very bad if [the Ngos' brother] Can were lynched." (As it turned out, Can was turned over by Lodge to the junta but enjoyed the benefit of a full trial. He was then shot by a firing squad in May 1964.) "Minh," Lodge worried, "seemed tired and somewhat frazzled. . . . Will he be strong enough to get on top of things?" In response to Washington's doubts about the new rulers, Lodge compared them favorably to the German plotters who botched their attempt on Hitler. Minh's group "didn't leave a slip of paper behind."[40] Lodge had advised Big Minh to drop in on a pagoda or two to sign autographs: even Asians liked to be patronized by politicians. Minh later declined this suggestion.[41]

From Cambridge, Massachusetts, John Kenneth Galbraith wrote speedily to congratulate Harriman for his management of the coup: "Dear Averell: The South Viet Nam coup is another great feather in your cap. Do get me a list of all the people who told us there was no alternative to Diem."[42]

In an executive session of the Senate Foreign Relations Committee four days after the coup, on November 5, 1963, Senator Frank Church, who had been a consistent enemy of the Diem regime, gave his estimate of the coup: "I think that what has happened in South Vietnam is the thing I certainly had hoped for, because it was becoming increasingly evident the incompetence and corruption of this regime was going to lose the war against the Communists. We can hope that the regime that follows can establish some rapport with the people and sufficient popular support to summon the will and resolution to win the war."[43]

While Washington was cautiously congratulating itself on the recent coup, Hanoi was exuberant. There Nguyen Huu Tho, president of the National Liberation Front, remarked to the Australian journalist Wilfred Burchett: "The fall of Ngo was a gift from heaven for us."[44] His vice president and chief of the military committee, Tran Nam Trung, added: "The Americans decided to change horses in mid-stream. They'll never find any one more effective than Diem."[45]

Ellen Hammer recounts Tho's further comments, which embraced the two successive coups, on November 1, 1963, and January 30, 1964:

> Our enemy has been seriously weakened from all points of view, military, political and administrative. . . . The military command has been turned upside down and weakened by purges. . . . The principal chiefs of security and the secret police, on which mainly depended the protection of the regime and the repression of the revolutionary movement, have been eliminated, purged. Troops, officers and officials of the army . . . are completely lost; they have no more confidence in their chiefs and have no idea to whom they should be loyal. . . . From the political point of view the weakening of our adversary is still clearer. Reactionary political organizations . . . which constituted an appreciable support for the regime, have been dissolved, eliminated.[46]

Hammer continues: "In the North, the Hanoi radio quoted the official newspaper *Nhan Dan:* By throwing off Ngo Dinh Diem and his brother Ngo Dinh Nhu, the U.S. imperialists have themselves destroyed the political bases they had built up for years. The deaths of Diem and Nhu were followed by the disintegration of big fragments of the . . . [government] machine."[47]

Two years later, Mao Tse-tung chatted with Edgar Snow about the events of November 1963. "Talking of South Vietnam, Mao said American forces there were still relatively small. Of course if they increased they could help speed up the arming of the people against them. But if he [Mao] should tell that to the United States leaders, they would not listen. Had they listened to Diem? Both Ho Chi Minh and he (Mao) thought that Ngo Dinh Diem was not so bad. . . . After all, following his assassination, was everything between Heaven and Earth more peaceful? . . . Diem had not wanted to take orders."[48]

On November 20 Lodge joined Rusk, McNamara, Bundy, Forrestal, and others in Honolulu. Lodge led off by warning his colleagues not to expect instant democracy in Vietnam and not to be overconfident about the staying power of the new government in Saigon. The record of the meeting states that:

Ambassador Lodge doubted the wisdom of the U.S. making sweeping demands for democratization or for early elections at this time. He believed that in Vietnam the technique of changing governments by violent means is not yet ready to be displaced in favor of changing governments by election. He emphasized that if we can get through the next six months without a serious falling out among the Generals we will be lucky. . . . Americans—whether in government or in the press—should not seek to guide them at every turn nor try to get them to act as though they were made in our image.[49]

His observations, both about the actuarial prospects of the Minh government and about the scenario of its replacement, turned out to rank among his most prescient observations as ambassador. His warning about the apathetic reception outside Saigon to the generals (which Harkins confirmed later) was chilling news.[50] Perhaps Minh's stern agenda, announced to Rufus Phillips on November 18, seeking to cure corruption in the countryside by executing a few province chiefs, may have cooled the peasants' enthusiasm about a military government.[51] For this and other reasons, all province programs had come to a virtual standstill, as Maxwell Taylor had warned before the coup. Peasants seemed to regret the overthrow and assassination of their president. At the Honolulu conference, these cardinal observations on the South Vietnamese national mood were then overwhelmed by detailed analyses of budgetary shortfalls, which McNamara called "political dynamite." The assembled officials then discussed a "fertilizer deficit" that had to be corrected to make Vietnam a regional granary. Rusk promised to take up the fertilizer question when he went on to Tokyo from Honolulu.[52]

While Rusk was flying on to Tokyo for this discussion, he was notified of Kennedy's assassination. In Washington, amid the grief, incredulity, and fear, Lyndon Johnson reflected with Hubert Humphrey, before moving to the White House, on the eerie echo of November 1–2. Pointing to a picture of Diem displayed in his home, the new president said: "We had a hand in killing him. Now it's happening here."[53]

AFTERSHOCKS

NOVEMBER 23, 1963, TO FEBRUARY 15, 1964

Ellen Hammer observes in the epilogue to her study of the Kennedy years in Vietnam that "the Vietnamese will to fight seemed to have died with Diem."[1] The reasons are not far to seek. The most obvious is that the hand that was guiding the war was now indelibly stained with the blood of the South Vietnamese president. When the French had from time to time decided to remove an emperor who was an obstacle to their goals, they at least did him the favor of granting him asylum.[2] The Americans, Vietnam now learned, had different sensibilities than the French: they removed heads of state "with extreme prejudice" and often in the name of virtue.

Almost equally salient as a cause of South Vietnamese demoralization in 1963 and 1964 was the abrupt transfer of political authority to a group of generals. As Frances FitzGerald remarks in her study of this period: "Traditionally the Vietnamese feared and disdained professional soldiers . . . out of the suspicion that they had not the moral or political authority to build up a government behind them. . . . The Saigon generals [in 1963] faced the task of creating an entirely new way of life, a new civilization for the Vietnamese. Trained and for so long dominated by foreigners, they had perhaps less capacity to undertake it than anyone in Vietnam."[3]

Jean Lacouture, who interviewed the members of the junta shortly after they came to power, described them as "the invisible government." Speaking of Saigon after November 2, 1963, Lacouture observed:

> It was a city in which one could not find the ruling powers. Here a void followed the detested regime. . . . In the great humid city, there was a strange absence. . . . The military were rather pleasant. But

what the devil was their program? . . . One must not oversimplify the matter and laugh at the "administrative committee," yet . . . one could not help noticing that the text adopted at the first meeting of the new regime's ministers ruled that it would no longer be necessary to make out medical prescriptions in triplicate. . . . After a first appeal to the people . . . the overthrowers of Diem . . . locked themselves in the general staff building and made their ideas and intentions known only by statements in the Saigon press or in interviews granted to New York or Paris newspapers. . . . Who were these invisible men who sealed the destiny of the Ngos but who would converse only with a few foreign journalists rather than the citizens of Vietnam?[4]

Lacouture here echoes Kennedy's anxious inquiry to his advisers on October 29, just twelve hours before the unleashing of the coup he had authorized two months earlier: "Who are these people?"[5]

While the Minh junta was consolidating and distributing its new power, Lyndon Johnson, too, was putting his stamp on Vietnam policy. In his first meeting on Vietnam, convened on November 24, the eve of Kennedy's funeral, Johnson made explicit what everyone already knew, that he had from the beginning disagreed with the Kennedy-Harriman-Ball peremptory demand that Diem reform his government to meet American standards. Meeting with Rusk, McNamara, Ball, Bundy, McCone, and Lodge, Johnson voiced his criticism of Kennedy's policies toward Diem. He then set out his own policy, in stark contrast to the policies leading up to the coup.

> He stated that he was not at all sure we took the right course in upsetting the Diem regime, but this was a decision he did not have to make as it was a *fait accompli.* . . .
>
> The President then said that . . . he did not think we had to reform every Asian into our own image. He said that he felt all too often when we engaged in the affairs of a foreign country we wanted to immediately transform that country into our own image, and this, in his opinion, was a mistake. He was anxious to get along, win the war — he didn't want as much effort placed on so called social reforms.[6]

John McCone, who was taking minutes at the meeting, added here his own reflections: "I received in this meeting the first 'President Johnson tone' for action as contrasted with the 'Kennedy tone.' Johnson definitely feels that we place too much emphasis on social reforms; he has very little tolerance with spending so much time being 'do-gooders.'"[7]

Lodge reminded the group that he and Kennedy had in no way been responsible for the deaths of Diem and his brother, who would still be alive if they had only followed Lodge's advice.[8] (Bundy later confided to Harriman, who had not attended the meeting, that Johnson had been unimpressed by Lodge's report but had never thought much of Lodge anyway.[9])

President Eisenhower, who had appointed Lodge to the United Nations, apparently did not share Johnson's critical view of him. Within days of Kennedy's assassination, Ike telephoned Lodge in Washington to suggest cautiously that the ambassador move his presidential plans forward from 1968 to 1964. After discreetly inquiring whether Lodge had had any role in the assassinations in Saigon (of "the King and his brother") and having been reassured that Lodge was in no way involved in this tragic denouement, Eisenhower urged him to resign his post immediately and open a campaign. Lodge's campaign opened on December 23, at the expiration of the mandatory month of mourning for Kennedy.[10]

Meanwhile, reports were coming in from South Vietnam. Some people were surprised to read on December 6 that bonzes were still burning themselves in Saigon, even though the presumed object of their protests had been dead for more than a month.[11] Hammer points out that there were more suicides by bonzes in the first four months after Diem's death than there had been in the nine years of his rule.[12] Other reports were hardy perennials of Saigon cables: Forrestal reported from Saigon on December 11 of inertia in the government, due to the wholesale replacement of Diem's regional officials. He also criticized the Minh government's indecisiveness. The government officials seemed too distant from the needs of the villages.[13] On December 16 the CIA echoed Forrestal in painting a picture of political paralysis.[14]

Concerned by these reports, McNamara bluntly asked Big Minh during his next trip to Saigon: "Who is the chief of state?" Minh claimed that role but offered to step aside. McNamara pleaded for Minh to get out of headquarters and give rousing speeches, as Johnson was doing at home. Minh pointed out that he had already held two press conferences.[15] On his return to Washington on December 21, McNamara reported to Johnson that "the new government is the source of greatest concern. It is indecisive and drifting. . . . We should watch the situation very carefully, running scared, hoping for the best."[16] McCone on December 21 concurred: "There is no organized Government in Vietnam at this time." The CIA director judged the present portents "ominous."[17]

After digesting these unpalatable assessments, Johnson ordered Lodge to speak bluntly to Minh about his failings. Predictably, Lodge declined Johnson's advice, just as he had ignored Kennedy's: "I really do not think it would be suitable for me to dash in on New Year's eve and repeat the advice I have already given. I think it would appear breathless and ineffective."[18] Rusk must have smiled when he read this rerun of the Kennedy-Lodge cables. Johnson's dispatch on December 30 of a New Year's message to Minh and Premier Tho in Saigon was symbolic of the distance between the two capitals.[19] It was, after all, not New Year's in Saigon. That festival would be celebrated in Saigon a month later by still another Vietnamese government.

On January 10 Lodge held his first substantive session with the Military Revolutionary Council (MRC). He read in French a long checklist of assignments for the new government, phrased as questions for the council's response. The central demand was the articulation of a political platform calculated to enlist popular support. As an example, Lodge proposed land reform. When Lodge completed his list of rhetorical questions, he was surprised that the junta's answers were chilly. Minh, for example, suggested that the Vietnamese had difficulty rallying around a program of land redistribution, for such schemes would look to them very much like "banditry." Lodge admitted the truth in this perception but urged Minh to view the schemes as an ideological program. Lodge reflected later that the new government was not inclined toward ideology.[20]

Earlier in the day Minh had warned Lodge that his suggestion of situating Americans at the village level was out of the question. That would make Americans look "more imperialistic than the French," substantiating Viet Cong propaganda that now Minh, like Diem, was an "American lackey."[21]

On January 21 Lodge and General Harkins jointly proposed to the MRC the initiation of a South Vietnamese military campaign against North Vietnam, including the mining of Haiphong Harbor and the destruction of petroleum reserves and naval installations. Lodge then revealed the American timetable, calling for the Vietnamese to launch their attacks on February 1. Lodge was assuming the generals' consent to the American plan. Consent was not in the cards. Tho suggested an alternative target: Cambodia.

Minh, on the other hand, whose reaction Lodge described as "thoughtful and constructive," was worried about world reaction to such an escalation of the war. Furthermore, Minh did not trust Johnson to follow through on supporting the new strategy. South Vietnam, Minh said, did not want to be "left holding the bag" if Ho Chi Minh retaliated. Suppose Ho unleashed a wave of refugees into the South, swamping the government by their arrival? Suppose Ho, or Mao, chose to retaliate with air attacks? Would Johnson be prepared to launch an American air assault on the North? Lodge conceded that such a development would be a "whole new war." Minh insisted he was not "trying to pick a plan to pieces" but was hoping to allow time to consider such eventualities. Lodge asked Washington for answers to Minh's questions.[22]

Part of the underlying Vietnamese hesitancy was the leaders' sensitivity to recent French overtures about neutralization of Vietnam. Since they were still having some difficulty distinguishing the Americans from the French, Charles de Gaulle's suggestions were clouding their readiness for further risky initiatives against Ho.[23]

FitzGerald compares the events unfolding after Diem's ouster to the destructive power of a river shattering a dam. "The fall of the Diem regime had come like the breaking of a great river dam, the political energy of the cities overflowing and using itself up in the act of destruction."[24]

That destructiveness burst forth in the bloodless palace coup of January 30. Truong Vinh-Le stresses the ease of this second coup: not a shot was fired to defend the Minh government.[25] General Nguyen Khanh emerged as the new leader, ruling with General Khiem and maintaining Big Minh as a figurehead chief of state. This government, which was destined to set a record of post-Diem longevity by lasting almost eight months, represented a radical decline in the personal distinction of the governmental figures. As FitzGerald notes:

> The Khanh coup, as it happened, marked a generational change in the army leadership. . . . Most of them [the members of the new junta] went straight into the army after leaving high school, and they did not

take on important rank until after Vietnamese independence in 1954. After that, they rose rocket-like to power. . . . Certainly the officers had no education to speak of. . . . While the professional military officers remained at the head of state there would be an almost total divorce between knowledge and power.

. . . Unlike the older officers, they had no formal education; unlike Ngo Dinh Diem and the Buddhists, they had no nationalist credentials whatever.

. . . Probity, a desire for social justice and equal opportunity for all—such virtues might more reasonably be expected in the heads of a Mafia ring than in those generals who had spent their formative years struggling to the top of the corrupt, inefficient, and demoralized army of the Diem regime.[26]

Khanh, a boundlessly ambitious officer who had been judged by Harkins "the strongest character in the military," had been outraged by Diem's assassination. Hammer claims that Diem, during the Minh coup, had urged Khanh to avenge his death.[27] But Khanh himself was merely a tool of the colonels who overthrew Minh. Summoned to a pre-coup meeting with the dissident officers on January 29, he was awaiting the transportation that the newly promoted brigadier general Nguyen Van Thieu had promised to dispatch for him. When the vehicle arrived, Khanh saw that it was the same armored personnel carrier in which Diem and his brother had been assassinated. After a terrifying trip to the coup headquarters, Khanh rushed into the meeting and threw himself on the floor pleading for his life. Breaking into laughter, the plotters told him to stand up: he was going to be their new chief of state.[28]

Wilfred Burchett, the perceptive Australian journalist who was on very close terms with Ho Chi Minh, suggests that the American effort to salvage an independent state below the Seventeenth Parallel died the day that Robert McNamara endorsed General Khanh following his coup. Burchett quotes Nguyen Huu Tho, the president of the National Liberation Front: "But the greatest gift for us was when McNamara came and toured the countryside, holding up Nguyen Khanh's arm and shouting, 'This is our man.' This saved our propaganda cadres a great deal of effort." Burchett continues: "McNamara felt it was necessary to come and 'sell' Nguyen Khanh to the population; to assure them in a dozen different variants that Khanh had the complete backing of the USA, precisely because Washington knew that he had no popular support at home. . . . 'He doesn't need your support, he's got ours,' was what McNamara was saying in effect to the South Vietnamese people."[29]

On January 30, the day of the Khanh coup, Averell Harriman was having lunch at the Pentagon when he was introduced to Lucien Conein, the CIA officer who had been at Minh's coup headquarters just ninety days earlier. Harriman, at a loss over the collapse of the government he had helped install in Saigon three months before in order to get on with the war, was reduced to asking Conein's predictions on the future of the U.S. presence in Vietnam. "Haven't got a clue, Governor. All bets are off now."[30]

Harriman's surprise was total. Just three days earlier he had sent a congratulatory cable to Lodge, in response to a message handwritten by Lodge on a news photograph of Big Minh barnstorming:

> Dear Cabot: I followed with interest the advice you have been giving Big Minh on campaigning and was delighted to see the newsphoto which shows that your pupil is learning from a real master.
>
> I remember when we first talked about your going out to Viet-Nam that you spoke of the need for training the people in political methods, particularly in getting down to the village level. I see you are working at that with the beginnings of some success, too. More power to you.[31]

Within two months Harriman had come around to Conein's view about prospects in Vietnam. By April 1964, when Harriman was interviewed by Arthur M. Schlesinger Jr. for the oral history of the Kennedy administration, the new Khanh government had already demonstrated that it was no improvement over the ninety-day reign of Big Minh. When Schlesinger asked Harriman for his retrospective judgment on Diem, he answered that "as you look back on it, Diem was better than the chaotic condition we have now."[32] Indeed, all bets were off now. Averell Harriman was one of the first to realize the dire consequences of overturning the Diem government.

The chaos deepened early in May, when Khanh proposed to Lodge a widening of the war against the North, with the accompanying warfooting measures of martial law, the removal of all politicians from positions of power, and initial preparations for the evacuation of Saigon's two million residents in the event of reprisals from the North. Lodge approved the proposed internal political rearrangements but voiced his instinctive apprehension about the risks of involving U.S. ground troops in an Asian land war.[33]

Later in the month, after Khanh ignored urgent U.S. requests to appoint an ambassador to the United Nations for the scheduled discussion in the General Assembly of Cambodian complaints about South Vietnamese incursions across the border that had occurred on May 7 and 8, Lodge abandoned his restrained neocolonial approach to Vietnam. He asked Rusk whether the time had not now arrived for Washington simply to take complete control of South Vietnam.

> This unhappy country emerged from colonialism ten years ago and has been trying to get along since then with help from us that is, in all truth, advisory and not at all colonial. The question clearly arises as to whether this "advisory" phase is not about to be played out and whether the United States will not have to move into a position of actual control. This time has clearly not arrived yet, but it may be approaching. Whether it means that we will have a High Commissioner or a Commissioner General, or a man who really gives the orders under the title of Ambassador, will have to be determined in the light of circumstances as they develop.[34]

Lodge abandoned his frustrating labors when he wrote to Rusk on June 18 announcing his immediate resignation in order to enter the Republican political fray at home. On June 23 President Johnson nominated General Maxwell Taylor to replace Lodge in Saigon.[35]

Taylor's first crisis in Saigon was grave. On August 16 Khanh announced the imposition of the martial law constitution that he had earlier proposed to Lodge and that Taylor had now approved.[36] The new proposal of absolute power for the military rulers unexpectedly triggered several weeks of violent civil and religious street battles. During one such confrontation, students forced Khanh to shout, "Down with military power, Down with dictatorships, Down with the army!" Describing Khanh's leadership of the younger officers, FitzGerald says he "floated like a cork on the whirlpool of their disputes." She compares the government of those days to "a Marx Brothers' movie."[37] Despite Khanh's rapid retreat on August 25 from the new authoritarian constitution, the riots continued on August 27 and 28, resulting in numerous deaths.[38]

Khanh responded on September 26 by appointing a twenty-member High National Council of elderly civilian and military "notables," who adamantly resisted pervasive U.S. efforts to influence their decision making. On October 24 the council, to the chagrin of the U.S. embassy, named as president Phan Khac Suu, an ineffectual and ancient figure. He in turn appointed as his prime minister Tran Van Huong, an aging high school teacher and former mayor of Saigon.[39]

After less than two months, the High National Council was dissolved without ceremony by the Military Revolutionary Council, which then swiftly arrested eight of the former council's members. When the outraged ambassador Taylor was unable to reverse this "illegal" procedure, he ordered General Khanh to leave the country. Khanh responded by urging President Suu and Prime Minister Huong to declare Taylor *persona non grata* in Vietnam.[40]

Taylor's evaluation of the stature of the South Vietnamese ally was manifest in his plea on February 2: "The . . . criterion . . . for a government [is] to exist and to have the strength of voice able to ask for U.S. help." That voice was heard unmistakably when Phan Khac Suu was ousted on June 9 and replaced with the rule of Nguyen Van Thieu and Nguyen Cao Ky, who promptly requested the deployment of two hundred thousand U.S. troops. Perhaps coincidentally, President Johnson on June 8 had approved the dispatch of additional ground troops to South Vietnam if the South Vietnamese government requested them.[41]

On July 28 President Johnson announced the dispatch of fifty-eight thousand troops. Another six months would pass before the requested force level of two hundred thousand American troops was attained. The maximum deployment of U.S. troops, numbering 543,000, would not be in place until April 1969.[42]

Johnson's dramatic wager was not made blindly. Before the July 1965 decision to escalate the conflict, the president gathered his advisers, pleading: "Now somebody answer me this . . . how can we fight a war under the direction of others whose governments topple like ten pins?"[43] The answer to that prescient question should have been ready enough: "We can't." War is, after all, a prolongation of politics. Johnson was no stranger to this commonsense analysis of U.S. war policy in Vietnam. During the summer and fall of 1963 he had opposed, at every rare opportunity the vice president was granted, the mounting pressure in Washington to back a coup against Diem. For he agreed with the analysis of the CIA and of former ambassador Nolting that such a coup would be an invitation to governmental chaos throughout South Vietnam and would ruin the war effort.

During the summer of 1964, after the second coup had displaced General Minh's inaugural junta, Nolting had a passing and fortuitous meeting with President Johnson at a ceremony in the Rose Garden. Recalling to the president their shared but futile opposition to the coup, Nolting inquired whether the president could not seize the opportunity of this second coup to retreat from Vietnam. After all, Johnson had predicted precisely such an ominous outcome from an American decision to topple the unsatisfactory but constitutional government of South Vietnam. Johnson's hurried but considered reply had almost the memorable cadence of a classic literary tragedy: "I cannot now repudiate my predecessor's commitments."[44] Johnson, of course, had not been among the handful of friends and advisers who knew of Kennedy's intention to quit Vietnam before he was overtaken by fate.

In 1976, the year after the final collapse of Saigon, General Maxwell Taylor reflected on the feasibility of the United States fighting a war under the direction of unstable governments in Saigon. Reviewing the parade of South Vietnamese governments with which he had been forced to deal during the war, he remarked on the spectrum of soldiers and civilians he had met during their brief moments of power: "[T]here were no George Washingtons among them."[45] Diem had predicted as much in his 1963 interview with Marguerite Higgins: "I hope . . . that your government will take a realistic look at these young generals plotting to take my place. . . . I am afraid there are no George Washingtons among our military."[46]

Administration officials in Washington had been too busy to take Diem's advice about scrutinizing the credentials of the insurgents whom they promoted on November 1, 1963, much less the members of the seven following governments. It had been a crucial oversight, which they had ample time to regret. Averell Harriman, whose initiative allowed Michael Forrestal and Roger Hilsman to have their initial coup cable sent to Lodge on August 24, 1963, came to rue the day he had yielded to their impatience.[47] In April 1964, while regretting the coup that had, as predicted, spawned chaos in Saigon, Harriman admitted to Schlesinger that his own impetuosity had deprived him of his control of Vietnam policy. In a handwritten notation on the typed script of his oral history interview, Harriman observed: "I am not consulted on Vietnam anymore."[48]

Two close associates of Harriman, the British journalist Henry Brandon and the former U.S. undersecretary of state for political affairs U. Alexis Johnson, agreed that Harriman never shook off the remorse he felt for the decisive reversal effected by that coup. Alex Johnson recalled that in the early 1980s, in the waning days of Harriman's active life, he brought up the painful topic: "Do you remember the cable to Lodge? There was plenty of time for Kennedy to recall it."[49] Indeed, there had been — more than two months. All it would have taken would have been a presidential judgment that coups are not an honorable alliance strategy. The president made that judgment, or at any rate a judgment to reverse the coup initiative, just minutes too late, after the initiative slipped out of his hands on October 29. Henry Brandon, a friend and frequent houseguest of Harriman's on weekends in Middleburg, Virginia, remarked that the coup was one of the few topics that Harriman would never discuss.[50]

Harriman may have recalled in the winter of 1964 some snatches of Rudyard Kipling's "Old World" realism about the bittersweet fruits of the raj. Kipling had penned "The White Man's Burden" in 1899 on the occasion of the U.S. Senate debate about the annexation of the Philippines. Now Americans, too, could taste the ambivalence of the colonial burden. Kipling's verses about the risks of civilizing the barbarian had been popular in Harriman's youth. Now, with his fresh wounds from the U.S. government's own experiment in civilizing, Harriman seemed to sense the shocks that would await the nation as it shouldered the burden of Kennedy's legacy in Vietnam. Kipling wrote:

> Take up the White Man's burden —
> Send forth the best ye breed —
> Go bind your sons to exile
> To serve your captives' need;
>
> .   .   .   .   .   .
>
> Your new-caught, sullen peoples,
> Half-devil and half-child.
>
> .   .   .   .   .   .
>
> Take up the White Man's burden —
>
> .   .   .   .   .   .

And when your goal is nearest
The end for others sought,
Watch Sloth and heathen Folly
Bring all your hope to nought.

.   .   .   .   .   .

Take up the White Man's burden—
And reap his old reward:
The blame of those ye better,
The hate of those ye guard—

.   .   .   .   .   .

Take up the White Man's burden—

.   .   .   .   .   .

The silent, sullen peoples
Shall weigh your Gods and you.[51]

THE PLAYERS

DEAN RUSK
An Embarrassment of Ethics

To imagine U.S. policy in Vietnam as a maze, with an inviting entrance and a tragically concealed exit, is to underestimate the complexity of the issue. In truth, only a very few especially conscientious statesmen could have found the opening into that doomed passage. Dwight Eisenhower and John Foster Dulles had declined the entreaty of the French to enter the fray. It is unlikely that the successors of Lyndon Johnson and Dean Rusk, Richard Nixon and Henry Kissinger, would have made the wager that Kennedy and Rusk staked in Southeast Asia. Only desperation could have driven two such cautious personalities as Kennedy and Rusk to commit U.S. prestige and resources to the cause of South Vietnamese independence under the fragile and anachronistic leadership of Ngo Dinh Diem. Their despair in turn was the work of conscience—their idiosyncratic and shared horror at the prospect of inaugurating nuclear war.

The Prologue above and chapter 14 below trace the route that led Kennedy and his secretary of state to resolve jointly never to fulfill the nation's pledge to its NATO partners to initiate nuclear war. Still committed to the policy of containing Soviet expansionism, they had to choose a conspicuous frontier between Western-allied nations and those sympathetic to the Communist cause. There they could safely display the resolve that would sap the Soviet willingness to use force in defense of its European sphere of influence. By historical accident, the American stake finally had settled in 1961 into the depression marked "Vietnam" on the wheel of fortune.[1]

After just a year in office, Rusk voiced his horror of nuclear war. Speaking in an interview with Theodore H. White, Rusk observed succinctly:

[I]f [European] war should break out, then the Northern Hemisphere will simply be burned up. That means that Kennedy and Khrushchev both live with the first question of the Westminster Catechism always in mind: "What is the Chief End of Man?"

This injects a new element into politics. . . . You don't, for example, use phrases like "massive retaliation." . . . Phrases like that are traps. I don't use them.[2]

Later, after retirement from office, especially in the 1980s, Rusk voiced this horror of nuclear war more frequently. Citing the foreseeable consequences for the American people of a U.S. president's decision to launch a nuclear strike, the secretary said:

More than one hundred million Americans would die in the first salvo. . . . [W]e knew that neither superpower could tolerate the effects of nuclear weapons. . . .

President Kennedy . . . occasionally brooded over whether it would be his fate to push the nuclear button. . . .

If any of us had held doubts, that 1961 briefing convinced us that a nuclear war must never be fought.[3]

In a 1989 interview with Robert McCloskey, Rusk recalled once more the 1961 resolution against initiating nuclear war in Europe: "Nuclear war could in no circumstances be a rational act of policy and 'must never be fought.'"[4]

But it is crucially significant that, while in office from 1961 to 1969, Rusk never mentioned this radical strategic corollary of his judgment about the extravagantly destructive consequences of nuclear war. Rusk had not said to White in 1962 that such a war "must not be fought." Criticizing the Eisenhower-Dulles doctrine of "massive retaliation," Rusk merely concluded that he *never used those words*, which could constitute a trap for U.S. officials. Rusk was wary of a trap that would lead a president eventually to act according to this irrational formula, initiating nuclear war.

Rusk's silence about his (and Kennedy's) resolve never to initiate nuclear war was simply the exacting requirement of nuclear deterrence, which demanded continual efforts to convince the Soviets that the United States would make good on its threat to meet overwhelming conventional military assault in Europe with an almost immediate launch of short- and intermediate-range nuclear warheads. If this credulity on the part of NATO's adversaries were to lapse, or even wane, the risk of armed confrontation in Europe would increase, posing an insoluble dilemma for U.S. leaders. Either they would escalate a crisis to nuclear confrontation, inviting the destruction of the Northern Hemisphere, or they would suffer the loss of eight hundred thousand Americans (military personnel and dependents) in Europe and risk the capture of their own unused nuclear arsenal on the Continent.

To avoid the intolerable choice between these unprecedented catastrophes, Rusk and his colleagues would, while in office, have to continue to talk tough, even recklessly, about their willingness to fight a nuclear war. But Rusk (and Kennedy) felt that such fighting words were not sufficient in themselves to maintain secure deterrence. They needed as well to *act* recklessly elsewhere, in a less volatile arena of world politics. That "elsewhere," as we know, was Vietnam.

As Rusk said repeatedly during the 1980s, his vigorous commitment to defending the divide between North and South Vietnam, that implausible outpost of democratic values selected as a showplace of resolve safely beyond the nuclear arena, was inspired by the need to keep Soviet planners off balance when estimating U.S. readiness for war. For example, in the interviews conducted by his son Richard, for *As I Saw It*, Rusk says: "I suspect that leaders in other capitals, when contemplating fresh adventures, might say, 'Now wait, a minute, comrades. We've got to be a little careful here, because those damned fool Americans just might do something about it.'"[5] Rusk did more than suspect such an effect on the minds of his adversaries. In a long conversation with Khrushchev at his Black Sea villa, Rusk had said bluntly to his host, "Americans were the only people who had ever dropped the bomb on other people, twice, and might do it again."[6] Rusk returned to this rationale for Washington's zeal in Southeast Asia in his 1989 interview with McCloskey. On that occasion he defined the message he intended by U.S. resolve in Vietnam as the need to retain an element of unpredictability in the American posture toward adversaries.[7]

It is wholly unsurprising that Rusk found it difficult to persuade historians and analysts of U.S. foreign policy of the logic of this tortuous strategy. For the policy was exceedingly subtle, the effort to convince the Soviets that the United States would honor its NATO pledge of first use of nuclear weapons in a European war, which the Kennedy administration had firmly determined *never* to do. It was thus a desperate determination to make credible a threat that was merely a bluff. To compound the political complexity of this subtle strategy, Rusk was unable to explain it to the public. For to explain that Vietnam was an arena of containment chosen precisely because containment in the primary theater of conflict—Europe—was unmanageable in the nuclear era would have been to alert the Soviets to the hollow NATO threats of the United States and thus to weaken further the fragile fabric of deterrence.

The wonder of this arabesque strategy is that it worked, at least in Europe. Rusk counted it as the greatest satisfaction of his years as secretary of state that nuclear war was averted. No one, of course, will now be able to say with certitude that the bluff in Europe succeeded because of the reckless bravado in Southeast Asia. Nor will anyone be able to deny it any more convincingly.[8]

Rusk remained, a quarter century after leaving office, content to let history judge the sagacity of this global, all-or-nothing wager that an unsurvivable war in Europe could be averted by fighting another one with vast, but supportable, expense and suffering on the other side of the globe. History is unlikely to judge Rusk favorably, for very few people understood at the time, and quite likely still fewer will understand in the decades to come, the imminent and apocalyptic risks attendant on any NATO–Warsaw Pact confrontation in Europe between 1961 and 1989, and thus the desperate need to deflect the spark of war away from the tinderbox of Eurasian nuclear rivalry. But Rusk's confidence of ultimate vindication stemmed from his own understanding of the impending global catastrophe, which happily was stillborn. His confidence arose finally from his conscience, which was also the driving force behind the new strategy.

Rusk's claim—that Kennedy had eschewed the reigning U.S. resolve to initiate nuclear war in Europe in the highly plausible context of a Warsaw Pact conventional assault that threatened imminent NATO defeat—has several times been confirmed by Robert McNamara.[9] The claim remains perplexing to many, who charge that it is counterintuitive and, quite likely, self-serving. This skepticism is understandable but open to challenge.

The principal positive element of Kennedy's foreign policy record, and its high point in many accounts, was his rapid and cautiously aggressive rejoinder to the Soviet installation of missiles in Cuba in the summer and fall of 1962. The "quarantine" option was finally selected by the president with the clear understanding that, if it failed, the resort to direct military confrontation with the Soviet forces was still readily available. Kennedy displayed, even privately, no reluctance to resort to the use of conventional military forces against the Soviets. From this record, some perhaps hastily conclude that he would not have shrunk from being the first to use nuclear weapons in Europe in accordance with the NATO doctrine of first use.

Careful analysis of Rusk's (and McNamara's) assertions reveals the unsoundness of the view that one can project Kennedy's response to an overwhelming conventional military assault in Europe by analysis of his response to the surprise installation of Soviet nuclear missiles in Cuba.[10] The first dramatic difference between the two situations is the total reversal of the correlation of conventional (nonnuclear) forces in the two separate theaters. In the Caribbean, the Soviets were totally—and unimaginably foolishly—unprepared for the eventual conventional showdown. Only people who still believe in the literal truth of David's triumph over Goliath will be likely to believe that either Kennedy or Khrushchev misunderstood the balance of conventional military forces available either on the island or in the surrounding waters.

Moreover, no one on Kennedy's Executive Committee or on the Joint Chiefs of Staff ever contemplated a U.S. inauguration of a *nuclear* exchange. While no one could rule out the possibility of a Soviet nuclear assault on the United States, or indeed on its invading forces, an action that might have forced Kennedy to respond in kind, no one familiar with the crisis has claimed that Kennedy even remotely contemplated a U.S. first nuclear use against Cuba, or elsewhere.[11] From the fact that Kennedy was willing to go to war over the Cuban missile installation, no logical inference can be drawn about his willingness to initiate nuclear war.

The second salient difference between the two situations—response to the installation of nuclear warheads and missiles less than one hundred miles from Florida versus a likely response to a conventional military advance by Warsaw Pact troops in Europe—seems to require little comment. Rusk has not claimed that Kennedy would not have used all the available military resources at his command, including nuclear weapons, in defense of his homeland, but rather that he would never risk the survival of the United States in response to a conventional war in Europe. The example of the Cuban missile crisis does not therefore contradict Rusk's understanding of Kennedy's strategic resolve but use-fully clarifies it.

In one decisively significant way, however, the Cuban missile crisis does complement Rusk's still controversial contention that Kennedy's resolve in Vietnam may have been the most overlooked factor in the suc-cessful NATO maintenance of global deterrence throughout the Cold War. For it should be obvious that Kennedy's actual preparations for the resort to force in Cuba must be counted at least as heavily on the scale of effective deterrent strategies against Soviet aggression in Europe as his high-profile, and higher-risk, anti-Communist stance in Vietnam.

A second threat of force issued by Kennedy, also to be counted seri-ously in the successful maintenance of global deterrence, was his re-sponse to the erection of the Berlin Wall in August 1961. That response to the overnight raising of the wall was tacit but swift: the dispatch of fifteen hundred men of the First Battle Group of the Eighth Infantry Division of the United States Army. No one, however, has claimed that the president contemplated responding with nuclear force, or even mak-ing nuclear noises, in this crisis.[12] The explanation of Kennedy's meek but effective reaction to this new challenge in Berlin was obviously the exact converse of Khrushchev's rapid retreat in Cuba: the correlation of military resources available to each of the adversaries in the respec-tive crises. Berlin was utterly indefensible for NATO using only con-ventional forces, as would Cuba have been for the Soviets the follow-ing year.

Both these supposed exceptions to Kennedy's (and Rusk's) resolve to eschew the escalation to nuclear war in Europe are thus fully consistent with Rusk's testimony about the logic of "flexible response."

Rusk's late effort to justify Kennedy's Vietnam policies as an initially enlightened application of "flexible response" came much too late to influence the definitive theoretical interpretations of the period. In his influential study *Strategies of Containment*, the dean of these specialized studies, John Lewis Gaddis, contrasts the Kennedy approach to strategy with that of Eisenhower, which he prefers. Gaddis raises the possibility that Kennedy's rhetoric may have actually exacerbated the U.S.-Soviet tensions by inviting Khrushchev's adventure in Cuba.[13] Recording, in-deed significantly understating, the Kennedy administration's sense of self-satisfaction with its handling of the Cuban crisis as a textbook dem-onstration of "flexible response," Gaddis then turns his scholarly attention to the Kennedy-Johnson experiment with applying the same (dubious) strategic innovations to Vietnam, which he judges a definitive demonstration of the inherent and insuperable deficiencies of the new theory:

> The American defeat there rather grew out of assumptions derived quite logically from that strategy: that the defense of Southeast Asia was crucial to the maintenance of world order; that force could be applied in Vietnam with precision and discrimination; that means existed accurately to evaluate performance; and that the effects would be to enhance American power, prestige, and credibility in the world. These assumptions in turn reflected a curiously myopic preoccupation with process—a disproportionate fascination with means at the expense of ends—with the result that a strategy designed to produce a precise correspondence between intentions and accomplishments in fact produced just the opposite.[14]

A less convincing, but still widespread, challenge to Rusk's interpretation comes from those who consider the entire scenario of a possible conventional military confrontation in Europe to be an illusion spawned by Cold War ideology. To those operating from this premise, any diversionary strategy to avoid a European nuclear war by pursuing a conventional war in Vietnam is nothing but an exercise in paranoia. Reasonable people may wonder, however, whether such critics have adequately addressed a contrary analysis, which saw as a source of dangerous instability any rapid shift in the balance of military and political power in the heart of Europe.

Defense ministries throughout the NATO nations (and correspondingly the Warsaw Pact) undoubtedly had analyzed dozens of such conceivable scenarios of destabilization. Such was their unhappy lot during the dismal period of the Cold War. One possible development that might seriously have challenged planners and political authorities on each side of the Iron Curtain was undoubtedly the potential of a significant civilian uprising within one of the Warsaw Pact nations (for example, in Leipzig, East Germany, as happened much later). The uncertainties with which officials would be required to reckon in such a circumstance would include the possible refusal of the local officials (for example, the internal security and military forces of the German Democratic Republic) to crack down on the insurgents, and the nature of a Soviet reaction to such an impasse, along with the possible involvement of forces from the Federal Republic of Germany on behalf of their eastern countrymen.

Another wholly imaginable scenario that might have involved a dramatic shift in the European balance of power during this period of tension would have been a possible military intervention by the Soviets outside their recognized sphere of influence, for example, on behalf of Serbia in a Balkan civil war, such as unrolled following the end of the Cold War. Even "doves" in Washington might have viewed such a military intervention as a source of European destabilization that could be ignored only with dire global consequences.

The distinctive strategic anguish of Kennedy's foreign policy team arose from its early awakening from the Eisenhower-Dulles declaratory deterrence policy, which apparently contemplated a nuclear riposte to such conceivable crises. (In the Berlin crisis of 1953 and the crushed Budapest uprising of 1956, however, that administration indeed settled for peaceful contemplation of the developments.) In an era when Washington had become accustomed to the deceptively simple strategy of massive nuclear retaliation against Warsaw Pact conventional aggression, determining that this strategy was a moral and military trap required a totally independent judgment. For its execution inevitably entailed the extinction of the American experiment.

Rusk, fortunately, had retained this bold independence from the conventional wisdom that deterrence would never fail. It was not fashionable in the Kennedy administration to make moral arguments about foreign policy.[15] Nonetheless, Rusk was candid in his 1962 interview for *Life* magazine about the religious and moral inspiration of his independent assessment of the prevailing superpower standoff called the balance of terror. He later echoed the apocalyptic assessment of this deterrence strategy once offered by Khrushchev: "In the event of nuclear war, the living will envy the dead."[16] Because Rusk knew that the strategy of deterrence was fatally flawed, because, that is, no one could guarantee that nuclear deterrence would never fail, he shrank from reliance on this strategy. Because Rusk was utterly unwilling to lend a hand in the annihilation of the Northern Hemisphere, he entered, at Kennedy's side, the maze of a diversionary containment policy surrounding Saigon. Only a statesman with no other viable strategic options available would have allowed himself the wild gamble of investing American prestige and power in Ngo Dinh Diem. For Rusk, reliance on the conventional wisdom of nuclear deterrence was forbidden by conscience.[17]

But making this wager in Southeast Asia took more than mere principled statesmanship. It also required an instinct for moral casuistry associated more readily with wily European Jesuits than with American Calvinism. For the global wager on the cause of Vietnamese independence under Diem was primarily calculated to convince Soviet leaders that the NATO threat to initiate nuclear war in Europe was a credible one, which our adversaries dare not underestimate. The hazardous Vietnamese commitment, however, was made precisely because that NATO pledge of "first use" of nuclear weapons was, under Kennedy and Rusk, merely a bluff.[18] Such an elaborate strategic shell game was thus the achievement of a very subtle Calvinist casuistry and a poker-faced penchant for deception. The 1961–69 American formula for the conduct of containment by "flexible response" constituted an exotic and novel interpretation of the national interest in the nuclear era.

The exceptional character of Rusk's retreat from nuclear brinkmanship to the unfamiliar terrain of counterinsurgency in Southeast Asia is especially remarkable in contrast to the apparent continuing confidence in nuclear deterrence displayed in 1990 by his counterpart in Kennedy's White House, McGeorge Bundy.[19] While it may be difficult to explain how Rusk (and Kennedy) managed to escape the dangerous illusion of security under the prevailing NATO strategy of the 1960s, the more baffling question is how those responsible for foreign policy—along with the professors, pundits, think tank writers, theologians, and editorialists—managed to remain morally complacent during this entire era about the manifest fragility of such flawed deterrence. Common sense, which acknowledged that deterrence could foreseeably fail, with catastrophic consequences, was rare indeed in those decades. In the 1960s and 1970s "weak nerves" about nuclear weapons were almost unknown among American political elites.[20] Only an exceptionally independent and conscientious statesman could have found his way in 1961 away from the nuclear standoff in Europe and into Vietnam.

Finding the exit from Vietnam, however, should have been comparatively simple, merely the routine exercise of statecraft: Was the $1.5 million-a-day investment in Vietnam paying, or at least promising, substantial dividends for American security? At the close of 1962 such auspices were good. But when, several months later, the auspicious indices swiftly changed into dire omens, Rusk (and the president) failed to read the obvious signs of danger. By overlooking these signposts toward an honorable withdrawal from Vietnam, Kennedy and Rusk slowly allowed what had been merely a maze to become a morass.

Henry Kissinger and Robert McNamara have recently echoed the earlier conclusion of Arthur Schlesinger Jr. that the Kennedy administration had a golden opportunity to quit Vietnam honorably, and therefore without compromise of its global responsibilities for containment. This was when Diem and Nhu pursued, from March to November 1963, surprisingly overt initiatives to establish a federation in Vietnam between North and South, with Ho Chi Minh as the northern leader and Diem as president in the South.[21]

Between March 15 and November 1, 1963, information was accumulating in different Washington offices to show that Kennedy's interests and Diem's misgivings had almost miraculously converged: both wished desperately to get the United States out of Vietnam. In February, Kennedy had decided to pull out of Vietnam after his reelection in 1964. His decision was triggered by Senator Mike Mansfield's bleak report on U.S. prospects in Vietnam. On February 26 the release to U.S. newspapers of some portions of the Mansfield report, those most damaging to Diem and most pessimistic about his prospects for victory, had persuaded Nhu (and later Diem) to beat a retreat from Kennedy before he could abandon the Ngos to their fate. As early as mid-March, Nhu was publicly demanding a reduction in U.S. force levels. By early April, Diem himself was notifying Ambassador Nolting that he was modifying his dependence on the United States by withdrawing a symbolic sum of Vietnamese war funds from U.S. control.

If President Kennedy or any of his principal advisers had grasped the convergence of resolve in the two governments to abandon one another, Kennedy could have moved his target date for withdrawal ahead from 1965 to 1963—and perhaps could have used the Buddhist crisis in May to announce his withdrawal. This abrupt reversal could have been presented by Kennedy to his right-wing, anti-Communist critics as a reluctant response to Diem's cowardly retreat. "Containment," the defense of freedom, had, after all, certain inherent limits: it could not be invoked to coerce unwilling allies to fight despite their own wishes. Moreover, repulsion at Diem's strong-arm tactics was widespread in Washington.

Rusk failed to bring this capital coincidence to Kennedy's attention at least partially because he had himself been left in the dark about the president's resolve to leave Vietnam in 1965. Indeed, as late as 1988 Rusk was arguing vigorously that Kennedy never made such an about-face on Vietnam. Rusk's argument against Senator Mansfield's frequent recounting of his February 1963 conversation with the president, in which Kennedy assured Mansfield that he would withdraw troops from Vietnam after his reelection, is a personal one. For Kennedy had never made such a statement to Rusk.[22]

Moreover, such a plan would have been in Rusk's mind dishonorable, because it would have involved sending troops into battle in a campaign carried on exclusively for U.S. domestic political purposes. As Rusk remarked to his son: "The important reason is that had he [Kennedy] decided in 1963 on a 1965 withdrawal, he would have left Americans in a combat zone for domestic political purposes. Neither Kennedy nor any other American president could live with himself or look his senior colleagues in the eye under those conditions. Had Kennedy said that to Bob McNamara or me in 1963, we would have told him, 'If that is your decision, Mr. President, you must take them out now.' John Kennedy was the kind of man who would have seen that point immediately."[23] Rusk's sense of honor among statesmen must here be weighed against Senator Mansfield's flatly contradictory claim.

The second obstacle to Rusk's timely receptivity to news about Diem's feelers toward Ho (and vice versa) was the gauge of his own diplomatic imagination. He apparently could not bring himself to believe that Diem could prefer the future risks of an alliance with Ho to the present risks of the alliance with the United States. In an August 29 cable to Lodge, Rusk warned against issuing further threats to Diem, who might respond with "some quite fantastic action such as calling on North Vietnam for assistance in expelling the Americans."[24]

Rusk's ability to assimilate the increasingly salient evidence of a North-South Vietnamese rapprochement was also blunted by his commitment to the independence of South Vietnam as an outpost of the free world. His commitment indeed had little to do with the historical situation or the national aspirations of South Vietnamese leaders but was rather a commitment to the principle of commitment itself. It was because the United States (against Rusk's earlier advice) had blundered into the SEATO guarantee to South Vietnam that Kennedy would have to honor that foolhardy pledge.[25] If great powers unilaterally reneged on such solemn commitments anywhere, Communist aggression might be unleashed in Europe. But if Rusk came to believe that Diem now really wanted to be released from his alliance, the Americans would have no further treaty obligation to Diem. Without any derogation of his values or strategic vision, Rusk could then have advised Kennedy to consider withdrawing from Vietnam in response to the Ngos' signs of retreat.

Unfortunately, Rusk was blinded to the unforeseen and propitious change in the alliance relationship between Saigon and Washington by his earlier dismissal of Diem's legitimacy as the ruler of South Vietnam. As he later explained to his son, Rusk believed that "[i]n the early 1960s President Diem lost touch with his own people. . . . [C]learly Diem lost the support of his people."[26]

On these grounds, and inspired by his own cherished belief that the universal hallmark of governmental legitimacy is the Jeffersonian axiom of "government by consent of the governed," Rusk had concluded that Diem no longer could claim to enjoy the consent of the people he governed in South Vietnam. Diem's intention, then, to forgo the American alliance for the sake of a federal alliance with Ho Chi Minh was insignificant to Rusk, because it represented only Diem's own dynastic preference and not the pursuit of the interests of the people of South Vietnam. The United States, Rusk had confidently concluded, would persevere in its commitment to the interests of the South Vietnamese people, rather than to their now discredited government. In such circumstances, replacing Diem with a more popular and representative (Buddhist) government was the appropriate U.S. response. The alternative option, of seizing the opportunity of Diem's retreat in order to abandon South Vietnam altogether, did not commend itself to Rusk because it would have required recognizing the legitimate authority of a proved and incorrigible autocrat. Such recognition was inconsistent with Rusk's Jeffersonian worldview.

Schlesinger, who regrets that Kennedy did not seize the unforeseen opening of Diem's negotiations with Ho to quit the Vietnam quagmire, observes that there is no record in the official documents that Rusk, or any other U.S. official, brought this auspicious development to the president's attention. It is, however, likely that no record exists of such an exchange between Rusk and the president about Nhu's talk of neutralization because it had been front-page news in the *New York Times* on September 2, 1963, and was therefore familiar to Kennedy. Robert Trumbull, writing from Saigon on September 1, had observed in his dispatch that "President De Gaulle's vision of a unified Vietnam is believed . . . to coincide with concepts voiced by Ngo Dinh Nhu. . . . Officials who have talked with Mr. Nhu . . . say he has often hinted that his intercession could end the nine-year-old split between the Communist North and the non-Communist South. Vietnamese unification . . . might well mean the departure of United States forces."

Another constraint on Rusk's opportunity to counsel Kennedy about this possible exit was his understanding of his responsibility as secretary of state, namely, that the president should be his own secretary of state, choosing his foreign policy course in the context of U.S. domestic politics. Since Kennedy had on these grounds turned over Vietnam policy to Averell Harriman, Rusk deferred to his own undersecretary, who had no knowledge or intrinsic interest in Vietnam and saw only the threat posed for Kennedy by Nhu and Diem.[27] That Diem and Nhu might have made some rational calculation to terminate the alliance, almost at the same moment as Kennedy himself, was too improbable a development to attract Harriman's attention. Harriman's deputy for Vietnam, Roger Hilsman—whom Rusk had not selected for the post[28]—was, however, acutely aware of the efforts of the Ngo brothers to escape Kennedy. Hilsman bellowed in outrage at their "treason" even while plotting their overthrow.[29]

Dean Rusk was one of a handful of Kennedy's officials who could have changed the course of policy after the coup cable (243) was dispatched in his absence on Saturday, August 24, by George Ball, acting secretary of state. The cable authorized Lodge to initiate contact with Vietnamese generals who might be amenable to leading a coup against Diem, if Diem proved unwilling to jettison his brother Nhu. The following day, Ball further simplified the instructions to Lodge, allowing him to bypass the step of negotiations with Diem about banishing Nhu. This covert shift of procedures on a highly significant matter, namely, the steps prescribed for the removal of a foreign government, was the cause of considerable confusion in the White House during the next two months, since Rusk was apparently never informed about the change in Lodge's instructions. Earlier in the summer Harriman had similarly usurped Rusk's authority by instructing the chargé d'affaires, William

Trueheart, to threaten Diem with U.S. withdrawal if he did not begin "acting like an American politician."

State Department control of Vietnam policy had thus slipped from Rusk's hands to those of two visceral enemies of Diem, Ball and Harriman. Rusk was left executing a policy he had not designed. But the ultimate failure of that impulsive policy will now rest partially on the shoulders of Rusk. For he could easily have avoided this historical stigma either by demanding the withdrawal of the coup cable at the White House meeting on August 26 or by dismissing either Ball or Harriman for usurping his authority. He might also have resigned in protest at such administrative chaos. He chose none of these options.[30] The reason for Rusk's patient tolerance of such decisive interference in his realm of responsibility is clear enough. To have protested Ball's or Harriman's actions publicly would have been for Rusk an unacceptably rude gesture, both to the president and to his colleagues at the State Department. Such rudeness was unthinkable, for Rusk was a gentleman to a fault.

Rusk's self-discipline in tolerating the meddling of Ball and Harriman in his own area of responsibility as secretary of state was perhaps also due in large part to his own apprenticeship in the profession of diplomacy, when he had served as an assistant secretary of state for international organization under Secretary of State George Marshall in 1948. After a bruising bureaucratic battle in which Marshall had resented Clark Clifford's meddling with U.S. policy concerning the recognition of Israel, several of Marshall's friends had urged him to resign when Truman followed Clifford's politically inspired initiatives in favor of Israel. Rusk quite likely remembered in this summer of 1963 Marshall's response to the suggestion of resignation: "You don't resign because the President, who has a constitutional right to make a decision, makes one."[31]

On August 29, 1963, Kennedy had cabled Lodge, adding his personal imprimatur to the August 24 cable and personally taking responsibility for the execution of the mandated change of government in Saigon.[32] Within a week, on September 2, Kennedy publicly avowed the same indifference to the fate of the Saigon government officials if they failed to pursue "changes in policy and perhaps in personnel." This unambiguous backing of the coup by the president himself effectively removed from Rusk's hands the policy formulated in the August 24 and 25 coup cables. Rusk's job would be confined to the policy's execution.

The record suggests, however, that Rusk was personally untroubled by the momentum toward a coup. Just days before the coup was unleashed, at a White House meeting on October 29, with the president present, a sudden stirring against the coup emerged after the attorney general blurted out that the coup "makes no sense on the face of it." Maxwell Taylor seconded Robert Kennedy's skepticism, as did John McCone. Rusk then warned that the only hope for winning the war lay in the removal of Diem. Although Kennedy himself disagreed with Rusk, echoing readily his brother's alarm, the meeting ended with a decision for still another cable of inquiry to Lodge rather than a cancellation of the coup.[33] Rusk seems then to have saved the day for Duong Van Minh's junta. The last dim glimpse of the exit from the maze had been overlooked.

Rusk's justification of his actions during this long interval between the initial coup cable, dispatched in his absence on August 24, and the unleashing of the coup on November 1 is an authentically American one. As late as 1988, when the ominous consequences of Kennedy's decision to overthrow the constitutional government of South Vietnam were inescapably evident, Rusk remained untroubled by that 1963 fateful turn in the road. He minimized Washington's role in the coup, arguing that the generals who led the coup were acting on their own.[34] Indeed, it was Diem himself who provoked the coup by his repressive policies. Implausibly, Rusk compared the junta leaders with Locke's idealized revolutionaries who act on their own conscience and in the name of God. Rusk recalled the dancing in the streets of Saigon at the news of the accession to power of the popular Big Minh.[35]

The argument on which Rusk relied for supporting the short-lived junta's ouster of Diem was a conscientious one: Diem "had lost the support of his people." Citing the struggle of the activist Buddhist demonstrators, Rusk recalled his own assessment of the American reaction to such repression: "I didn't feel that the United States could acquiesce in Diem's repression of the Buddhists."[36] This judgment arose from the political philosophy that Rusk consistently articulated for the conduct of foreign affairs. The first principle of that philosophy is the eminently American criterion that "we believe that governments derive their just powers from the consent of the governed." Rusk told Theodore H. White in 1962 that this principle of consent was the key to American foreign policy, as he always explained to new ambassadors presenting their credentials in Washington.[37]

Still more tellingly, Rusk argued in 1989 that the American credo of government by consent of the governed was not merely our own national heritage but rather a sort of natural law of human development. People everywhere want to enjoy the blessings of Lockean democracy. "All my adult life I have believed that Jefferson put his finger on the ultimate political truth when he said, 'Governments derive their just powers from the consent of the governed.' All other forms of political organization—rule by an aristocracy, dictatorship of the proletariat, the divine right of kings—must contend with those yearnings for freedom seemingly *ingrained in human nature.*"[38] Here Rusk echoed the commonplace American assumption that our historical experience is an epiphany of universal human aspirations. Thus he had had no qualms in 1963, and no regrets in the late 1980s, about the Kennedy administration's decision to promote "government by consent" in Saigon by supporting a military coup that overthrew the government. This paradoxical formula, attaining government by consent through an externally stimulated military takeover, sprang from conscience, as Rusk's memoirs make indelibly clear.

Just as a conscientious fear of nuclear catastrophe had led in 1961 to the secret entry point of a U.S.–South Vietnamese military alliance, so conscience later required that Washington remove an incorrigible autocratic ally rather than allow Diem to pursue his own quixotic quest for a federal alliance with Ho Chi Minh. For Rusk, as for Kennedy, Diem's constant appeal to the universal right of sovereignty had been unpersuasive. For the anachronistic claim of sovereignty had now been eclipsed by the universal natural right to government by consent. The Vietnamese government was dismissed by Rusk and others because it contradicted irreconcilably their own ascendant Enlightenment formula of democracy.

Less than three weeks before the coup, in a Columbus Day address at Hebrew Union College in Cincinnati, Rusk spelled out a nuanced and culturally sensitive formula for relating the American political philosophy of "consent by the governed" to American policies in Southeast Asia. For Rusk, the specific heritage of the American experiment was not a univocal and rigid universal model, but merely one successful formulation of the ancient and worldwide perception that government cannot be understood merely as a matter of coercion and obedience but must remain always a form of social contract, with reciprocal rights.

The ancient sacred books of the Hindus contain coronation oaths which show that in Vedic times the king usually was elected and bound by compact with the people. . . .

In ancient China likewise: Even the authority of the Emperor is not a divine right, but is conditioned by the wish and consent of the people. . . .

Mencius, the great disciple of Confucius, said 2,250 years ago: "The people are the most important element in a state. . . ." He advanced the view that both the ministers and the people had a right to depose a wicked king. . . .

. . . We recognize also that there are many possible forms of democratic institutions, and that those that are best for a particular country may differ considerably from our own and from the various parliamentary forms of Western Europe. But we feel deeply about the difference between democracy and dictatorship, between constitutional government and rule by raw force.[39]

Dean Rusk was blessed with a long life that allowed him to witness the unraveling of the Soviet empire and indeed the Soviet Union itself. This natural process of disintegration of the Soviet totalitarian and imperial order was an unexpectedly early denouement to the Cold War struggle, which ended without a nuclear catastrophe. Characteristically, Rusk declined to claim victory in the protracted struggle, preferring to underline the natural dynamics of the Lockean drive to attain government by consent as the power that finally undermined the Warsaw Pact.[40]

But other Americans will continue to inquire whether Rusk's policies were not at least partially to blame for the fruitless prosecution of the war in Indochina for a full decade after the overthrow of Diem. To many of them, it may seem reasonable to conclude that Rusk's stewardship as secretary of state was historically tragic in its Vietnam policy even though it was consistently high-principled. For none of Rusk's decisions about Vietnam were merely a reckless resort to realpolitik. Each was forged rather in the crucible of conscience. And therein lies the unique puzzle at the heart of the American experience in Vietnam: How could the consequences of a policy so unambiguously dictated by conscience be so morally repugnant?

Perhaps no one has framed this provocative question more clearly, examined Rusk's career more meticulously, or drawn conclusions more bitterly critical of him than Warren Cohen, the dean of American historians of U.S.-Asian diplomatic relations. In an illuminating and remarkably forthright preface to his study of Rusk, Cohen announces that he undertook this exacting inaugural diplomatic biography of Rusk because he was intrigued by the ironic destiny of such an able American who garnered a worldwide reputation as a "sinister" statesman.[41] Later, at the conclusion of the study, in a brief but equally trenchant evaluation of Rusk's legacy as secretary of state, Cohen concludes that the secretary's undoing was his liberal conscience. Throughout the study Cohen frequently lauds Rusk for his universal vision of liberal politics, which differed from the perspectives of other influential American statesmen of the Cold War, such as Dean Acheson and George Kennan, by insisting that the vision of Locke, Jefferson, and Madison was a legacy for all mankind of whatever race and on whatever continent.[42] Until the closing paragraphs of the study, then, the reader is led to believe that Cohen shares Rusk's universalist liberalism. Thus there is a surprise on the final page of this definitive account, where Cohen faults Rusk for his ethical consistency: "In the mid-1960s, some liberals shed their universalism and recognized the irrelevance of liberal democracy and a Eurocentric peace system for much of Asia and Africa. They concluded, as more radical thinkers had long before, that anti-Communism was senseless when Communism might be the best alternative offered a people. Rusk, however, remained loyal to his President and to an earlier vision. He thus betrayed his own better instincts, the interests of his country, the principles of the UN. Much may be said in mitigation, but never enough."[43] Finally Cohen concludes that Rusk's "sinister" reputation was earned at least partially by his unbending commitment to liberalism when much of the American liberal community had consigned Africa and Asia to the tender mercies of communism. Such consistency, Cohen observed quizzically, was a betrayal of liberalism.

Cohen's learned complaint that Rusk clung to his universal liberal philosophy when others were consigning peoples of color to the experiment of materialistic totalitarianism is one that Rusk likely bore in good humor. But the incomprehensibility of Cohen's conclusions may have triggered in Rusk some misgivings about his own 1961 resolve not to write his own memoirs.[44] After the appearance of Cohen's study in 1980,

Rusk generously welcomed interviews with other authors, who might present an alternative philosophical and ethical critique of his diplomacy.[45] Rusk was, as Cohen amply documents, committed to the global relevance of the American experiment. Persuasive arguments can be made against this culturally univocal philosophy of diplomacy. Some, for example, have argued that political institutions and mores are a function of culture and therefore legitimately may, and perhaps must, differ from one culture to another.[46] This cultural pluralism, demanding diversity of political institutions around the globe, was Diem's own viewpoint, voiced in his insistence on the right of sovereignty, which Rusk conscientiously dismissed.

From 1961 onward, Rusk resisted the momentum in the Kennedy White House to "make major additional commitments of American prestige to a losing horse." He recalled the role of the Kennedy administration officials who wished "[t]o nudge Diem into retirement or even conspire with other elements in South Vietnam to bring about a coup d'état. I was personally repelled by Diem's repressive rule but uncomfortable with talk about trying to replace him, thinking this was not a decision for Americans to make."[47] Nevertheless, when George Ball sent the coup cable, which obviously represented a decision made by Americans to replace Diem, Rusk did not demand its recall. Indeed, months later, just two days before the coup, Rusk was the only cabinet member who shielded the coup planning, now finally nearing execution, from Kennedy's own anxious misgivings. For the imminent coup was directed by Ball, Harriman, and Hilsman, who acted more precipitately but with precisely the same feelings of revulsion that Diem evoked in Rusk.

It was, then, a thoroughly conscientious coup, unleashed out of moral repugnance at autocracy, in the Wilsonian confidence that democracy can grow out of the barrel of a gun.[48] The fruits of this high-minded meddling in Vietnam were, however, predictably bitter: eighteen months of low-scale civil war, punctuated by eight successive and increasingly comic coups. Rusk never directly confronted his own responsibility for this downward spiral of Vietnamese politics, which quickly drew Washington into its vortex. He merely observed: "The immediate result of Diem's downfall was positive . . . but the bloom soon wore off."[49] Rusk tentatively attributed the factionalism and ineffectuality of the eight bimonthly Saigon dynasties to the French legacy of political instability. He appears not to have wondered whether the abrupt American overthrow of the constitutional government of South Vietnam might have severed the nerve of government in Saigon.

Rusk's moral composure while presiding over a coup against a nine-year ally seems to have arisen from his confidence that democracy was the natural instinct of people everywhere. Thus, the ousting of an autocrat would likely presage a spontaneous and noble flourishing of popular government. Rusk seems not to have been puzzled by the philosophical paradox of such liberal intolerance for alien forms of government abroad. Proud of the unique American achievement of constitutional pluralism, that legal formula that had allowed Americans to adjudicate creatively the radical diversity of the different regions, economies, and cultural loyalties in their far-flung states, Rusk followed in Wilson's footsteps to conclude that this eighteenth-century American constitutional formula was the sole legitimate structure of authority in the modern world, East or West. Dictators like Diem must be forced to reform or be set aside. Thus the internal pluralism enshrined in the U.S. Constitution now ironically required global uniformity of constitutions fashioned in conformity with the image of American democracy.

To those less univocally minded about the spectrum of political cultures and the possible range of political imagination, it is no surprise that the Wilsonian fundamentalism of twentieth-century American liberalism came a cropper in Vietnam. Americans were misled by their recent political triumphs: U.S. leadership had just guided the re-creation of Germany and Japan in the American image after those nations' own political traditions had led them to shame and defeat.[50] But the young American leaders who savored this triumph were naturally unprepared for their encounter with an oriental mandarin tradition whose image of authority was that of a divinely sanctioned autocracy, presiding over an immutable social hierarchy. Diem stubbornly preferred the ancient traditions of the Confucian empire, fashioned on the Chinese model, to the legacy of Jefferson. Here the narrow limits of the American tolerance for diversity rapidly asserted themselves. For autocrats, many Americans believe, have no rights in the modern world.

Rusk personally shared this narrow vision of political legitimacy. He had consistently counseled since 1961 that Kennedy should make U.S. assistance to Diem contingent on "reform," that is, the abandonment of Confucian autocracy in favor of the American formula for democracy. But he was driven finally to take the enormous risk with Diem by prin-

ciples other than his liberalism. If Rusk had been merely a liberal statesman, he would almost surely never have found the elusive entrance to
the maze of Vietnamese politics that welcomed Kennedy's advisers and
troops.

Rusk had confided to Theodore H. White that there were considerations decisively more important than politics, liberal or otherwise. In the
1962 *Life* interview, he indicated that for him the realm of politics was
not an end in itself but an instrument of human betterment. Politics is
not the whole of human existence but a splendid chapter in the book of
life. Beyond politics lie the physical, social, and cultural treasures of life.
Politics must then remain an instrument of the human experiment, not
its goal. Political struggles, such as the Cold War confrontation between
democracy and communism, must be held bound within the clear borders of politics, which constitute a province of man's domain but not its
entirety. Recalling to White the hemispheric threat of nuclear annihilation, Rusk suggested that "Kennedy and Khrushchev both live with the
first question of the Westminster Catechism always in mind: 'What is
the Chief End of Man?'" Neither Khrushchev, of course, nor Kennedy,
nor for that matter White, had likely ever heard of the Westminster
Catechism. Nevertheless, Rusk's point is clear: political struggles that
dare to make their own ephemeral rivalries the justification for destroying the earth have overrun their natural boundaries and must be tamed.
Conscience, according to Rusk, is the metapolitical compass that defines
the perimeters of politics and challenges the political assumptions that
make politics an end in itself.

By 1962, and most dramatically during the Cuban missile crisis
months after Rusk's *Life* interview with White, the political rivalry between Washington and Moscow had crossed this forbidden border.
Rusk, like Kennedy, was determined to change course in the Cold War
and return the conflict to its proper role as a struggle of human pro-
portions rather than an all-out, all-or-nothing wager at the precipice of
extinction. Perhaps never has so ominous a threat to humanity been
successfully deflected by so few people (on each side of the Iron Curtain), clinging to the commonsense view that politicians have no right to
play God.

If Rusk had been merely a liberal statesman, he almost certainly
would not have steered Kennedy into a cautious commitment to Ngo
Dinh Diem. It was his moral repugnance at the risks of the fragility of

nuclear deterrence that drove him to seek such a change of venue for containment. If he had been a less consistent liberal, he might not have condoned the overthrow of this same government in Saigon on grounds of moral revulsion. But as it was, Rusk was both a Calvinist, who shrank from sitting in judgment over the fate of the Northern Hemisphere and its peoples, and a liberal, who shrank from association with a dictator. If he is remembered, as Warren Cohen pictures him, as a "sinister" statesman who refused to consign two-thirds of humanity—the Asian and African nations—to the illiberal embrace of communism, he will be only half-remembered. For Rusk consciously ushered himself into the dilemma of deposing an allied head of state in the name of conscience precisely because of that other, and more inescapable, imperative to do all he could on his watch to stave off nuclear annihilation. Rusk's definitive success, the avoidance of nuclear war, will nevertheless forever be clouded by his partial failure, namely, to find a democratic future for a confused and Confucian people in the midst of civil war.

Rusk's failure was a very American one. We are a nation seemingly incapable of implementing a morally neutral political settlement for a people in the midst of an armed struggle for independence. We were dissatisfied supporting mere containment of Communist aggression; we must confer salvation by elections.

Just as it took a poet, Robert Frost, speaking at the hour when Kennedy took the oath of office, to prophesy unerringly the exact lineaments and fatal virtues of the Kennedy administration, so it was a novelist, Graham Greene, who foresaw as early as 1955 the trajectory of U.S. policy in South Vietnam.[51] Sketching the young American protagonist of *The Quiet American*, Alden Pyle, as a salesman for democracy in a half nation recently carved out of the colonial wreck of Vietnam, Greene indicts the reckless innocence of the United States. After Pyle has killed and maimed civilians in Saigon with bombs intended to disrupt a non-democratic military parade, Greene's persona, the British journalist Fowler, explodes in anger: "God save us always from the innocent and the good." But Fowler insists that the OSS/CIA agent, Pyle, was a good man in his own Yankee eyes. His crime was his innocence, that is, his determination to act on the warrant of a U.S. political strategy tract on the promotion of democracy in Asia, written by the fictional York Harding.[52] Innocence, the tragic virtue that would soon lead to the downfall of the U.S. democratic crusade in Vietnam, was the American assumption that the bitter French and British experience in Southeast Asia was no precursor of doom but rather a confirmation of Washington's hopes, because Americans could accomplish what no tainted "old colonialists" had achieved. The fatal virtue of innocence was the American inability to accept the permanence of political diversity as the law of the human condition. With the cynical Greene, just as with the innocent Yankee Robert Frost, the literary imagination here crystallized the decisive U.S. error in Vietnam.

Greene's only blind spot in plotting American prospects was his premise that the inspiration of the strategy was found in some faddish anti-Communist tract by York Harding. In reality, the democratic strategy pursued so fatefully by resolute Americans had been scripted, as at least Rusk sincerely believed, by Thomas Jefferson. It was not to some feverish McCarthyite imagination but to the "natural law" of democratic rule, voiced authoritatively by Jefferson, that Rusk had looked for guidance. If he was misguided in removing an autocratic Confucian leader in the innocent expectation of easily making space thereby for a spontaneously democratic government, he was still manifesting a thoroughly American confidence in the "democratic form of right divine" to which Frost had appealed in his Inauguration Ode on January 20, 1961.[53]

Rusk's leadership in sheltering the coup strategy dictated by his subordinates Ball and Harriman was due, not to the panic of anticommunism that had seized Washington in the 1950s, but to the late-eighteenth century's serene confidence that history had then begun anew in Philadelphia.

Rusk stands apart from, and above, the other American secretaries of state who managed the Cold War. For he vetoed the standing orders to risk hemispheric destruction in order to contain Communist aggression. Neither his two immediate predecessors, John Foster Dulles and Christian Herter, nor his two immediate successors, William Rogers and Henry Kissinger, are yet known to have made such a bold stand against the nuclear bravado that surrounded the years of Rusk's service.

Yet in the logical course of his determination to reverse Cold War strategy, Rusk unhappily indulged in another illusion, which Graham Greene reasonably labeled insanity. "What's the good? he'll always be

innocent, you can't blame the innocent, they're always guiltless. . . . Innocence is a kind of insanity."[54] Having boldly sidestepped the insanity
of "massive (nuclear) retaliation," Rusk had inadvertently stepped onto
the adjacent slope of the "democratic form of right divine," the democratic imperative of reform. Rusk's reputation will always be marked by
his singular destiny among the statesmen of his era: an embarrassment
of ethics.

NGO DINH DIEM
Mandarin to an Empty Throne

In his 1995 memoir, Robert McNamara admits that he never understood Diem. "Diem was an enigma to me. . . . He appeared autocratic, suspicious, secretive and insulated from his people. . . . Even today I do not know what long-term objectives he envisioned for his nation and his people."[1] McNamara's present mystification about Diem's purposes is in sharp contrast to his views in October 1963, when he told the Senate Foreign Relations Committee in executive session that the overwhelming political, military, and social odds against Diem could easily explain "the brutal repression that that government has applied during the period May to August (and . . . theretofore). . . . But there is at least the beginning of the elements of democracy."[2] At that time Diem was no enigma but an embattled autocrat struggling for survival.

The odds against Diem were indeed daunting. As McNamara assessed the situation for the committee, Diem had been besieged for almost a decade by both foreign and internal forces. Under such circumstances, South Vietnam's slow progress toward a modern political structure was comparatively impressive. Yet McNamara's unvarnished assessment of Diem in October 1963 was factually uncontroversial.

A catalog of historical studies of the Diem government has come to the same unflattering conclusion.[3] Evidence is ample that Diem eliminated all opposition to his regime through imprisonment or censorship.[4] An influential critic, Joseph Buttinger, describes Diem's post-1959 rule as a brutal dictatorship.[5] Buttinger had once been an enthusiastic supporter of Diem, but later, in 1962, he undertook a campaign, in cooperation with Diem's ambassador in Washington, to turn Kennedy against Diem. Buttinger is careful, however, to recall that before 1959 Diem was universally acknowledged to have enjoyed popular support.[6] But

Robert Scigliano, a sympathetic student of South Vietnam, observed that by 1962 Diem's government had unhappily replicated many of the repressive features of Ho Chi Minh's totalitarian state.[7] In a similar vein, Stanley Karnow published an unflattering assessment of the regime in the September 28, 1963, issue of the *Saturday Evening Post*, calling Diem's family "a cross between the Borgias and the Bourbons . . . devious, obstinate, imperious . . . neurotic and sanctimonious."[8]

Many of the same critics who meticulously cataloged Diem's ineffaceable failings have likewise faithfully portrayed his undoubted stature in Vietnamese eyes. Buttinger, for example, on the next to last page of his thousand-page text about the early years of the Vietnam wars, concludes that Diem "was the only outstanding leader in the anti-communist camp."[9] William Duiker likewise underlines the early lofty stature of Diem in Vietnamese eyes. When Bao Dai took power and dismissed the former Council of Ministers in 1933, his appointment of Diem to his cabinet had been widely approved. Diem's sudden resignation after three months in office, in protest against French interference, caused a public furor.[10] Scigliano agrees: Diem's abrupt resignation from Bao Dai's 1933 cabinet in protest against French interference earned him the lasting aura of "unsullied opposition to colonialism." Diem was the best known of the small group who had refused to collaborate with the French.[11] Discussing Bao Dai's renewed choice of Diem in 1954 as premier of the new state of South Vietnam, Buttinger observes: "Bao Dai . . . realized that Diem was virtually without competition. There was no serious contestant of his stature and political acceptability. . . . Diem was the only one who was talked about in Saigon as a future prime minister."[12] Scigliano, too, concludes that Diem's investiture as premier in 1954 "seems in retrospect altogether natural."[13]

Earlier, in 1945, Bao Dai had tried to appoint Diem prime minister on the virtually unanimous advice of all those whom the emperor consulted.[14] John McAlister Jr., a student and colleague of Paul Mus, the legendary French specialist on Vietnam, traces to this moment in 1945 the unique authority of Diem among his non-Communist contemporaries. In March of that year Bao Dai had abrogated French control, accepting instead Japanese protection for the moment as a prelude to independence. He offered the premiership to Diem, who had steadily resisted collaboration with the Japanese. Clinging to his autonomy, and his decade-long animosity to Bao Dai, Diem declined the emperor's offer.[15]

One of Diem's salient credentials for this nomination was his legitimate claim to be the authentic link to Vietnam's monarchical tradition. His father, Ngo Dinh Kha, had successfully vindicated some of the claims of earlier emperors under the French. Diem himself was close to Prince Cuong De until the prince's death in 1950.[16] Public standing for Vietnamese politicians was largely a function of their record for resistance to, or at least noncollaboration with, the French overlord. Such stature was frequently linked to pro-royalist activities, since early resistance efforts tended to coalesce around the traditional indigenous rulers of Vietnam, the imperial dynasties. Mandarins and other scholars were prominent in such doomed movements.[17]

The earliest overt rebellion against the French occurred in 1885, when the French-imposed child emperor Ham Nghi was taken from court by the regent, Ton That Tuyet, and hidden in the nearby hills. Three years later Ham Nghi was captured by the French and deposed. They replaced him with his more docile brother, Dong Khanh.[18] Early in the twentieth century other rebel scholars selected Prince Cuong De as their leader. Cuong De established a school of resistance in Japan, where he spent the rest of his life as head of the Modernization Society. The leader of this Western-oriented society was Phan Boi Chau, who had earlier rallied to the support of Ham Nghi.[19] Chau was kidnapped in 1925 by the French and subjected to house arrest until his death in 1940.[20]

The leading Vietnamese rivals of the royalist Modernization Society were the conservative Constitutionalists. Seeking accommodation with the French, the Constitutionalists hoped to combine the advantages of French education (and wine) with traditional Vietnamese royalist and religious values.[21] Phan Quynh, their spokesman, warned against the wholesale westernization of Vietnam and the risk of cultural suicide. Though he welcomed the French presence with its opening to modernity and science, which he felt should be blended with Confucian heritage, he insisted on the indispensability of the traditions of religion, including Buddhism, and the monarchy. Blind to the ineradicable tensions between traditional hierarchy and religion on the one hand and the Enlightenment humanism of Europe on the other, Phan Quynh bequeathed a legacy of cultural ambivalence to the next generation.[22] While Diem would later pick up this legacy of cultural struggle and restoration, he was not blind to the contradictions between Eastern and Western values.

Ngo Dinh Diem had early elected the domestic role of a mandarin moralist. An able scholar, he declined an offer in 1918 of a scholarship to complete his studies in Paris, opting instead for the Vietnamese School of Administration. He graduated to an administrative position as province chief in Phan Rang and later Phan Thiet. But Diem was dreaming of a higher calling: to restore the Confucian religious and political heritage that Vietnam had absorbed from its Chinese conquerors more than a thousand years before, but that was being undermined by the French.

This Confucian legacy had offered Vietnam a venerable tradition of order and justice that had definitively changed the earlier civilization. It was an order linking nature and society, where the emperor served as mediator between heaven and earth, keeping the two in harmony through meticulous ritual and imperial virtue.[23] From the imperial court in Hue had radiated the aura of virtue through the mediation of mandarins, a disciplined cadre of officials selected on the basis of competitive intellectual merit.

In a long interview with Marguerite Higgins of the *New York Herald Tribune* on August 7, 1963, Diem sought to communicate to Washington officials some central Vietnamese cultural realities that inspired his government. Regarding the constant critique in American editorials that he was a mandarin, he countered: "I know that some Americans try to tarnish me by calling me a mandarin. . . . But I am proud of being a mandarin. . . . It may not be similar to anything that you Americans have experienced — this mandarin-Confucian system. But it has its merits and its own inner democracy."[24]

Although the neo-Confucian model of society in Vietnam was a millennial institution, Diem's effort to revitalize it in the wake of French colonialism was almost certainly a utopian illusion, hardly more realizable than Ho Chi Minh's competing Marxist vision of a classless society. For the invasion of French civilization, which followed military conquest, had virtually undone the whole of the Confucian antiprogressive worldview. As French commentator Jacques Dalloz argues, the traditionalist and ritualistic system that concentrated all power in one (mandarin) class had been rejected much earlier in the twentieth century by the young Vietnamese intellectuals' Eurocentric cultural revolution (1919–39). The traditional role of the mandarin had been jettisoned, although the precepts of Confucianism continued to prevail in society. The professional classes had by then become gallicized, striving, always unsuccessfully, to be fully integrated into the French community. Diem's efforts to recall these political elites to the anachronistic order of Confucius were no more auspicious than his parallel effort to bypass French-tainted officials by appointing Americans to administer his government.[25]

As Diem turned his eyes to the monarchical Confucian past, he stared soberly into the void. For the apex of that order, the imperial dynasty itself, had been systematically dismantled and discarded by the French in a series of depositions and exiles beginning in 1885. Removing independence-minded emperors and installing more accommodating ones had been a central tenet of French imperial strategy in Vietnam. When the last of the imperial line, Bao Dai, was restored in the South after the Geneva Accords, he had been uniformly advised to appoint Diem as premier. Then, in a burst of irony, Diem deposed Bao Dai because of his record of guarded accommodation with the French.[26] With this deed Diem completed the work of the French, smashing the last symbol of Confucian order. Now he was the chief mandarin to an empty throne.

At the same time, Diem rejected all the other trained administrative personnel who had been tainted by their love of France. To the despair of the Americans, he resolutely excluded from office the French-educated political classes of the South. These politicians were by and large an immature, fractious, anarchic cast of characters whose behavior in office after Diem's ouster vindicated his low opinion of them.[27] Isolated from potential political collaborators and deprived of an educated electorate by a century of French asphyxiation of the vigorous Vietnamese educational tradition, Diem nevertheless somehow presided over almost a decade of impressive economic and educational recovery.[28]

The forces gradually undermining Diem's effort at restoration included the relentless campaign of terror waged by North Vietnam.[29] Buttinger puts the toll of assassinated South Vietnamese officials between 1957 and 1964 at thirteen thousand, evenly distributed among corrupt and responsible officials.[30] Bernard Fall summarized perhaps most tellingly the assault on Diem's officialdom, recalling the results of his 1959 study: "Saigon was deliberately *encircled* and *cut off* from the hinterland with a 'wall' of dead village chiefs."[31] National anti-Communist leaders, including Diem's brother Ngo Dinh Khoi, were likewise systematically assassinated at Communist Party direction between 1945 and 1946.[32] Khoi and his son were buried alive.[33]

The assault of the North Vietnamese against the South recalled their earlier ideological campaign to motivate their own peasants for the struggle ahead by punishing and murdering "large landholders." This harrowing story of the 1953–55 "mass mobilization movement" was modeled precisely on the earlier Chinese Communist paradigm. Owners of as little as two acres were branded "landlords" and put on trial in the villages. Between ten thousand and fifteen thousand landowners in the North were killed in this campaign and perhaps one hundred thousand imprisoned. In August 1956 Ho Chi Minh confessed that "errors" had been committed in the program and regretted that "one cannot wake the dead."[34]

This massacre marked perhaps the nadir of Ho's career. Ho had returned to Vietnam after decades in Moscow and in China at Tet in 1941. He took up residence in a large cave at Pac Bo, near the Chinese border, eventually constructing there a bamboo hut. He remained there for a year, naming a mountain Karl Marx and a nearby stream Lenin. There he presided in May 1941 at the Eighth Party Plenum, which founded the Viet Minh.[35]

This revolutionary party at first sought accommodation with France, while reprimanding the French for refusing to export their political heritage of freedom and equality to Indochina. Ho appeared so gentle and personally deferential to French officials that Jean Sainteny, the principal French negotiator, compared him with Gandhi, who had eschewed violent confrontation during his own struggle for independence from Great Britain. Jean and Simonne Lacouture, however, suggest that Ho resembled the warrior Mao more than Gandhi.[36]

Frederick Dupont, a French financial official who had been responsible for the military budgets of the French forces in Indochina, depicted these contrasting faces of Ho Chi Minh in his *Mission de la France en Asie*. Dupont defined the unique characteristic of the doomed Indochina war as the triumph of psychological warfare, that is, of "the smiling terrorist." Ho Chi Minh, for example, the night before his slaughter of French soldiers in Hanoi, wrote an amiable letter to an old friend in Paris, Monsieur Moutet, asking for the latest news from Moutet's son. Similarly, the day after he ordered the elimination of the whole body of

the traditional North Vietnamese francophile political class, Ho issued a
call for a renewal of civil dialogue in the country.[37]

In 1945 Ho put out feelers to the victorious Americans, symbolized
by his generous borrowings from Jefferson in his September 2, 1945,
proclamation of independence, which he read to an audience of half a
million Vietnamese.[38] After 1954 Ho relinquished all involvement in administration or military strategy, devoting himself exclusively to the symbolic role of personifying the new political order. He made himself into
the living "ancestor" of the revolution in his own lifetime.[39] Frances
FitzGerald observed:

> Ho was perfectly conscious of his role. He orchestrated his own pub-
> lic gestures just as carefully as the emperors had performed the rites
> in order to *show* the Vietnamese what had to be done. . . .
>
> Quite consciously, Ho Chi Minh foreswore the grand patriarchal
> tradition of the Confucian emperors. Consciously he created an "im-
> age" of himself as "Uncle Ho," the gentle bachelor relative who has
> only disinterested affection for the children who are *not* his own sons.
> As a warrior and a politician he acted ruthlessly upon occasion, but in
> public and as head of state he took pains to promote that family feel-
> ing which the Vietnamese had often had for their leaders.[40]

In the struggle for independence in Vietnam, Ho's carefully contrived
avuncular image was matched by the equally artificial self-image portrayed by Diem. Just as Ho had delegated care of the political struggle to
his party, so Diem delegated to his brother Nhu all the coercive responsibilities of government. As FitzGerald noted:

> Diem neither formed nor joined a political party, where the real
> training for independence might be had. He saw himself as a man of
> destiny, responsible for the nation by right of birth and superior
> virtue. . . .
>
> . . . It was as if he [Diem] had made an image of himself—an image
> that was static, two dimensional, like an icon hung in a museum
> whose significance has long been forgotten. For Diem was not truly a
> traditional ruler—he was a reactionary, and like so many reaction-
> aries, he idealized the past and misconceived the present. His whole
> political outlook was founded in nostalgia—nostalgia for a country
> that did not exist except in the Confucian texts, where the sovereign

governed entirely by ritual and the people looked up to him with a distant filial respect. Diem realized that Vietnam had changed. But he saw it as his duty to restore the old society and preserve it from the corrupting influence of the West, not by efficient measures but by moral example.[41]

The tantalizing question of the prospects for a stable alliance between Ho and Diem, which the two began to explore in July 1963, will remain a matter of permanent speculation. Amid the many formidable indications of the eventual failure of such federal cooperation, there remains one slender hint that they might have succeeded in such a sudden shift of tactics. That hope lay in an ardent aspiration for independence that they shared. In choosing a joint path to that independence, they also harbored one additional shared belief: that the key to the renaissance of Vietnam lay in the villages, not in the urban areas where the contagion of colonialism had been internalized by the francophile city dwellers. For both Diem and Ho, extremists respectively of the right and the left, sought to recapture the traditional ethos of the autonomous village that antedated the two millennia of Chinese cultural influence.

Diem, for example, was planning for democratic reform on a different scale and calendar than his American (and Vietnamese) critics. His first priority was village self-government.[42] Dalloz observes: "The power of the emperor stops at the bamboo hedge [of the village]." The national government therefore dealt not with individuals but with the village elders.[43] At the village level, Diem was already engaged in preparing for elections. By October 7, 1963, he would be able to announce with satisfaction that villagers had elected executive committees and village councils with constitutional charters in almost nine thousand villages.[44] The unique salience of the village in Vietnamese culture is stressed by André Masson, a former colonial finance official and later an archivist in Paris for the Indochina Archives and Libraries, in his academic manual *Histoire du Vietnam*. Contrasting Vietnamese culture with that of France, Masson argues that European individualism is antithetical to the worldview of the Vietnamese, whose identity derives from the family and the village. Each village, for example, has its own deity and its inherited sense of the sacred character of village life. Moreover, the essential dynamic of traditional Vietnamese religion (onto which have been grafted both Confucianism and Buddhism) is animism, the communal bond be-tween the living and the deceased spirits of the village.[45]

Diem's insistence on instituting change at the *village* level is easier to appreciate in light of the sociological analysis of Paul Mus, the Vietnamese-born and -reared son of the founder in 1907 of the first French-language lycée in Vietnam. There Paul Mus studied with the class of Vietnamese students being prepared for posts in the colonial adminis-tration. During World War II Mus was parachuted into Japanese-held Indochina by the Free French Associates of the British Intelligence Ser-vice in order to assess Japanese military strength. There, hiding in the villages, he discovered what no Frenchman suspected at the time: to the grassroots-level Vietnamese, the French, who had been militarily routed by the Japanese, had lost their aura of invincibility and now could be challenged for independence. Mus was thus later able to interpret in-cisively the meaning of Ho Chi Minh's bold declaration of indepen-dence in August 1945. The Viet Minh's confidence rested on their con-viction that the mandate of heaven had passed from France to some future rulers.[46]

Mus's effort to share these insights with the French colonial administra-tors was unavailing, and he eventually retired from his government posts. While still in government employ, however, he had been sent on a daring solo mission to Ho Chi Minh, bearing the French demand of un-conditional surrender. He finally was brought to meet Ho in his forest hideaway early one day in May 1947. Unsurprisingly, Ho pointed out that surrender would be a cowardly act of which he was incapable. Re-buffed and certain now of the future of Indochina, Mus returned with-out harm to Hanoi.[47] In 1952 Mus published his study *Viet-Nam: Socio-logie d'une guerre*, which remains a classic, if nearly impenetrable, study of the struggle between Indochinese city dwellers (one quarter of the pop-ulation in Vietnam) and the peasants (the other three-quarters).[48]

Mus had observed the marginality, in relation to the future of Viet-nam, of some of his own lycée classmates from among the French-speaking (and -thinking) Vietnamese elites. Many of his former class-mates, for example, returned with their advanced degrees from Paris only to find themselves unable to express the basic concepts of their pro-fessional fields in Vietnamese. This linguistic ineptitude was a function both of their worldview and of their cultural preference for France.

Mus insisted that the worldview that would govern the future of Vietnam would not be the scientific and cosmopolitan perspective of Paris (and of French-trained elites in Hanoi and Saigon) but the mythic and religious worldview of the countryside. Ho was seeking to enlist the peasants in the struggle for independence by instilling a radically novel belief in the popular wisdom of the peasantry. Mus believed that Ho would be the victor in the struggle between the peasants and the French rulers (and their surrogate, Bao Dai).[49] Unknown to Mus, Diem was likewise seeking to rekindle the respect for Confucian values among the same villagers.

Ho had targeted for destruction the entire Confucian system, which rested on hierarchy and ritual, a comprehensive worldview constructed on hoary traditions. Since this entire hierarchical culture was imported from China, it was alien and vulnerable, as were the French. Ho was retreating to Vietnam's pre-Chinese culture, the rice-rhythm culture of the village.[50] While Ho, therefore, sought to extirpate both Chinese and French influences, his rival Diem sought to preserve the Chinese Confucian influence as well as the uniquely Vietnamese village-centered social order, while eliminating all traces of French influence.

The French, who had sought to break the mythic hold of Confucianism in order to install their own "advanced" cultural forms, had not managed to fill the consequent spiritual void in the villages, though they had their zealous adherents in the cities. The cities were now populated with the new bourgeoisie, who had acquired wealth by developing large tracts of the newly drained rice land created by French administration and technology. But such redistribution of land resources conflicted with the egalitarian, communal, and ancestor-oriented Confucian order. The economic struggle between the countryside and the city, as Mus predicted, would eventually turn in favor of the peasants. This struggle would include terrorist tactics employed by the peasant forces and justified by the need to overcome the Western-induced alienation of the city dwellers from their native culture.[51]

Diem's insistence in his interview with Higgins on the political renewal already under way in the villages, which had never captured the enthusiasm of *New York Times* reporters, echoed unwittingly the earlier independence strategy of Mahatma Gandhi.[52] After his return from South Africa, Gandhi quickly dissociated himself from the numerous prominent anglophile attorneys in Bombay and New Delhi. When setting off on his year-long pilgrimage throughout India to familiarize himself with his people, he explained to the constitutional debating groups in New Delhi: "India is seven hundred thousand villages. It is not several hundred lawyers in Delhi. Until we represent India, we will not be able to challenge England as one nation."[53] The twin but antagonistic village-centered strategies of Ho and Diem in Vietnam were as hard for American politicians to understand as Gandhi's early successes in *satyagraha* had been to successive British governments. Diem, in seeking to inform American public opinion about the purity of restoring village life, was working against enormous odds of Western assumptions about the status of urban dominance in the modern world.

In light of this instinctive consensus shared by Ho and Diem that the path to the future lay through the village, it is faintly possible that a rural renaissance might have blossomed in Vietnam.[54] The rivalry and new alliance efforts between the two icons of independence were finally resolved when the Americans smashed the Confucian image, leaving only the revolutionary one in place.

The potential federation between Ho and Diem, ideological adversaries who nevertheless were equally extreme independence seekers, was foreclosed by "one of the strangest episodes in the annals of American foreign policy and practice," as Karnow describes the nine-week joint American-Vietnamese maneuver that led to the coup on November 1.[55] Twenty years after the event, when Karnow was completing his encyclopedic history of the Vietnam wars, the orchestration of the coup had indeed begun to look bizarre to many observers, who grasped from that vantage point the anarchic consequences in Vietnam to which the coup predictably led. But ample evidence suggests that in the years and months leading up to the coup, such a strategy was considered a counsel of Cold War common sense. For example, the sober political analyst and later tenacious opponent of the Vietnam War Hans Morgenthau published in *Commentary* for May 1962 a forthright appeal for a military coup to remove Diem. Morgenthau had met Diem in 1955 in Saigon and had then generously counseled the Vietnamese leader to undertake political reform. Labeling Diem a "totalitarian" ruler, Morgenthau in the 1962 article called for a military junta to replace him.

But certainly the United States could, if it had a mind to, find a general who could take over the reins of government and through whom the necessary political, economic, and social reforms could be effected.

The United States has two alternative policies to choose from: political reforms as a precondition for the restoration of peace and order in South Vietnam, or purely military means. The former policy requires the elimination of Diem and demands of American officials in the field great manipulative skills and exposes them to considerable short-term political risks, while it is likely to require of the United States but a limited military commitment. On the highest level at least, the government of the United States seems to have recognized the need for such political reforms, but there is no indication that this intellectual recognition has been transformed into effective political action in Saigon. Thus we have been forced to choose, half-heartedly, and almost by default, the other alternative of a purely military solution.[56]

A little further to the left on the American intellectual spectrum, Americans for Democratic Action (ADA) debated in the summer of 1963 "a resolution calling for a coup in Saigon to advance international democracy and the conduct of the war." John Roche, later an adviser to Lyndon Johnson on the war and at this time the national chairman of the ADA, considered the resolution, which was narrowly defeated, "bizarre."[57]

The swift execution of this surgical intervention in Saigon, promoted by many segments of elite political sentiment as well as by crucially placed U.S. government officials, was effected because there was a ready instrument at hand, the Buddhist protesters who had appeared in Saigon and a handful of other cities and whose urgent cries were echoed in the American press. To quiet their grating chants, Kennedy authorized the accelerated pace of contacts with military officers long sidelined by Diem because of their openly seditious designs.

The unsuspected irony of this denouement was that both of the instigators of the coup, Kennedy himself and the activist monks who set out to topple Diem, unknowingly shared the common resolve to get the Americans out of Vietnam. Heightening the irony is the reality that Diem sought exactly the same goal and was indeed actively negotiating to bring about the expulsion of the U.S. presence. But none of the three parties deemed any of the others worthy of candid communication. For both the Buddhists and Kennedy, the successful coup was thus a Pyrrhic victory, eliminating the only person in South Vietnam able to carry out their wishes without a war. The coup then postponed for a full decade the inevitable retreat of the Americans, carrying with them their haunting sorrows. For Diem, the coup was his final liberation from the Sisyphean task of liberating his land from the foreigners.

HENRY CABOT LODGE JR.
An American Raj

On June 12, 1963, the morning on which newspapers worldwide carried Malcolm Browne's appalling photograph of the self-incineration in Saigon of the elderly monk Thich Quang Duc, Lodge happened to be in President Kennedy's office for a long-scheduled meeting concerning plans for the Atlantic Institute, of which Lodge was director. The president almost immediately turned the conversation to Vietnam and the looming threat of a public relations disaster arising from the protests by activist Buddhists. Singling out Saigon as his most significant press relations challenge, Kennedy asked Lodge to accept nomination as ambassador to Saigon, with personal and primary responsibility for solving the neuralgic problem of Diem's image in the American press.[1] Kennedy knew his man, who would on October 28 explain to Diem's secretary, Thuan, that "the trouble between Vietnam and the United States was largely one of public relations."[2]

After consulting his wife, Lodge readily accepted Kennedy's high-risk offer. What Kennedy may not have appreciated was that Lodge harbored a somewhat broader definition of public relations than Kennedy as he set out on this task. For Lodge was beginning to think about his own presidential prospects in 1964 or, more likely, 1968. On the basis of Lodge's personal diaries, his "Confidential Journal," Anne Blair has focused attention on the salience of Lodge's personal electoral ambitions as one of the controlling elements in his singular diplomatic strategy in Saigon. The Saigon spotlight and his own instinct for press relations offered him an unexpected opportunity to position himself for a draft nomination in the future.[3]

Lodge brought a certain personal luster to the task of public relations diplomacy. Grandson and protégé of Senator Henry Cabot Lodge Sr.,

he had been especially close to that senatorial leader after his own father's death in 1909, when Lodge was only seven years old. Lodge inherited his grandfather's mantle as senator from Massachusetts in 1936,
when he was thirty-four. Before receiving that early honor, he had prepared for public life by stints at the *New York Herald Tribune* and, between 1924 and 1932, at *Time*.[4]

Lodge left the Senate, where he admittedly was bored, voluntarily.
First in 1941, before Pearl Harbor, he took up active duty with a tank division serving in Libya with the British Eighth Army. Later he resigned
his seat in the Senate to join the regular army; he was the only senator to
have done so since the Civil War. He then served in France as liaison
officer to General Jean de Lattre de Tassigny. Later de Tassigny was the
French commander in Vietnam until his death in 1952. Reelected to the
Senate in 1946, Lodge helped marshal Republican votes for the Marshall Plan and NATO.[5]

Lodge's forced departure from the Senate was caused by his defeat at
the hands of Kennedy in 1952, a defeat that Lodge attributed to his
own overinvolvement in the successful "Draft Eisenhower" effort. In
return, perhaps, for this costly effort by Lodge, President Eisenhower
appointed him his permanent representative to the United Nations, admittedly an ironic post for the grandson of the architect of the U.S. Senate defeat of the League of Nations.[6] At the UN, Lodge immediately
displayed the ambassadorial independence that would later turn out to
be the undoing of Kennedy's troubled relations with Diem. As Blair recalls in her study,

> When Henry Cabot Lodge II was United States ambassador to the
> United Nations in 1953, a question arose during debates over the
> Korean conflict on which the vote promised to be closely divided.
> After much discussion, the U.S. Department of State advised Lodge
> to vote yes. But the next morning Robert Murphy, head of the U.N.
> section of the Department of State, read in the newspapers that
> Lodge had voted no. He put through an urgent call to Lodge in New
> York. "Apparently our instructions failed to reach you?" he asked.
> "Instructions?" queried Lodge. "I'm not bound by instructions from
> the State Department. I am a member of the President's cabinet, and
> accept instructions only from him." Murphy protested, "But you are
> also the head of an Embassy, and our ambassadors accept instructions

from the Secretary of State." After a pause, Lodge replied, "I take note of the department's opinions."[7]

The narrative of his ambassadorial record at the United Nations foreshadows almost literally his later refusal to treat with Diem, in defiance of seven insistent demands from Kennedy and Rusk. Only someone wholly unfamiliar with that United Nations diplomatic record would be surprised by Lodge's autonomous diplomacy in Saigon. Apparently no one in the Kennedy administration had inquired about Lodge's record in his only previous ambassadorial post.

True to his conception of diplomacy as a form of public relations, Lodge paid little attention between mid-June and mid-August to State Department briefings on the situation in Saigon, but he obtained the president's permission to inform Henry Luce, of *Time*, of his appointment and was allowed to review the *Time* files on Vietnam. He was especially struck by correspondent Charles Mohr's May 2, 1963, description of the impasse in Saigon between the U.S. ambassador, Fritz Nolting, and Diem as "a game of chicken." Nolting, Mohr reported, routinely "chickened out" rather than risking a collision with Diem. (Mohr's sources did not include Nolting's own classified cables to Rusk, which Lodge might profitably have read at the State Department, in addition to the *Time* files. These cables give ample evidence of the showdown Nolting staged with Diem in April. Mohr apparently believed that what was not reported by an ambassador to the U.S. press corps had never taken place in private.[8])

Lodge, fortified with his introduction to the press coverage of United States–Vietnam relations, set off for Honolulu, for a stopover on the way to Saigon. Alarmed by Nhu's August 20–21 crackdown on the Buddhists, Kennedy urged Lodge to abbreviate his planned stop in Japan and to proceed immediately to his post. Lodge left Japan complaining about the air transport provisions made for him by Kennedy (a mere propeller plane) and worried that the extensive television equipment on board might be too heavy a load for the plane.[9] For he had invited along numerous representatives from the media, including four press reporters chosen to serve as a pool for the American press corps. This gesture of State Department reconciliation with the press was a genuine promise of closer personal diplomacy between the new ambassador and the representatives of the media, which immediately resolved Kennedy's problem of press relations in Saigon.[10]

Public relations were not, however, without their own peculiar perils. Not wasting a minute on embassy business after arrival, Lodge accepted a request for a rare "photo op" of the new ambassador for a photo essay scheduled to appear soon in *Life*. Lodge drove with his wife and the photographers to the Saigon zoo, where the prize exhibit was a large male tiger. As the patrician Lodge and his elegant wife posed by the tiger cage, the tiger greeted them with a warm stream of traditional feline welcome for the two newly installed exhibits. The ambassador's embarrassed Vietnamese hosts rushed to assure him that in Vietnam this was considered a very good omen. Despite such reassurances, *Life* did not publish the exposures.[11]

The equation of diplomacy with public relations held unforeseen risks for Kennedy as well. Pressured by Forrestal and Hilsman as early as February 4, 1963, to downplay diplomatic relations with the government in Saigon in favor of improved relations with the resident U.S. press corps, the president finally yielded to this novel approach to diplomacy on June 12, under the intolerable provocation of a bonze's self-immolation, portrayed on the front pages of the world's newspapers.[12] His charge to Lodge was to calm the storm of press coverage of the religious repression by the Diem regime. Kennedy's gamble on Lodge to solve this problem was made, however, without taking account of the crucial consideration of *whose* public relations Lodge would assure. As it predictably turned out, Lodge was more solicitous of his own image in the press than of a meticulous observance of Kennedy's continuously frustrated orders cabled to Saigon. Public relations is a two-edged sword, as Michael Forrestal had warned the president when he announced his choice of a new ambassador for Saigon.[13]

On a second diplomatic front, namely, the choice of the appropriate posture for an American ambassador accredited to the court of a mandarin autocrat, Lodge showed a good deal more acuity than his traditionalist predecessor, Fritz Nolting. While Nolting failed to see the symbolic significance of Diem's April 4 demand for total control of South Vietnam's own small financial contribution to the war effort, Lodge grasped immediately the symbolic dimension of Vietnamese politics. Sensing that actions speak louder than words in Saigon, Lodge almost from the outset adopted an attitude of proconsular aloofness from Diem.

The only flaw in Lodge's symbolic approach to diplomacy was that he preferred the symbols of another century, like those of Kipling and his own grandfather, who had urged the annexation of the Philippines.[14] The symbols were those of oriental obeisance. Despite seven separate, explicit pleas from Washington to meet with Diem and to demand the removal of Nhu from power, Lodge stood his ground. Requests to meet Diem were sent to Lodge on August 24, 28, and 29, September 3, 6, and 11, and October 5. The last order, from Rusk, was obeyed.[15] Finally, Diem capitulated and asked for a meeting on October 27. In his cable reporting that seemingly fruitless conversation, Lodge revealed his own self-conscious strategy toward Diem. He would make the oriental despot-client kowtow.[16]

During the meeting at Da Lat on October 27, Lodge graciously offered to let Diem himself select the "reform" he would introduce to placate U.S. public opinion. Unsurprisingly, Diem declined the offer. The only flaw in Lodge's approach to an oriental politics of symbolism was that Lodge's one requirement, that Diem beg for largesse from Washington, was the one symbol Diem could not grant.

For all of Lodge's remarkable range of experience, added to the advantages of a privileged place in society, his record in Saigon has not escaped well-informed criticism, for example, from Arthur Schlesinger Jr., whose intimate familiarity with these events is unparalleled.[17] This disappointing, and some might say tragic, gap between Lodge's promise and his achievement in Saigon may partially be explained by still another axiom of Lodge's concerning the conduct of diplomacy. He believed, as Blair recounts, that health and good looks count for more in diplomacy than brains.[18] Some of his critics perhaps felt that this was a theory very well adapted to the thinker responsible for it.

Many colleagues, interviewed shortly after Lodge's death in 1985, felt that the soul of Henry Cabot Lodge Jr. was the brevity of his wit.[19] This quip, while unkind, is not far off the mark. Remembering it is indispensable to understanding the drama of the autumn season of 1963. The impasse between Kennedy and Diem cannot be grasped without taking account of the intellectual vacuity of Kennedy's hand-picked ambassador for this crucial post. Consider, for example, Lodge's response when Stanley Karnow asked about his reaction to the November 1, 1963, unleashing of the coup that he had carefully nurtured for ten weeks: "Well, I couldn't say I was surprised. I had been sort of living with this for months. But, well, it's always interesting to see people shooting one another."[20] Equally revealing was his apparently serious assessment of the generals' effort to portray the Ngos' deaths as suicides. "The [unimpeachable] source . . . said both [Diem and Nhu] were shot in the nape of the neck. . . . This definitely disproves rumor of suicide."[21]

The dominant assessment of Lodge's intellectual frailty seems confirmed with the recent publication of his October 30 memorandum on a solution to the Vietnam impasse, drafted just hours before the coup that he had been orchestrating finally occurred. At this late stage, while waiting for the coup to hatch, Lodge finally found time to do some of the thinking he found preferable to meeting with Diem.[22] The fruit of these tranquil reflections, even as the troops of Minh's sedition forces were encircling Saigon, is genuinely sui generis in the annals of American diplomacy: a proposal to encourage Ho Chi Minh to undertake a process of self-neutralization in return for U.S. food aid. If Ho accepted this bargain, Lodge reflected, the United States could claim credit for the emergence of "a sort of Tito" to "roll back" Chinese Communist influence, while continuing to support Diem's (or, soon, Big Minh's) close alliance with the United States. Lodge's own words capture the subtlety and nuance of the proposal, which he suggested be sent to Ho through the good offices of the Italian ambassador and the Polish representative to the ICC group overseeing the implementation of the Geneva Accords, Mieczyslaw Maneli:

> Is it not doubtful that the SVN [South Vietnamese] can ever know true peace and tranquility without neutralization of NVN [North Vietnam]? What follows is also not a scheme to unify North and South Viet-Nam; it is still less a scheme to neutralize South Viet-Nam. On the contrary, it aims at a ChiCom rollback; it is a move towards neutralizing NVN alone; it should tend to strengthen the anti-Communist position in SVN; it seeks to contend with the Communists over what they (the Communists) have rather than contending with them over what we have.
>
> I do not visualize a neutralized and united Viet-Nam; on the contrary, I look for a militantly anti-Communist SVN with a Yugoslavia-like neutralist nation to the north.[23]

Bill Bundy later kindly categorized these reflections as "a bizarre aberration."[24]

Another striking vignette of Lodge's diplomatic acuity is recounted by Maneli. On August 25, when Maneli had already been shuttling for weeks between Saigon and Hanoi bearing messages designed to arrange a neutralized federation between North and South Vietnam, Lodge approached this key player during a reception to ask a question. Maneli had suddenly hoped that Lodge would make inquiries about the progress of his diplomatic efforts, signaling American interest. Maneli records their brief exchange:

> This was the first party at which Ambassador Lodge appeared after his arrival in Saigon. He had a superior air about him. . . . The scene was strongly reminiscent of relations in the capitals of the people's democracies: many Soviet ambassadors behaved like Lodge, and their lesser brothers like schoolboys during an inspection by the visiting superintendent of schools. . . .
>
> At some point Ambassador Lodge found himself next to me, and I was introduced to him. . . . He said: "That is very interesting. And what is the time difference between Warsaw and Vietnam?"
>
> I answered: "The same as between Warsaw and New York." . . . He moved on right away.[25]

At this potentially crucial juncture, when Lodge could have learned first-hand of Nhu's active negotiations to escape from Kennedy, Lodge settled for comparing time zones with Nhu's intermediary, Maneli. Good looks were apparently unavailing in this critical diplomatic démarche.

The same would be true through the remaining days until the ambassador's first resignation from Saigon. The final straw for Lodge was his failure to get General Khanh, Big Minh's successor, to appoint an ambassador to the United Nations in time for the scheduled General Assembly debate on May 21, 1964, that would consider Cambodian charges that the United States and Vietnam were jointly violating Cambodia's borders. Responding to Rusk's frustrations with Khanh, Lodge was proud to say that U.S. influence in Vietnam had never been colonial. But he warned the secretary of state that it might soon be necessary to exercise straightforward colonial control, for example, by appointing a high commissioner, as the United States had once done in the Philippines.

Less than a month later Lodge informed Rusk and Johnson that he was resigning in an effort to play a role at the Republican convention that summer. The convention turned out to spell the end of Lodge's presidential ambitions.[26]

Lodge once more nominated himself to be ambassador to Saigon on March 24, 1965. He was apparently bored at home in Beverly, Massachusetts. His nomination was announced on July 9. Johnson at the time had decided to send in a dramatically increased U.S. military contingent of fifty-eight thousand troops. Lodge's contribution to the strategic planning for this new engagement of American forces was to insist that the United States take advantage of its maritime superiority by fighting an exclusively naval war against the Viet Cong, rather than "getting trapped in the jungles." He was sworn in by Johnson in the Rose Garden on August 12, 1965, almost precisely two years after his final meeting with Kennedy before leaving for his first stay in Saigon. The ambassador's proposal for an exclusively naval response to the guerrilla forces of the Viet Cong appears to have been too innovative to win support from the Joint Chiefs. Lodge nevertheless soldiered on in Saigon until April 25, 1967.[27]

THE *NEW YORK TIMES*
Tragic Chorus or Protagonist in a Tragedy?

The twentieth anniversary of the "fall" of Saigon to the forces of General Vo Nguyen Giap went largely unobserved in the United States on April 30, 1995. *Time* broke the silence with a special report, "Vietnam: Twenty Years Later, It Haunts Us Still." Along with a stunning portfolio of photographs, some published for the first time, it offered somber reflections capturing the unbridgeable gap between American memories of the war and its abiding meaninglessness: "Vietnam may be the war that passeth all understanding . . . a place where memory burns, but darkness still prevails." Further on, looking futilely into "lessons from the lost war," Bruce Nelan quotes Seth Tillman, a distinguished professor of international politics who himself participated in the antiwar struggles while serving on the staff of Senator Fulbright. Tillman advises: "The lesson of Vietnam is to forget about Vietnam."[1]

This counsel of amnesia, widely heeded across the land, never seemed to reach the Vietnam Memorial on the Mall, where throngs of veterans, family, friends, and citizens once again gathered on Veterans' Day, November 11, 1995, precisely to remember. That gathering coincided with two notable disruptions to the American preference for forgetfulness. The two events, which occurred accidentally at the same moment but were striking in their incongruity, were a news release from Hanoi and the publication of William Prochnau's long-awaited study of the American resident correspondents who were in Saigon between 1961 and 1963.

The *Washington Post* carried on that Veterans' Day the report of an interview with Robert McNamara, who was in Hanoi on a visit to arrange a joint Vietnamese-American conference for late 1996 on the lessons of the Vietnam War, to be sponsored by the Council on Foreign

Relations. One of the striking features of McNamara's report of the planning session was the evaluation of the origins of the U.S. defeat, offered during the session by many senior Vietnamese officials, including apparently General Giap, the mastermind of North Vietnamese strategy that routed the French and Americans. McNamara observed that he found it "fascinating that several former high-level Vietnamese Communist officials here told him that [Ngo Dinh] Diem was a nationalist and that had he lived, Diem would probably not have accepted the U.S. buildup and the Americanization of the war that eventually cost 58,000 American lives."[2]

McNamara apparently found the Vietnamese praise of Diem as a nationalist determined to resist Americanization of his country, by war or any other means, fascinating, not because it was news to anyone but because it echoed the emergence of a consensus among American scholars and former Vietnam-policy officials. McNamara has now added his own practitioner's judgment to the earlier conclusions of the scholar-statesman Henry Kissinger and the historian Arthur Schlesinger Jr. that the overthrow of Diem was Kennedy's fatal mistake in Vietnam. For Kennedy knew in the autumn of 1963 that Diem was negotiating with delegates of Ho Chi Minh to explore the possibility of forming a North-South Vietnam federation, after expelling the Americans. The coup scuttled these auspicious all-Vietnamese negotiations. The current Vietnamese assessment of the American folly of overthrowing their own ally in the midst of a civil war is likewise an echo of the North Vietnamese views expressed at the time, which regarded the American-led coup as an unimaginable windfall for the North. The Vietnamese are now once more on record in drawing the lesson, shared by Kissinger and Schlesinger, that the American orchestration of the 1963 coup was the prelude to a tragedy for both the allies.

So far, no news. But the same week did produce some genuinely new information about the personalities and institutions that decisively influenced Kennedy to opt for the coup against Diem. That news appeared in the book by Prochnau, a former *Washington Post* correspondent in Vietnam. Prochnau's study investigated the early American resident correspondents in Saigon, including David Halberstam of the *New York Times*. The news about Halberstam in Prochnau's study is that the now middle-aged former reporter is still boasting about his successful effort to overthrow Diem. Prochnau himself applauds Halberstam's role (along with those of his colleagues, especially Neil Sheehan and Malcolm Browne) in the coup. Relying on more than a hundred interviews with Halberstam, Prochnau concludes that "to a rare degree the historical role of a handful of young reporters approached that of many government officials."[3] At another place, Prochnau searches for a comparable display of journalistic power in the history of American foreign policy, reaching all the way back to the Spanish-American War to find a genuine power parallel.[4]

An initially puzzling aspect of Prochnau's comparison between 1898 and 1963 is the contradictory outcome of the two wars. The United States after all won the Spanish-American War, while it clearly lost in Vietnam. Boasting today about having played a decisive role in shaping that loss, which became a national (and bilateral) tragedy, seems ironic. But the boast itself is unambiguous enough.

Prochnau quotes from a memo prepared for Kennedy in July 1963 by Robert Manning, the assistant secretary of state for public affairs, whom Kennedy had sent to Saigon to inquire about the impasse between the press and the Saigon regime. Reporting on his conversation with Ngo Dinh Nhu, Manning told Kennedy: "Mr. Nhu said that these young [American] reporters want nothing less than to make a government. This was, indeed, an exalting ambition. It was a stimulating pastime indeed for three or four of them to get together on a concerted effort to overthrow and to create governments."[5]

Manning's conclusion to Kennedy on press relations in Saigon was uncompromising and perceptive:

> The correspondents reflect unanimous bitterness toward, and contempt for, the Diem government. They unanimously maintain that the Vietnamese program cannot succeed unless the Diem regime (*cum* family) is replaced; this conviction, though it does not always appear in their copy, underlies all the reports and analyses of the correspondents. . . .
>
> The Buddhist activists, and whoever on the Viet-Nam scene is encouraging or supporting them, premise their potential effectiveness to a large extent on exploitation of the American correspondents. . . .
>
> The GVN, on the other hand, knows full well that its life is at stake, and considers the American correspondents to be an essen-

tial and enthusiastic element in the attempt to bring down the Government. . . .

They [the American correspondents] have formed a closed group, cemented together by a sense of maltreatment from the GVN and the Embassy. They have convinced themselves that they are the only ones who know or will recognize the truth about the situation in Viet-Nam. Any contrary views from Embassy-MAC/V [Military Assistance Command, Vietnam] officials are dismissed as untruthful and deceitful.[6]

Manning's harshly critical views of the reporters' untraditional policy advocacy in 1963 had always until the present remained just that: the analysis of a senior official of the government, whose primary allegiance was to the president, not to the press (although he himself was a former reporter). Now Prochnau confirms the accuracy of Manning's complaint about the self-conscious politicization of the reporting in Saigon, by relying on his recent interviews with Halberstam and the other Saigon correspondents. Referring to Manning's July 1963 memo, Prochnau comments: "None of the correspondents would have taken offense at that. They had become total and unabashed advocates. 'Halberstam and I and the other reporters had seized on the Buddhist crisis . . . ,' Sheehan wrote later. 'We had been holding it up as proof that the regime was as bankrupt politically as it was militarily.'" Returning to the Buddhist crisis, Prochnau continues: "None of them could afford to abandon the Buddhist story. It was cresting. It could bring down Diem, and they would help it bring down Diem. They did not delude themselves about their goals. The Buddhist crisis had become the second half of their personal offensive. . . . It was the kind of raw-boned advocacy that in 1963 shook cages."[7]

In the course of his 1963 anti-Diem campaign, Halberstam did not hesitate to reiterate misrepresentations of easily verifiable facts. For example, during the spring and summer Buddhist crisis in several major cities (but not in the countryside), David Halberstam "explained" the religious makeup of the South Vietnamese government.[8] On June 17, July 17, and July 20, his front-page articles repeated: "The President [Diem] and most government officials are Roman Catholic." The actual religious profile of Diem's government was much less easily schematized.

According to the president of the South Vietnamese National Assembly in 1963, Truong Vinh-Le, Diem's cabinet ministers were quite diverse: five Catholics, five Confucians, and eight Buddhists, including the vice president, Tho, and the minister of foreign affairs, Vu Van Mau. Moreover, the religious affiliation of the province chiefs was equally mixed: of the thirty-eight governors, twelve were Catholic and twenty-six either Buddhist or Confucian. Similarly, in the military command the three Catholics were outnumbered by sixteen Confucians or Buddhists.[9]

Gradually, a decade or more after his departure from Saigon, Halberstam began to admit some of his misrepresentations of the political situation in Vietnam. Writing in his 1979 study of the impact of the media on contemporary politics, *The Powers That Be*, Halberstam himself observed:

> It was an irony of Vietnam that their [Halberstam's and his colleagues'] military reporting was generally a good deal better than their political reporting. They had the best possible military sources in the country, but their political reporting was limited by the absence of serious skilled Asia experts in the American embassy. The McCarthy era had taken care of that. Thus the historical perspective was often lacking, as well as an understanding of how deeply rooted the political sickness was. Reporters are rarely very much better than their sources and their political sources in Saigon were regrettably limited in their larger vision.[10]

In 1983, at a symposium at the University of Southern California, Halberstam reiterated his mea culpa: "I am enormously proud of the military reporting we did. I am not nearly so proud of my political reporting. I don't think it was nearly so profound. . . . Slowly, and only by late 1963, did we begin to understand that the failings of Diem were not so much causes as symptoms of a leadership that had stayed on the sidelines during the French-Indochina War."[11] Halberstam's candor about his own mistaken reading of Vietnamese politics, which curiously is wholly overlooked in Prochnau's otherwise definitive study, makes puzzling his presently self-proclaimed satisfaction about the achievement of overthrowing the government of Vietnam, carried out while he was admittedly still laboring under such fundamental misconceptions.

Keyes Beech, who represented the *Chicago Daily News* in Saigon during this period, believed at the time that Diem was "the only true

Vietnamese nationalist of stature in South Vietnam," and therefore he regretted the "lopsided" reporting of his fellow correspondents in the spring of 1963.[12] This critical judgment was echoed later by the scholar Daniel Hallin in his balanced defense of the press and especially the *New York Times* against those critics who blamed it for "shaping events rather than reporting them." Hallin, however, nevertheless admits the tendentious character of reporting during the Buddhist crisis of 1963. "But from mid-1962 until the end of his regime, there is no doubt that a strong hostility toward the Diem regime was building up among American journalists."[13]

At the time, Halberstam and his colleagues did not escape the critical attention of rival editors. The editors of *Time*, for example, would soon detect an almost conspiratorial spirit among the correspondents in the inner sanctum of Saigon's Caravelle bar. Throughout the summer *Time* had voiced a vigorous counterpoint to the anti-Diem resident U.S. press corps in Saigon. In their "Press" section for September 20, the editors published a broadside charging that the correspondents, uniformly hostile to the regime, were at the center of America's problem in Vietnam, contributing to U.S. government confusion by their ill-informed and inbred diatribes against Diem. (The *Time* analysis corresponded entirely with the private report Kennedy had received from Robert Manning on July 17.[14]) On October 11 *Time* named names, including Halberstam of the *New York Times*, Malcolm Browne of the Associated Press, and Neil Sheehan of United Press International. *Time* added that its own Southeast Asia editor, Charles Mohr, had resigned to protest the earlier September 20 *Time* critique of the U.S. reporters.

Earlier, Mohr had been assigned by *Time*'s editors to do a cover story for the August 9 issue on the notorious "Dragon Lady," the wife of Ngo Dinh Nhu. Mohr, perhaps to his surprise, had found her the most interesting of the ruling troika in Saigon. Mohr portrayed Madame Nhu as the most inflexible of the Ngo family, never yielding to any doubt about the insincerity of all dissident bonzes. The reporter had learned that Madame Nhu had herself been imprisoned with her daughter by the Viet Cong and had survived for four months on two bowls of rice a day. Her inflexibility on the subject of communism was thus the genuine fruit of terror. Attempting to mute other press attacks on the Ngo family, *Time* pointed to the Saigon government's achievement of a certain fragile order in Vietnam, where chaos had long been king.[15]

In striking counterpoint to the reporting by *Time*'s own Hugh Sidey, whom Kennedy had known since 1958, the editors at *Time* were among the earliest critics of the White House efforts to square the circle, namely, to coerce Diem into conformity with Washington without tarnishing his stature by making him act like an American "lackey." *Time* excoriated the Labor Day Kennedy-Cronkite interview, quoting James ("Scotty") Reston of the *Times*, who was appalled at this television diplomacy, as well as the *New York Times* Hong Kong correspondent Robert Trumbull, who reported the shock among European diplomats in Saigon at Kennedy's ineptitude. The *Time* editors also pulled back the curtain to report on State Department "leaks" to reporters, including their own, concerning the Kennedy administration's receptivity to coup plots.[16]

Kennedy himself, especially after being alerted by Manning's July 1963 memorandum, was sharply critical of Halberstam's influence on the fragile alliance between Washington and Saigon. For example, in a crisis meeting in the Oval Office on August 26, 1963, immediately following George Ball's August 24 dispatch of the cable authorizing a coup, Kennedy warned Roger Hilsman, who had authored the text of the Ball cable, not to let Halberstam determine any more policies. In the official record of the White House meeting on August 26, the note taker recorded: "The President observed that Mr. Halberstam of the *New York Times* is actually running a political campaign; that he is wholly unobjective, reminiscent of Mr. Matthews in the Castro days. He stated that it was essential that we not permit Halberstam unduly to influence our actions. . . . The President observed that Diem and his brother, however repugnant in some respects, had done a great deal along the lines that we desire and, *when we move to eliminate this government*, it should not be a result of *New York Times* pressure."[17]

Kennedy was so nettled by Halberstam's dispatches — and the echoing editorials that often, presumably independently, followed Halberstam's front-page exposés — that the president was still seeking, just a week before the November 1963 coup, to have Halberstam transferred away from Saigon. Meeting in the Oval Office with officials of the *Times* on October 22, Kennedy suggested a change of assignment for Halberstam. The new publisher of the *New York Times*, Arthur Ochs ("Punch") Sulzberger, after consulting Washington Bureau chief Reston, refused.

Kennedy's request even stiffened editorial support for the *Times*'s Saigon correspondent.[18]

It would, of course, be unfair to criticize Halberstam's reporting without taking into account the need that such an inexperienced reporter in an Asian war zone felt for more seasoned veterans of war and of wartime journalism. The senior military officer to whom Halberstam and the other correspondents instinctively turned was Colonel John Paul Vann, the then legendary, and now thoroughly discredited, military adviser. It was only in 1988 that the secret of the self-confidence of the three influential young reporters in Saigon—Halberstam, Sheehan, and Browne—became known to the public. It had been Vann who consistently had contradicted the military briefings of General Harkins at the headquarters of the Military Assistance Command, Vietnam.[19]

When Neil Sheehan finally published in 1988 his Pulitzer Prize–winning *Bright Shining Lie*, he cited Vann as the reporters' source, revealing that they had accepted his version of battlefield activities because of his obvious courage and idealism in openly risking a "promising military career" by continuing to talk to dissident reporters against Harkins's orders.[20] In the same volume, however, Sheehan obliquely acknowledged that the three reporters had been partially misled by Vann. For Vann was not a rising star in the military with everything to lose by his candor, but rather a cashiered soldier, whose regular army career had ended in 1958 when he impregnated a minor and was nearly court-martialed.[21] Recently confronted by Prochnau with the evidence that Vann had lied to the reporters in 1963 about his personal and professional status, thus leading them to dismiss systematically any official military briefings from Saigon or Washington, Halberstam dismissed this challenge to the reliability of his reporting, not pausing to acknowledge the possibly grave political consequences of providing Vann with a national and international forum for his views.[22]

Still more decisive in Halberstam's journalistic formation in Vietnam was the influence of Homer Bigart. Bigart was Halberstam's predecessor, who had left Saigon just before Halberstam's arrival but had left for the young reporter a memorial of his own interpretation of the war for Halberstam's reading.[23] Bigart was a legendary, Pulitzer Prize–winning war correspondent, having covered World War II and Korea. But as much as generals prepare for, and seek to fight, the last war, so Bigart apparently sought to cover the last war. He found, apparently to his distress, that there was no (conventional) war going on in Vietnam. He resented being required to cover the dull dedication of schools, agricultural improvements, and fish pools, which certainly had not been part of the coverage of earlier wars. His published criticism of the Diem regime caused that government to cancel his visa, which Ambassador Nolting was able to have restored by intervening personally with the government. Bigart was infuriated by this change, because his expulsion by Diem would have been for him a badge of honor.[24]

Bigart's contempt for his assignment in Saigon and for the government he was reporting on was well expressed in the lead he filed to report on the February 27, 1962, bombing of Diem's palace: "After yesterday's thrilling bombing of the Presidential Palace, Saigon slipped back into its usual state of apathy today."[25] At the close of his tour in Saigon, in July 1962, Bigart wrote of the Diem regime: "[V]isions of ultimate victory are obscured by the image of a secretive, suspicious, dictatorial regime. American officers are frustrated and irritated by the constant and whimsical meddling of the President and his brother, Ngo Dinh Nhu, in the military chain of command."[26]

After his return from Saigon, Bigart published in the *Times* on July 25, 1962, a summary of his experiences and conclusions about the low-level conflict in Vietnam. His final paragraphs were prophetically incisive:

> Washington insists there is no alternative to President Ngo Dinh Diem. United States official policy is tied to the status quo. This policy is doomed in the long run, some feel, because the Vietnamese President cannot give his country the inspired leadership needed to defeat the Viet Cong. . . .
>
> By last year the Communists controlled most of the countryside. . . . Should the situation disintegrate further, Washington may face the alternative of ditching Ngo Dinh Diem for a military junta or sending combat troops to bolster his regime.[27]

Only the disjunction posed by Bigart was illusory, for the alternative of "ditching Ngo Dinh Diem for a military junta" rapidly escalated to the policy of "sending combat troops to bolster" a successor regime. Perhaps Bigart's published call for a military coup was reflected in the memorial that he had left in Saigon for Halberstam's guidance.

Halberstam prided himself on writing copy that Bigart would applaud. "To our generation in Vietnam, I don't think his [Bigart's] importance can be over-estimated. We were his lineal descendants in the sense that someone of such consuming integrity had preceded us, and in the kind of honor he represented. I was aware every day that he was going to read my story." [28]

Long before Halberstam arrived in Saigon, the *New York Times* was criticizing Kennedy's Vietnam policy. As early as November 28, 1961, the *Times* had warned that Diem's obstinate failure to adopt American political practices could lead to his downfall. In an editorial entitled "Ngo Dinh Diem's Responsibility," the editors had commented:

> Washington's urgent new program for assisting South Vietnam is now well advanced. . . . Still lacking, however, is the basic requisite for success—government reform in Saigon.
>
> It has become increasingly evident that the inadequacies of the Government of President Ngo Dinh Diem are the weakest component in South Vietnam's struggle against Communism. Aloof and rigidly dictatorial, the President's personal and family regime has become generally unpopular. . . .
>
> Dispatches from our correspondent in Saigon report that President Ngo is resisting new American pressure for a change in the nature and methods of his regime. . . .
>
> President Ngo would add immensely to his stature as a courageous patriot if he moved to make the necessary reforms himself. If he stubbornly refuses, he risks personal downfall and failure in his long effort to defeat the Communists. The situation is a delicate and dangerous one and could lead to disaster in South Vietnam.

The *New York Times* editors sought once more to budge Diem from his autocratic ways on February 20, 1962, under the lead "Reform Still Needed in Saigon": "It is evident from recent official American statements that Washington is now de-emphasizing the need for reform by the South Vietnam Government. . . . President Ngo should constantly be pressed to associate himself and his officials more closely with popular needs and aspirations, to modify his aloof domination and broaden his use of able and reliable Vietnamese now outside the Government." By March 1, 1962, the editors had lost patience, declaring: "The

[February 27] attack on President Ngo's palace by two South Vietnam Air Force planes represents no organized conspiracy against Mr. Ngo, but does reflect serious discontent. The attack only emphasizes the necessity — to which we have frequently pointed — of correcting defects of policy and leadership in the Ngo regime." After a fortnight, on March 14, a more measured comment on South Vietnamese military unrest appeared in the *New York Times*, headed "President Diem and His Critics":

> As the elected constitutional Chief of State, President Diem is determined not to be violently and illegally displaced. He obviously fears that free criticism and political activity in South Vietnam at this time would weaken his authority, give rise to intrigues against him and undermine resistance to the Communists. . . .
>
> There is much evidence to indicate, however, that the scope of political repression in South Vietnam far exceeds the bounds of necessity and of political wisdom. . . . Many out-of-office political figures in Vietnam are chronic, self-seeking opportunists; but many are imbued with a broad spirit of national service, and they should be allowed to participate in public life. Mr. Diem could do much to expand the popular backing of his regime if he permitted a role in national affairs for all those Vietnamese willing to collaborate loyally in constructing a free, independent and democratic South Vietnam.

On August 22, just after the August 20–21 crackdown on the Buddhists, a *Times* editorial observed:

> The crisis in South Vietnam is rooted in the oppressively dictatorial character of the Ngo family government and its widespread unpopularity. . . .
>
> If stiff-necked President Diem and the power-intoxicated members of his family had acted promptly to redress justified Buddhist grievances and carry out long-needed general reforms, dangerous repercussions might have been avoided.
>
> [Diem] . . . has sent troops into their temples, killing some and arresting many others. . . . It may be that he struck to forestall a coup or a mass demonstration against him timed for the arrival of Ambassador Lodge. Whatever temporary repression his troops may inflict, he cannot remain in power indefinitely without changing the unpopular

posture of his regime and satisfying the just complaints of the Buddhists.

Halberstam, then, was not singing out of tune with the choir in his complaints against Diem, for the editors were voicing in the stately syllables of their own page very consonant criticisms.[29] Inexplicably, Harrison Salisbury claims in his history of the *New York Times* in the 1960s and 1970s that the *Times* editorials on Vietnam between 1961 and 1964 were "each one as like the latest government pronouncement as one sausage resembles another."[30]

Prochnau unflinchingly reminds his readers of Kennedy press secretary Pierre Salinger's question about the legitimacy of the correspondents' open assault on the government of the United States' ally: "It is a deep question of reportorial ethics whether the destruction of a government is within the legitimate framework of journalistic enterprise." Prochnau's own answer to Salinger's question is revealing. For he cites, as the legitimating precedent for the coup-rattling dispatches from Saigon in 1963, the nineteenth-century case of the distinguished British war correspondent William Howard Russell, who returned home a hero from covering the Crimean campaign after bringing down his own government by his dispatches from the field.[31] The most revealing facet of Prochnau's reply to Salinger's question lies in his own assumption that Russell's undermining of *his own* government is a relevant criterion by which to judge Halberstam's (and the *New York Times* editors') dismissal of Diem's government. For there is no logical corollary from the Russell story about the role of the British press in overturning a British government for the case of the *Times*'s leverage in overthrowing the government of *another nation*, namely, Vietnam.

Prochnau's unconscious colonialism in assuming the existence of such a right on the part of the American press is not singular. Halberstam himself evidenced the same equally unconscious imperialism with his 1979 defense about the political convictions of the early 1960s correspondents in Saigon. He reflected a wholly proprietary air concerning the Diem government. Describing the political consensus animating the small band of reporters, Halberstam recalls that they were unanimous in their conclusion that Diem was unworthy of the huge investment that the United States was making in him: "There was remarkably little disagreement over the essential direction and facts of the story, over how badly the war was going, how incompetent and hostile *an instrument of American policy* the Ngo family was." [32]

In this apparently unconscious but revelatory articulation of his own earlier judgment about the government of Diem, Halberstam overlooked the central issue of the United States–South Vietnam alliance and the cause of its decay, namely, the American assumption that Diem's governmental raison d'être was to promote American interests on Vietnamese soil. While this assumption—only tacit in 1963 but explicated by Halberstam in 1979—accounts for the severity of this reporting from Saigon, it begs the question of the propriety and the plausibility of an alliance of independent states organized to pursue the interests of only one of the partners.

Halberstam's judgment on the intractability of Diem in the face of American Cold War imperatives explains the root of the correspondent's mounting dissatisfaction with Diem. That root was the assumption that some (non-Western, weak) states exist to serve the interests of the white, powerful nations of the West. Is this perhaps the reemergence, in the proud era of decolonization, of the ancient (Eastern and Western) logic of colonialism? Perhaps, then, the Kennedy administration might have been shrewd to challenge the editorial and reportorial ethos that covertly shaped the *Times* interpretation of Vietnam.

Kennedy had had the foresight to commission Manning's perceptive July 1963 analysis. Once he had digested it, however, the president had no excuse for accepting at face-value any longer the reporting from Saigon. Nevertheless, he never publicly challenged the correspondents and their editors. Nor did the State Department, which seemed more inclined to enlist correspondents in the assault on Diem than to correct the obvious factual misrepresentations in the press coverage. From mid-July on, Kennedy bore the responsibility of being knowingly intimidated by the crusading press, whose understandable outrage at Diem's autocracy was elevated by George Ball, Averell Harriman, and Dean Rusk into national security policy. [33]

Until the spring of 1963, the *Times* had maintained a more traditionally journalistic role of informing readers of developments abroad and the complementary function of drawing attention to dangerous developments abroad that could threaten U.S. interests. Up until the Buddhist crisis, the editors had confined themselves to a monitory role reminiscent of the stately prescience of the choral odes in a Greek tragedy. After May, the paper assumed a different role, striding onto the stage as a new protagonist in the tragedy. It was certainly understandable at the time that American reporters would react with instinctive horror at Diem's brutal repression of revolutionaries, especially monks. It was more difficult to grasp how a president, who had been amply informed of the subversive goals of Tri Quang's monks, would make his own policy, and ultimately his historical record, hostage to such an overt journalistic engagement in a coup d'état.

Still less easy to understand is the recent vindictiveness of some of these same journalists—including David Halberstam and Max Frankel, the latter of whom was in 1963 a Washington correspondent of the *Times*—as displayed in their high-handed dismissal of McNamara's effort to shoulder personally some of the blame for the tragedy of Vietnam. The editorial board of the *Times* on April 12, 1995, too, observed of McNamara's mea culpa icily: "Such sentences break the heart while making clear that McNamara must not escape the lasting moral indictment of his countrymen." Frankel, in his review of McNamara's *In Retrospect* in the *Times Book Review* on April 16, 1995, concludes that the lesson of Vietnam for Americans is that "a respectful skepticism [of government] is essential and is rarely wrong."[34] No one could fault this lesson, which has for centuries been written into the American ethos and is enshrined in the Constitution.

What the current editors, and the former correspondents Halberstam and Frankel, consistently overlook is the decisive role of the *Times* itself in the Vietnam tragedy. On any fair reading of the Kennedy administration buildup to a coup in Saigon, the pressure of the press on Kennedy to reform Diem or to remove him is dramatically evident. When he unleashed the coup, Kennedy was simply following the conventional wisdom of the journalism of the day.

On April 29, 1975, the American ambassador, Graham Martin, made a hasty escape from the roof of the Saigon embassy—which Henry Cabot Lodge Jr. had had the foresight in November 1963 to have redesigned as a helicopter landing pad.[35] Before his departure, Martin had sought once more to save the day by still another shuffle of government personalities in Saigon, ordering President Thieu to resign in favor of Duong Van Minh, whom the United States had once before chosen as president to replace President Ngo Dinh Diem.

Big Minh turned out to be no more malleable at the last moment than he had been in his earlier brief and ineffectual rule, from November 2, 1963, to January 29, 1964. He gave Ambassador Martin twenty-four hours to leave Vietnam with whatever Vietnamese he wished to rescue. Minh in turn surrendered the next day to Colonel Bui Tin, the North Vietnamese official who was covering Saigon's surrender for the army newspaper, but who happened to be the North's highest-ranking official present for this anticlimactic moment.[36] When Big Minh announced that he was turning over his power to Bui Tin, the journalist-victor observed incontrovertibly: "You have no power to surrender."[37]

This denouement, in which a journalist was all it took to wrest power from a general still commanding the world's third-largest Air Force, will seem ironic only to those who have not studied the first act of this drama. The final scene on April 30, 1975, which gives new meaning to the expression "the power of the pen," is almost literary in its imaginability. For the first act of the tragic U.S.–South Vietnamese alliance was decisively shaped by correspondents in Saigon and editors in New York.

Time's claim in 1995 that Vietnam remains a place "where memory burns, but darkness [incomprehension] still prevails" may be already anachronistic. For the observation by senior Vietnamese officials meeting in Hanoi with Robert McNamara sheds new light on that realm, too soon consigned to meaninglessness. General Giap and his colleagues pointed in November 1995 to another November when the United States overthrew their adversary, Ngo Dinh Diem. President Diem, widely viewed in Washington and New York at the time as the principal obstacle to a viable national future for South Vietnam, would, Giap argued, never have permitted the accumulation of American dead on his soil. He would likely have dismissed them from Vietnam early in 1964 if Kennedy had not preempted this option by the November coup.

Our somber memories, then, may not be doomed to meander endlessly, like so many unburied corpses in the world of ancient mythology, in search of meaning. The lesson of Vietnam is now increasingly inescapable: the fate that befell the American intervention in Vietnam was the ever-bitter fruit of colonialism. For the self-complacent American rush to remake Vietnam's government in a Western democratic image was a blind violation of the prerogative of sovereignty, the right of self-determination. Less abstractly, Kennedy's coup vainly sought to extinguish in Vietnam the flame of freedom in the name of an alien political ideal, democracy. But the eternal and universal drive for independence is more natural and therefore more enduring than any hallowed monument on a hill. Finally, Kennedy's place in history will always be shadowed by his own, perhaps unconscious, colonialism, which mirrored the colonialist ethos of the correspondents and editors of his time.

14

JOHN FITZGERALD KENNEDY
Selective Conscientious Objection

Richard Reeves's study of the presidency of John F. Kennedy is reminiscent of the artistry of the early twentieth-century American portrait painter John Singer Sargent. Reeves adds subtly to the likeness he sketches of the president his own interpretation of his subject, for the most part simply letting Kennedy speak for himself. The writer's signature is dramatically understated, showing principally in a detached passage on an unnumbered page, just before the title page. The passage has so far been overlooked by reviewers, some of whom complain that Reeves has failed to offer an interpretation of Kennedy.[1] That interpretation is offered by Reeves in his prefatory remarks:

> John F. Kennedy's favorite book was *Melbourne* by David Cecil, the biography of William Lamb, Viscount Melbourne, who was prime minister of Great Britain for seven years, from 1834 to 1841, serving as the political mentor of Queen Victoria. The book was published in 1939 and this is part of Cecil's description of the young William Lamb: . . . .
>
> He had studied a great many subjects, but none thoroughly; his ideas were original, but they were fragmentary, scattered, unmatured. This lack of system meant further that he never overhauled his mind to set its contents in order in the light of a considered standard of value — so that the precious and the worthless jostled each other in its confused recesses; side by side with fresh and vivid thoughts lurked contradictions, commonplaces, and relics of the conventional prejudices of his rank and station. . . . Like so many aristocratic persons, he was an amateur.

His amateurishness was increased by his hedonism. For it led him to pursue his thought only in so far as the process was pleasant. He shirked intellectual drudgery. Besides, the life he lived was all too full of distracting delights. If he felt bored reading and cogitating, there was always a party for him to go to where he could be perfectly happy without having to make an effort. Such temptations were particularly hard to resist for a man brought up in the easygoing, disorderly atmosphere of Melbourne House, where no one was ever forced to be methodical or conscientious and where there was always something entertaining going on. If virtue was hard to acquire there, pleasure came all too easily.[2]

In these words Reeves distills the heritage and the spirit of the young president: self-indulgent, episodically attentive, effortlessly influential. The rest Reeves lets readers gather for themselves: the clues that reveal the full personality are amply scattered throughout the text. Reeves's portrait is perhaps the best likeness yet published. For it highlights the chiaroscuro character of Kennedy's conscience, which has been neglected by many critics, including Thomas Reeves, who concludes that Kennedy was an unconscionable and irresponsible person, a "chip off the old block" of Joseph P. Kennedy.[3]

Richard Reeves does not shrink, of course, from portraying the ruthless side of Kennedy. Most concisely, it was a ruthless empathy that distinguished Kennedy from all his advisers on Vietnam who were struggling to deal with Ngo Dinh Diem. The president had been surrounded for months by advisers who either loathed Diem (Harriman, Ball, Forrestal, Hilsman, and Lodge) or, on the contrary, generously empathized with Diem's own intractable responsibilities (McCone, McNamara, Nolting, Colby, and Taylor). Kennedy was able to assimilate partially the views of both these camps. He then personally directed a coup against the South Vietnamese president even while speaking understandingly of Diem's straitened situation. Reeves recalls Kennedy's comment several days after the ouster and assassination of Diem. "At six o'clock that Saturday evening, Kennedy flew by helicopter to meet his wife and children in their new horse-country house on Rattlesnake Mountain. At dinner there, a friend, Mary Gimbel, said of Diem and Nhu: 'They were just tyrants.' 'No,' the President said, 'they were in a difficult position.

They did the best they could for their country.'"[4] None of Diem's Washington enemies expressed or, very likely, experienced such empathy. Kennedy's steady and successful resolve to remove Diem from power, unlike that of many in his entourage, was wholly unemotional.

Yet the president acted ruthlessly to deliver himself from the stigma of alliance with Diem. He directed the coup to change governments in Saigon, even though he had already resolved to abandon Vietnam, now leaderless, after his own likely reelection in 1964.[5] Kennedy's empathy for Diem, then, was not matched by any concern for the destiny of Vietnam. In the October 29 last-minute White House meeting concerning the imminent coup, the president showed his political hand unashamedly. The note taker, Bromley Smith, observed: "The President commented that he was not so concerned now about the kind of government which would exist after the coup as he was of the correlation of pro- and anti-Diem forces."[6] At the meeting, probably only two of the participants, Harriman and Forrestal, realized that this sangfroid about the risk of anarchy in Saigon was caused by Kennedy's intention to quit Vietnam in early 1965.

The same opportunism is evident in Kennedy's earlier conversation with Charles Bartlett at Hyannisport. Bartlett spent a weekend with the president there in September 1963, several weeks after the coup cable went out to Lodge and just after Kennedy's August 29 cable personally accepting responsibility for the imminent change of government in Saigon.[7] During what turned out to be a gloomy spell of weather on Cape Cod, Kennedy repeated to Bartlett his promise (made earlier to Senator Mansfield) to quit Vietnam after his reelection: "We have no future in Vietnam. They're going to kick our asses out of there. I can't give up on Vietnam before 1964. I couldn't go out there and ask for reelection after giving up two pieces of territory [Laos and Vietnam] to Communism." But after the election was won, he would be free to disengage.[8]

Some close friends of Kennedy, including Roswell Gilpatric, remained until recently puzzled by Kennedy's indifference to the sort of government that might follow Diem. The revelation of Kennedy's post-election plans for Vietnam resolved the "enigma" of the president's insouciance but heightened the shock concerning his ruthless ambition. What seemed to some close associates an enigma turned out to be merely a scandal. The resolve to hand over Vietnam to unknown (and possibly ineffectual and autocratic) leaders, without fear of the consequences, was undisturbing to Kennedy because he would soon be free of Vietnam. His only concern was the possibility of an abortive coup, which might evoke memories of his miscalculations on the Bay of Pigs.

Bartlett later commented about his friend Kennedy: "He identified the national interest with his reelection."[9] Therefore, the repugnant, despotic image of Diem in the American press was neuralgic to Kennedy because it continually obscured Kennedy's own carefully burnished press image. To contain that threat to his reelection, Kennedy had allowed Diem one last chance for survival: to banish his brother and to make whatever political concessions were required to pacify, if possible, the Buddhist activists. On Labor Day, when Kennedy broadcast this ultimatum on television, he understood that these two changes — "of policy and perhaps of personnel," as he had specified to Walter Cronkite — were tantamount to Diem's surrendering his ability to rule.

Michael Beschloss has argued incisively that Kennedy's repeated private claim that he would disengage from Vietnam following his reelection may have been ephemeral and unreliable. For he may have been led too into bombing the North, just as Johnson later was under the direction of Kennedy's advisers Rusk, McNamara, and Bundy.[10] Additional factors that may have persuaded Kennedy to extend his "limited" intervention there might have included the rampant chaos, effectively a state of anarchy, introduced by his precipitate removal of the Diem regime. Kennedy's sensitivity to his own image, permanently marred by his identification as the producer of the "Marx Brothers' comedy" of eight Saigon governments between 1963 and 1965, along with his own explicitly acknowledged sense of responsibility for the fortunes of the first post-Diem regime, might have forced him to salvage the situation by remaining longer.[11] Others might respond that Kennedy might have taken advantage of the second (Khanh) coup, on January 30, 1964, to wish Vietnam "sayonara." These possibilities all dwell permanently, however, in the land of speculation, which will nevertheless be constantly revisited in the years to come.

For the purposes of this study, such speculation is idle, since it lies beyond the realm of fact. The uncontrovertible reality that does require explanation — and that invites the formulation of possible moral, diplomatic, and military lessons — is that Kennedy, while apparently sincerely intending to abandon Vietnam to its own fate sometime early in his second term, personally supervised the elimination of the troublesome but legitimate government of Diem. He did so even though he had been amply (and, as it turned out, accurately) warned that the most likely consequence of the coup would be military and political chaos in the midst of a highly unpredictable civil war. Efforts to divine what might have happened without Lee Harvey Oswald's own later intervention should not then be allowed to distract us from the historical and moral reality of Kennedy's actual choices.

Many who came to realize the power that the prospect of reelection held over almost all Kennedy's first-term deliberations were shocked at the opportunism displayed in his personal direction of the coup. Some of those closest to him were even led later to seek a constitutional amendment that would limit the presidency to one term of six or seven years. Such an amendment, they hoped, would cut the nerve of ambition and free the president to govern strictly in the national interest. But such an amendment seems at present a very remote possibility. For the foreseeable future, therefore, citizens will have to live with the realization that ambition is at the helm of the ship of state. Accepting this reality should serve as a preliminary "lesson of Vietnam," which is not specific to this tragic failure but endemic in a republic such as ours.

Accepting the republican law that the lure of power will invariably affect the compass of presidential conscience, at least during the first term in office, is simply a first step toward realism in American foreign policy. For democracy does not claim to exorcise from politics the lust for power but only to make that drive ephemeral by assigning a term to its enjoyment or, in the American case, two terms at most.

Power is identical in its lure, whether it is driving autocrats or democrats. Ambition is the face that the love of power turns to democrats, just as absolutism is its other, autocratic face. Electoral ambition is the price democracy pays for overturning autocracy. Ambition is thus a shrewdly selected alternative to the evils of autocracy, its eternal twin.

To observe, then, that the first lesson from a study of the Year of the Hare is the peril of presidential ambition is unexceptionable, but unenlightening. It is merely to admit that democracy is a form of politics, a system for channeling power, not an exercise in transcendental meditation. Hence, any planning for the future of American diplomacy that does not reckon with the inexorable ambition of the president will prove futile. If reckless electoral ambition is the democratic face of power-lust and the only available alternative to autocracy, then it is written into the destiny of democracy. John Kennedy's illusion of identifying his reelection with the national interest is a dramatic illustration of this law of the dynamics of democracy.

Richard Reeves, however, has captured another and equally decisive facet of Kennedy's conscience: his absolute aversion to any European security policies that might entail the probable risk of triggering a nuclear war. The singularity of Kennedy's anguish over the responsibility that the United States had once assumed—and Kennedy himself had reiterated in Berlin in June 1961—arose from his awareness that the defense of Berlin, and indeed of Western Europe, was wholly contingent on the American president's willingness to escalate any conventional military conflict to the level of nuclear war. But neither Europe nor the United States would survive such a war.

Shaken by his first meeting with Khrushchev in Vienna on June 4, 1961, Kennedy had returned to Washington depressed and anxious about Khrushchev's saber-rattling over Berlin. Convinced by this bluster, the president was worrying about his unique responsibility in the eventuality of a Soviet assault on West Berlin. He could order NATO forces to stand down, or he could authorize the release of nuclear warheads against the Warsaw Pact forces and territories. There was no alternative military response available for the foreseeable future.

In preparation for his report to the leaders of Congress and to the nation on his trip, he asked first from the Pentagon an estimate of American casualties in any probable scenario of nuclear war. The answer was swift: 70 million deaths. Reeves recounts the progression of Kennedy's inquiry: "How many would die if just one enemy missile got through and hit somewhere near a city?" The answer this time was 600,000. "That's the total number of casualties in the Civil War," Kennedy said. "And we haven't gotten over that in a hundred years."[12]

An hour later, in a meeting with congressional leaders in the White House, Kennedy lost his temper when he heard from Gilpatric, McNamara's deputy, the articulation of NATO plans to respond to an attack on Berlin with nuclear weapons. "Goddamn it, Ros. Use your head. . . . What we are talking about is 70 million dead Americans." Regaining his composure, the president voiced to the congressional leadership his new alarm about his role as commander in chief. "I'm the one who has to push the button if it goes that far. I'm convinced it won't go that far, but I can't guarantee it." Kennedy was deeply preoccupied for days with the American dilemma of defending Berlin at the risk of national suicide. Shortly afterward, seeing a friend's wife who was pregnant, he remarked, "I question whether it's really right to bring children into this world right now."[13]

Earlier, on his June 5 flight from Vienna to London, he had been anguishing out loud to his friend Kenneth O'Donnell:

> So we've got a problem. . . . We have to see what we can do that will restore a feeling in Moscow that we will defend our national interests. . . . And we have to confront them. The only place we can do that is in Vietnam. We have to send more people there.
>
> If you could think only of yourself, it would be easy to say you'd push the button. . . . You can't just think about yourself. There are generations involved. It really doesn't matter as far as you and I are concerned. I've had a full life. What really matters is all the children.[14]

Fifteen months later, when the dreaded nuclear crisis arose in Cuba, rather than in Berlin, Kennedy was still acutely conscious of his unique moral responsibility at that moment. On October 27, 1962, Kennedy remarked: "It is insane that two men, sitting on opposite sides of the world, should be able to decide to bring an end to civilization."[15]

Kennedy's conscience, then, was not so thoroughly malleable as many of his critics argued. Though he was prepared to compromise on most uncomfortable decisions, Kennedy did have a moral sticking point: the unthinkability of launching nuclear war. This rigid resistance to risking the future of the world's children is a quality that places Kennedy in the front ranks of conscientious statesmen in the nuclear era.

If it had not been for this singular aversion to the risks of nuclear war, Kennedy would almost certainly never have fallen into the trap of Vietnam. Because he would do almost anything but initiate nuclear war, Kennedy felt impelled to risk transferring the struggle of containment from Europe, where it was prohibitively risky, to Southeast Asia, where the shoals still lay hidden in 1961. The link in Kennedy's mind between the nuclear trap in Europe, which he was determined to escape, and the apparently low-risk alliance in Vietnam is clear both from Dean Rusk's recollections of this moment and from James Reston's quizzical account of his conversation with Kennedy immediately after the 1961 showdown in Vienna.[16] A less conscientious commander in chief, who could easily tolerate the inherent and hemispheric risks of the strategy of flexible response, would almost surely not have sailed into the uncharted waters of a Vietnamese civil war in 1961.

Having taken the drastic step of diverting the Cold War from Europe to Southeast Asia, Kennedy could sleep more easily. Unfortunately, this diversion left him strangely unable to think clearly about the implications of such a radical change of course in the policy of containment. Reeves captures the complexities of this radical shift in speaking of Kennedy's futile efforts "trying to find the way to . . . persuade President Diem to save his country the American way."[17] Kennedy never succeeded in solving this puzzle. Indeed, one of his greatest admirers and closest students, Arthur Schlesinger Jr., judges that Kennedy never understood how problematic this change would become. For the president always assumed that American standards were applicable to Vietnamese politics. Schlesinger attributes this misconception to the distorting lens of sustained and unquestioned American power from 1945 to 1960.

> The Kennedys had a romantic view of the possibilities of diplomacy. . . . This view had its most genial expression in the Peace Corps, its most corrupt in the mystique of counterinsurgency. . . .
>
> But action diplomacy was easier to advocate than to execute. . . . [John Paton] Davies [the "old China hand"] was not surprised that the Foreign Service did not win the confidence of the New Frontier. "Crusading activism touched with naiveté seldom welcomes warnings of pitfalls and entanglements."
>
> The professionals were right to question New Frontier activism in execution of policy. . . .
>
> Counterinsurgency faced still deeper problems. . . . The regimes most severely challenged were those most suicidally determined to hold onto despotic power and privilege. Modernization and reform might well undermine whatever stability the regime had.[18]

Schlesinger's analysis of this ill-fated chapter in American diplomacy adds this dismal note: "As a weapon, counterinsurgency was turning cruelly in the hand of the user. In the end it was a ghastly illusion. Its primary consequence was to keep alive the American belief in the capacity and right to intervene in foreign lands. God save us always from the innocent and the good."[19]

Examining the impact of the counterinsurgency craze of the New Frontier on Vietnam, Schlesinger remarks:

The Harriman group felt on the contrary that Diem was lost unless he relaxed his despotism and broadened his base.

The critique was persuasive. Alas, the remedy was not. . . . The very idea of democratization was unintelligible to Diem. . . . The oriental mandarin regarded reform talk as typical American simplemindedness. He was right.[20]

A more forgiving interpretation of the foibles of U.S. Cold War presidents, who all seemed to a greater or lesser extent at times out of touch with political reality, is that of Jonathan Schell. Schell sought to interpret the surreal and self-destructive later days of Nixon's rule by recalling that an American president's tangible power to destroy the universe in the twinkling of an eye had dazzled the holders of that power so that they could not reliably evaluate other risks that beset them. The overwhelming compulsion to avoid nuclear disaster at any cost had skewed their consciousnesses. Schell's analysis applies equally to Kennedy's judgment, and that of his cabinet, concerning South Vietnam. While this moral disorientation does not absolve American presidents of consequent diplomatic and moral lapses, it goes a long way toward explaining policies that would be otherwise incomprehensible. The taboo of nuclear war relativizes, or mutes, all other moral inhibitions and prohibitions, as Schell argues.

> For the advent of nuclear weapons has done nothing less than place the President in a radically new relation to the whole of human reality. . . . If Presidents in recent years have lost touch with reality, bringing disaster to their Administrations and to the nation, may it not be because their grip on what is literally human reality—on the continued existence of mankind—is so tenuous and shaky? . . . And, measured against the extinction of the whole, almost anything that does not contribute directly to the current scheme for survival may seem to be a detail. . . . For what right, what law, what fact, what truth, what aspiration could be allowed to stand in the way of the imperative of human survival, in which all rights, laws, facts, truths, and aspirations were grounded? The first question of the age was how to guarantee survival.[21]

Kennedy's radical miscalculations in Vietnam, with which his name will ever be associated, are partially the understandable reverberations of the weapons-shock that drove him shrewdly away from turning Europe into humanity's final battlefield. A president less sensitive to his responsibility for the future of humankind could have made much more ruinous mistakes than the doomed detour through Vietnam.

Yet the mistakes that Kennedy made in unhurried calculation over two months in 1963 will eddy in the destinies of Vietnam and the United States as far as memory will reach. Reeves's portrait catches every facet of the personality of John Kennedy, including his conscientious horror of nuclear war. The whole personality is there, from the courageous flight from self-destruction in Europe to the fatuous crusade of self-duplication in Asia, the folly of seeking to superimpose the image of Washington on the reality of Saigon.

The passage from David Cecil's life of Melbourne that opens Reeves's portrait of Kennedy falls short of our expectations. But that analytic failure was almost inevitable. No Victorian statesman such as Melbourne can serve as an adequate model of a Cold War president, for the starkness of Kennedy's choices fortunately knew no genuine parallel in the nineteenth century. Since ours is a more exacting age, Kennedy must be judged in comparison with the presidents from 1945 to the present. For they were at the helm through straits wholly uncharted by history. During the Cold War, the challenge of diplomacy for American presidents and their Soviet counterparts was to confront and contain one another without direct military engagement.

The passage that Kennedy discovered between this modern Scylla and Charybdis lay, implausibly, through the South China Sea and the Gulf of Tonkin. As the costs of the American shipwreck there are now gradually understood in the context of the catastrophic risks of a third European war—a war that Kennedy successfully avoided—perhaps a more balanced and lasting interpretation of the Kennedy legacy in foreign policy will be possible.

AN AMERICAN MORALITY TALE

LESSONS OF THE YEAR OF THE HARE

The fog of defeat is lifting. As Americans approached the twentieth anniversary of the fall of Saigon, they began to discern in the distance the shape of the wreck that was their policy in Southeast Asia.

The fall of Saigon on April 30, 1975, has assaulted American self-esteem as mercilessly as the soldiers of General Giap then swept over Saigon in a storm of victory. Jonathan Schell, writing at the time in the *New Yorker*'s "Talk of the Town," captured the imminent collapse of South Vietnam in words that will be read as long as citizens are curious about the wager of war.

> The victory of the revolutionary forces in Vietnam has been something like a certainty for years now; indeed . . . it has been something like a certainty for more than a quarter of a century. . . . Events have unfolded more swiftly than thought could follow. At the heart of the South Vietnamese collapse there seems to have been a vacuum: the Saigon government. One moment, it was there, with its one million one hundred thousand men under arms and its gigantic Air Force — the third largest in the world — and the next moment it was gone. . . . City after city was falling without a battle. The North Vietnamese invasion, swift as it was, could not keep pace with the South Vietnamese collapse. Cities fell; days later, the foe approached. . . . [N]o one had foreseen this bloodbath: the massacre of civilians by the disintegrating South Vietnamese Army. . . . Something deeper than the collapse of an army's discipline — deeper, even, than the collapse of a body politic — was taking place. It was the disintegration of a society that had been pulverized by war and corrupted by foreign invaders for thirty years. A society that had lost all sense of self-respect and that

despised itself for its subservience to one foreign master after another—was tearing itself apart in a frenzy of self-destruction. . . . And
President Thieu summed up the general feeling when . . . he said,
"Many Vietnamese now have the feeling that they actually have been
lured into all this and then abandoned." And so they had. For more
than a decade, the United States had imposed an American fantasy on
Vietnamese reality. Then we had left, and now the South Vietnamese
government was fading like the mirage it had in fact always been.[1]

Shocked by the photos of Ambassador Graham Martin being rescued
from the roof of the embassy by helicopter, and of the rescue helicopters
rising from the Saigon compound while Marines crushed the desperate
hands of clinging Vietnamese allies, Americans closed their eyes to the
consequences of their doomed crusade in Southeast Asia. Only the epi-
sodic coverage of the plight of boat people, and their eventual reluctant
reception in American cities, broke the spell of amnesia.

On the occasion of the tenth anniversary of the fall of Saigon, two
clear-eyed analysts, David Fromkin and James Chace, writing in *Foreign
Affairs*, sought to examine the lessons that had so far been drawn in the
American literature on the war in Vietnam. They reported that there
were no lessons to be drawn.

> The Indochina War was surely the most tragic episode in the his-
> tory of the United States in this century. If we could all look at that
> terrible experience through the same pair of eyes, it could teach us
> much. But we cannot, so it cannot. That may be the final tragedy of
> the Vietnam War.
>   . . . The truth about Indochina is not self-evident; we all have our
> own views, but they are evident only to ourselves. The authors of this
> article also hold strong views about the Vietnam War, but no longer
> believe they can prove they are right to someone who holds contrary
> views. It is not because of any doubt as to the truth of the matter; it
> is for lack of objective evidence that cannot be controverted by the
> other side.[2]

Yet while some scholars still cling to this curiously obscurantist conclusion, others, including American presidents and generals, have drawn
their own conclusions. Both in the 1983 rapid invasion of Grenada and
in the more deliberate and less controversial campaign of "Desert

Storm," Presidents Reagan and Bush seemed to be guided by two intuitive lessons from Vietnam: Never go to war without an insuperable military advantage, and Keep the press on a short leash. Without specifically challenging these perhaps overcautious corollaries of the defeat in Vietnam, it now seems possible to delve more deeply into the roots of the American defeat in Vietnam. Perhaps such an inquiry will reveal that the 1975 debacle was merely the long-delayed consequence of earlier political and moral mistakes that could no longer have been corrected in the 1970s, no matter how much force was applied, even without the long shadow of the camera across the battlefield. Perhaps the fundamental lesson of Vietnam is political and moral rather than strategic or journalistic.

The present inquiry is guided by the hypothesis that Kennedy, in deciding to overthrow his ally, President Ngo Dinh Diem, chose a path that eventually led to disaster. When Kennedy cast his lot with the coup plotters, who responded to U.S. initiatives for such a betrayal, the American crusade to secure the independence of South Vietnam was doomed. From the moment that the United States committed itself to securing the independence of a wholly controlled ally, it had entered on its perilous march of folly.[3] For independence has its own exacting dynamism, which is displayed in resistance to control by foreigners.

The banality of this lesson of Vietnam — its seemingly uncomplicated clarity — is now at last being registered by a surprising, and therefore persuasive, chorus of commentators. Two of these analysts who share a conviction about the cardinal importance of the choice by Kennedy to overthrow Ngo Dinh Diem probably agree on little else about American foreign policy. They are Arthur Schlesinger Jr. and Henry Kissinger.

In the spring of 1995, during the twentieth anniversary of the fall of Saigon, Robert McNamara likewise confirmed and fortified this consensus in his memoirs. Arguing that the United States could, and should, have abandoned Vietnam after the coup against Diem, McNamara's perspective adds to the force of the judgments by Kissinger and Schlesinger the authority of one who had the principal operational responsibility for the war in Vietnam. He regrets that Kennedy and Johnson failed to seize the moment of heightened instability in Saigon during 1963–65 to terminate an assistance program that already appeared futile.[4]

Schlesinger's early (but too little noticed) analysis of the weight of the decision to elicit, and support, a coup against Ngo Dinh Diem is found in his study *Robert Kennedy and His Times:* "Still, a Diem-Ho deal could have been the means of an American exit from Vietnam in 1963. . . . An opportunity of some sort was perhaps missed in the autumn of 1963."[5] Earlier Schlesinger had observed:

> The irony is that Diem and Nhu, without Kennedy's knowledge, were engaged in secret negotiations that could have resulted in somewhat the situation Kennedy had in mind [to quit Vietnam]. The Ngo brothers were, in their anachronistic fashion, authentic Vietnamese nationalists. They were reluctant about American troops and resistant to American interference. . . . In May 1963 Nhu proposed publicly that the United States start withdrawing its troops. In the summer he told Forrestal in his "hooded" way that the United States did not understand Vietnam; "sooner or later we Vietnamese will settle our differences between us." "Even during the most ferocious battle," Nhu said to Mieczyslaw Maneli . . . : "the Vietnamese never forget who is a Vietnamese and who is a foreigner."[6]

Schlesinger here suggests shrewdly, if somewhat tentatively, that an opportunity to quit Vietnam with honor may have been missed in the autumn of 1963, when Diem was negotiating with Ho Chi Minh for a neutral, and federal, state of Vietnam.

Henry Kissinger states more assertively: "In retrospect, the last moment at which America could have withdrawn from Vietnam at tolerable — though still heavy — cost would have been just before or just after Diem was overthrown. The Kennedy administration was correct in its assessment that it could not win with Diem. . . . In light of what followed the coup, it would have been easier for America to disengage by letting Diem collapse of his own inadequacies or, at a minimum, by not standing in the way of the negotiations he was suspected of planning with Hanoi."[7]

The reasons Kissinger proffers to prove that the United States could not win its containment struggle in Indochina with Diem as an ally are persuasive. He reflects on two facets of Diem's personality and predicament that made it inconceivable for him to restructure his society along democratic lines in the midst of civil war. Diem was a lifelong crusader for independence and thus constitutionally unable to reform his society along Western lines, especially at the noisy behest of a Western government. "Leaders of so-called freedom movements are typically not democratic personalities; . . . Humility is rarely one of their attributes; if it were, they would not be revolutionaries. Installing a government that makes its leaders dispensable — the essence of democracy — strikes most of them as a contradiction in terms."[8]

Kissinger then sharpens his portrait of Diem by sketching in the cultural background of Vietnamese Confucianism.

> Diem's personality traits were compounded by the Confucian political tradition of Vietnam. . . . Its quest for truth does not treat conflicting ideas as having equal merit, the way democratic theory does. Since there is only one truth, that which is not true can have no standing or be enhanced through competition. Confucianism is essentially hierarchical and elitist, emphasizing loyalty to family, institutions, and authority. . . .
>
> A mandarin, he [Diem] held as a model the Confucian ruler governing by virtue, not consensus, and who achieved legitimacy, the so-called mandate of heaven, by success. Diem recoiled instinctively from the concept of a legitimate opposition.[9]

According to Kissinger, the United States miscalculated about the odds of winning with Diem, hoping simultaneously to execute two antithetical strategies: democratic reform and enhanced security against an unprincipled but shrewd adversary. "The Kennedy administration took for a truism what would turn out to be one of Indochina's many insoluble dilemmas; the insistence on simultaneous political reform and military victory set up a vicious circle. . . . Trapped between fanatical ideologues in Hanoi and inexperienced idealists in Washington, Diem's government froze into rigidity and was eventually ground down."[10]

This emerging consensus on Kennedy's miscalculations in Vietnam, independently argued by Schlesinger, McNamara, and Kissinger, stressed the misfortune of Kennedy's failure to quit Vietnam when Diem was negotiating with North Vietnam. The same regret has been voiced by the journalist and historian of the Vietnam wars Stanley Karnow: "Looking back with 20–20 hindsight, it seems to me that the great Vietnam tragedy really began with the overthrow of Ngo Dinh Diem in 1963. I think it was true, as those of us who criticized him at the time said, 'We can't win the war with Diem.' Having been involved in his ouster, however, the United States assumed a responsibility for Vietnam that was to lead inexorably to the American combat intervention." Karnow labels the U.S. struggle in Vietnam "the most avoidable war in our history."[11] He does not think that this "avoidable war" could have been won by the alliance between the United States and Diem.

For Karnow, the only road that might have escaped the quagmire was the road not taken in 1963, when Ngo Dinh Diem was cut down on the very eve of negotiating a peace settlement between North and South in Vietnam. In the 1983 Wilson Center Conference, Karnow made only an oblique reference to "lost opportunities" that were diplomatic, rather than military.[12] It is in another, much earlier article, published in 1974, that Karnow identifies the diplomatic escape route that was tragically overlooked, namely, the imminent negotiations, to be opened on November 15, 1963, between Diem's new ambassador to India, Tran Van Dinh, and Ho's diplomatic representative, Le Duc Tho, who would in 1973 be Henry Kissinger's interlocutor in the Paris Peace Accords.[13] By 1973 it had taken ten years and an avalanche of mutual misfortune to open the negotiations that might have ended the war in 1963 with South Vietnam's dream of independence still intact. When Le Duc Tho finally negotiated instead with Kissinger, the dream of Saigon's independence was already a memory.

Why did Kennedy and his counselors miss the only exit from the maze? Henry Kissinger has compared the Kennedy years in Vietnam to "a classical tragedy in which the hero is led step by imperceptible step toward his destiny by seemingly random events."[14] Kissinger is correct in evoking the tradition of classical tragedy in an effort to comprehend Kennedy's failure. For this tradition sought to explain doom, not as a random and incomprehensible event, but as the consequence of some character flaw that inexorably sets the hero at odds with the gods, who ultimately determine the fate of man.

In his study of Sophocles' *Antigone*, for example, H. D. F. Kitto traces the undoing of the rule and house of Creon to the king's transgression of the limits imposed on mankind by the nature of reality. In condemning Antigone, his son's fiancée, to prison for the pious, if unpatriotic, act of burying her fallen rebel brother, as the "unwritten laws of nature" commanded her, King Creon offended Aphrodite, the powerful goddess of love. Creon then compounded his guilt by refusing the plea of his son, Haemon, to pardon Antigone. When Haemon found that Antigone had hanged herself, he too committed suicide, leading to his mother's suicide in turn. These serial suicides are presented by Sophocles not merely as misfortune but as tragedy, focusing the admonitory tale of Creon's punishment by the gods for his transgressions of the prerogatives of Love, which the gods had fixed as the core of human experience.[15]

Is the story of Kennedy's missed opportunities the stuff of such tragic drama? Are the consequences of Kennedy's choices tragic in the classical literary sense of being linked fatefully to the hero's character flaw? If we can identify in retrospect some human frailty that entailed such dire consequences, we may be able to draw lessons from Vietnam that might be posted as warning signs in future U.S. foreign policy crises.

Fortunately, both Schlesinger and Kissinger have incisively identified certain characteristics of Kennedy and his administration that blinded these leaders to the risks inherent in the decision to overthrow Ngo Dinh Diem. Personal traits and philosophical attitudes hid from them the opening for Kennedy to withdraw from Vietnam as soon as it was known that Diem was negotiating with Ho. The only frustrating feature of Schlesinger's and Kissinger's respective analyses is that they are apparently contradictory. For Schlesinger sees the root of Kennedy's errors in the dynamics of American power, while Kissinger on the contrary attributes Kennedy's oversight to the excessive weight of American ideals in the Kennedy foreign policy.

There is a good case to be made, as Schlesinger urges, that it was the dizzying effect of America's sudden elevation to the new rank of superpower that misled successive presidents in dealing with smaller nations. But Kissinger is equally persuasive in arguing that the decisive factor in Kennedy's miscalculation in Vietnam was not the sudden surge of American power but his administration's exaggeration of the relevance of American ideals to its objectives in Southeast Asia.

Kissinger criticizes Kennedy for carelessly assuming that the strategy of containment could be picked up from its original European milieu and set down in Southeast Asia without a self-conscious effort to adjust that policy for the dramatic change of venue. Kissinger underlines the radical shift of diplomatic sensibilities required in 1963 for supporting Diem, a non-European, indeed anti-European, ally ruling in a deeply antidemocratic culture. "In the post–World War II period, America had been fortunate to have never had to choose between its moral convictions and its strategic analysis. All of its key decisions had been readily justified as both promoting democracy and resisting aggression. South

Vietnam, however, could by no stretch of the imagination be described as democratic."[16]

The Vietnamese alliance of convenience would require Kennedy to make a clear disjunction between military assistance to an Asian nation resisting Communist expansion and the distasteful imperative of political association with a ruler of unquestioned autocratic pedigree. The distinction would not be an easy one to maintain. Kissinger continues: "Imbued with the belief in the universal appeal of its values, America vastly underestimated the obstacles to democratization in a society shaped by Confucianism. . . . American idealism had imbued both officials and critics with the misconception that Vietnamese society could be transformed relatively easily and quickly into an American-style democracy. When that optimistic proposition collapsed. . . disillusionment was inevitable."[17]

Other, European, democracies might have sustained such a two-tiered alliance — of military assistance to Diem without political agreement or moral approval — but American "exceptionalism" precluded this strategy for Kennedy. Kissinger defines American exceptionalism as "the belief in the universal applicability of American values." He writes, "Basically, the Kennedy Administration was implementing Wilsonian assumptions. Just as Wilson had believed that American notions about democracy and diplomacy could be grafted onto Europe in the form of the Fourteen Points, so the Kennedy Administration sought to give the Vietnamese essentially American rules by which to govern themselves. If despots in the south could be deposed and good democrats installed, the conflict raging in Indochina would surely subside." Kissinger concludes: "American exceptionalism had sustained one of the great eras of American policy with its idealism, its innocence, and its dedication; now it turned relentless in demanding the same perfectionism of America's allies, and the absence of ambiguity in America's choice. Failing these, it envisaged only shame for America and doom for its ally."[18]

These two critiques of the Kennedy policies in Vietnam, argued by Schlesinger and Kissinger, seem at first to identify antithetical causes of our failure there. Schlesinger lays the blame on the dizzying influence of power over Kennedy's judgment, while Kissinger laments the moral zeal that drove the administration to depose Diem with catastrophic consequences. But the analyses are complementary. Schlesinger is correct in blaming the administration for romantic illusions about its power to remold other societies in the American image.[19] Kissinger indicts American exceptionalism for mandating such a radical social transformation in the midst of civil war. The tragic flaw of American diplomacy, they seem finally to agree, was the midcentury American illusion of the malleability of allied nations under American influence.

But Vietnam was by no means the first instance of this reckless rejection of other societies' social and political customs in favor of a new political culture to be imported from the United States. Such messianism has been pervasive throughout "the American century," evident as early as the Spanish-American War. This adventure revealed the instinctive attitude of Americans in their dealings abroad, which Stanley Karnow delineates in his study of U.S. leadership during the Spanish-American War:

> They were intoxicated by stirring parades, martial music, and flamboyant oratory—all flushed with a sense of high moral purpose. In contrast to the Europeans, who merely lusted for power, Americans would mobilize their might to spread the blessings of their exceptional civilization to the world. . . .
>
> When war with Spain broke out in April 1898, [Jeremiah Beveridge, a young lawyer and future senator,] designated the Philippines as "logically our first target" and the Pacific "the true field of our earliest operations." His speech to a Boston audience marked a milestone in xenophobia: "We are a conquering race: . . . American law, American order, American civilization, and the American flag will plant themselves on shores hitherto bloody and benighted, but by those agencies of God henceforth to be made beautiful and bright."[20]

This spontaneous spiritual imperialism, sparking the drive to "annex and christianize" the Philippines, was later echoed in the stirring phrases of Woodrow Wilson, who found himself in the position as president to exercise his enthusiastic convictions about American "exceptionalism." American moral superiority calls for control of far-flung peoples in order to civilize them.[21] Arthur Link observes that the intellectual and moral logic of Wilson's foreign policy leads to "the conclusion that democracy must some day be the universal rule of political life."[22]

Harley Notter focuses on the same messianic zeal in Wilson's foreign policy, appearing as early as 1913, when Wilson "preached America's mission to . . . set up constitutional liberty and government in Puerto Rico and the Philippines." Citing Wilson's July Fourth address of 1914, Notter recalls the prophecy that "the United States would be privileged to pilot the world to that point," namely, the point of democratic self-government based on the ideals of the American Revolution.[23]

Link's summary of the Wilsonian diplomatic vision confirms this analysis by Notter: "The American people, he believed, had a peculiar role to play, indeed a mission to execute in history, precisely because they were in so many ways unique among the peoples of the world. They were unique politically, not because they alone possessed democratic institutions, but because they had succeeded in organizing diverse sections and a hundred million people into a federal system such as one day . . . must provide a structure for a world organization." Thus America's mission to the world was unique: not to attain wealth or power but to fulfill the divine plan by service to humanity, by leadership and moral purposes, and above all by advancing peace and world friendship.[24] Wilson's confidence about transforming alien political cultures is perhaps the archetypal American political illusion. For such "idealism" is by nature the enemy of other peoples' dreams and ideals.

If America has a tragic flaw, it is perhaps this heedless zeal to improve its allies. Understandably, it was a poet who captured the boundless American enthusiasm for creating democracy abroad. Robert Frost had been moved by President-elect Kennedy's invitation to read at the January 20 inauguration his hymn to the American revolution, "The Gift Outright." Unable to still his imagination on such an auspicious occasion for the arts in the United States, Frost scribbled away the evening of January 19, 1961, on a new dedicatory ode, and then borrowed a hotel typewriter to make a copy. Unfortunately, the brilliant sun of that snowy January morning blinded Frost's aging eyes. After a chivalrous effort by Lyndon Johnson, who attempted to use his black top hat to shield the pages of the fresh text from the glare of the sun, Frost surrendered to his temporary blinding and recited his older revolutionary ode from memory.[25]

Frost's newly crafted inaugural ode read like a prophecy of Kennedy's priorities during his sparsely numbered days in the White House. In the lines hastily scribbled for the occasion, Frost rivaled Kennedy himself in the apt articulation of the ambition of the New Frontier. More incisively than any historian who followed (except Schlesinger), Frost captured the ethos of the era.

> This verse . . .
> Goes back to the beginning of the end
> Of what had been for centuries the trend;
> A turning point in modern history.
> Colonial had been the thing to be
> As long as the great issue was to see
> What country'd be the one to dominate
> By character, by tongue, by native trait,
> The new world that Columbus found. . . .
>
> .   .   .   .
>
> So much those heroes knew and understood—
> I mean the great four, Washington,
> John Adams, Jefferson, and Madison—
> So much they knew as consecrated seers
> They must have seen ahead what now appears.
> They would bring empires down about our ears
> And by the example of our Declaration
> Make everybody want to be a nation. . . .
>
> .   .   .   .
>
> *They are our wards to some extent*
> *For the time being and with their consent,*
> *To teach them how Democracy is meant.* . . .
>
> .   .   .   .
>
> A democratic form of right divine
> To rule first answerable to high design.[26]

Mistaking it for a virtue, indeed for America's singular claim among the great historical powers, Frost rhapsodized on the march of progress, with Kennedy in the lead. Surely no one could have foreseen in that blinding light of the inauguration the self-destructive course that such proud ambition would soon choose. Even sober critics such as Kissinger continue to identify the reforming zeal of American presidents, from Wilson to Kennedy, as a virtue, the characteristic mark of American

idealism in foreign policy. But the time may have come for a more critical evaluation of this destructive messianism, a latent xenophobia mas-
querading as benevolence.

It is time to call this reforming instinct a tragic flaw, rather than an
ill-starred flight of idealism, as Kissinger does. What the narrative of the
Year of the Hare reveals unmistakably is the distortion of political judgment generated by American frustration at the intransigence of its ir-
reformable allies. The destructive force in such crusades is the rage that
they generate in the American policy makers, after these leaders have
searched in vain for progress in democracy among their "wards" in the
developing world.

The shock of the New Frontier approach to Vietnam is the profile in
rage that marked the fulminations of William Trueheart and Henry
Cabot Lodge Jr. in their formal meetings with Diem and in the cabled
recollections of these "diplomatic" démarches. The same rage marked
George Ball's reminiscences of Diem, even at the distance of twenty-five
years. Rage triggered the outbursts of Averell Harriman in White
House meetings during the summer and fall of 1963.[27] And rage was evident in the daily front-page dispatches and matching editorials of the
New York Times throughout the year.

This rage is a characteristically high-minded, if philosophically quizzical, one. American insistence on the universality of its political dreams
is more striking when one compares this view of politics with any other
field of human achievement. For a claim that there is one definitive work
of art — sculpture, drama, symphony, painting, ballet, architecture —
that constitutes self-evident perfection, by which all other achievements
in these disciplines can forever and everywhere be objectively measured,
would seem to most educated people an implausible, even possibly de-
ranged, attitude. But in politics, many Americans believe precisely that:
no political theorist or leader, past, present, or future, could legitimately
claim merit for a society that was structured on principles other than
those of Jefferson and Madison.

If Sophocles or Michelangelo had made such an unimaginable claim
for his work, believing that it would remain the definitive achievement
of its field forever, his fame would deservedly have been effaced in mock-
ery. Many Americans, however, expect to be taken seriously when they
claim such timeless and global political primacy for their own political heritage. Diem, like many other non-Americans, may have harbored doubts

that humanity's millennial quest for the meaning of justice had come to an end once and for all in the writings—profound as they are—of two Virginia neighbors, Jefferson and Madison, both conscientious yet slave-owning republican aristocrats.[28]

Jefferson would himself have been the first to reject the twentieth-century effort to bind foreign governments to the mold of the immediate postrevolutionary ethos of the United States. For he had observed in a letter to Thomas Law on June 13, 1814: "The same actions are deemed virtuous in one country and vicious in another. The answer is, that nature has constituted *utility* to man, that standard and test of virtue. Men living in different countries, under different circumstances, different habits and regimens, may have different utilities; the same act, therefore, may be useful, and consequently virtuous, in one country which is injurious and vicious in another differently circumstanced."[29] Perhaps because his six years as ambassador in Paris in 1783–89 had allowed him to compare France's prerevolutionary turbulence with the American march toward revolution a decade earlier, or perhaps simply because he was able to read history and literature in six or more ancient and modern languages, Jefferson was innocent of the moral myopia of many of his successors in government, who insist that all nations must march to the same two Virginia drummers.

Even in his own nation, Jefferson insisted that every generation had a right to its own revolution. As early as 1789 Jefferson wrote to Madison insisting that each generation should write its own constitution, since "the earth belongs to the living."[30] Later he was to write from Monticello that each generation needed to have its own revolution; he meant that a reconstitution of the national life should occur every twenty years.

Hannah Arendt recalls Jefferson's radical revolutionary (and anticonstitutional) worldview:

> On the American scene, no one has perceived this seemingly inevitable flaw in the structure of the republic with greater clarity and more passionate preoccupation than Jefferson. His occasional, and sometimes violent, antagonism against the Constitution and particularly against those who "look at constitutions with sanctimonious reverence and deem them like the ark of the covenant, too sacred to be touched," was motivated by a feeling of outrage about the injustice that only his generation should have it in their power "to begin the

world over again"; for him, as for Paine, it was plain "vanity and
presumption [to govern] beyond the grave. . . . Nothing is unchange-
able but the inherent and unalienable rights of man," among which
he counted the rights to rebellion and revolution. When the news
of Shay's Rebellion in Massachusetts reached him while he was in
Paris . . . he greeted it with enthusiasm: "God forbid we should ever
be twenty years without such a rebellion. . . ." For "the tree of liberty
must be refreshed, from time to time, with the blood of patriots and
tyrants. It is its natural manure."[31]

The American political and editorial cliché, whereby officials worldwide
are judged by their resemblance to Jefferson, is then as historically ill informed as it is philosophically myopic.

   In the mirror of Vietnam policy making, we learn who we are. We are,
it seems, a self-adulatory people, whose mead is imitation and whose
rage is our indignation at the stubborn idiosyncracy of others. Such rage
is no ideal, *pace* Henry Kissinger, but an irrational aversion to the
stranger and thus the enemy of diplomacy. Eclipsing reason, such rage
creates a surreal landscape of shadowy and eerie shapes, masking friends
and enemies alike. Since rage is no climate for discernment, it is little
wonder that the Vietnam policies generated by that mood defy rational
analysis. For this curious alchemy turned our single fragile ally, Ngo
Dinh Diem, into our most threatening adversary.

   Rage is the political posture that thinks well of the strategy of reform
by means of coup. Such strategies have understandably all the allure and
substance of a rainbow, but at the end of that rainbow lies always another despot, another provocation, another storm of rage. Finally it was
rage that blinded some of Kennedy's advisers to the exit from the maze
of his alliance with Diem. After half a year of branding Diem as the de-
mon, it was difficult to identify him in his August machinations as the
providential deus ex machina, who might himself release Kennedy from
his unsustainable commitment to Vietnam.

Rage predictably begets rage. When Fritz Nolting was allowed to return
to Saigon on July 11, 1963, in the faint hope of reestablishing diplomatic
relations with Diem, his first cable to Rusk evoked the incendiary rage
of the Buddhist monks launched on a suicidal campaign: "Diem's in a
martyr's mood himself."[32] The fire of independence now blazed as dan-

gerously in Diem's eyes as in the flames consuming the sacrificial monks. With Diem's open defiance, even of his friend Nolting's last effort to rebuild the alliance, the moment of rupture was approaching. Diem's fatal response to the two months of hectoring by William Trueheart and relentless denunciations by the *Times* was wholly unsurprising.

For all his clairvoyance about the American spirit, Robert Frost had revealed in his inaugural ode an American insensitivity to the independence of other nations, whom Kennedy would be seeking to elevate to America's revolutionary heights. Two verses of the inaugural ode crystallize the American conscience abroad. The first telling words are "a democratic form of right divine." By borrowing, in his description of Kennedy's imminent rule abroad, the consecrated phrase "of right divine," Frost here stood political history on its head. For the words *right divine* had always previously stigmatized the tyrannical ruler's violation of the rights of his subjects. Here Frost reverses that process by authorizing the democratic government of John Kennedy to indulge in absolutism abroad, teaching rulers of developing nations such as Diem "how Democracy is meant." Democratic absolutism, which Frost evoked only to applaud it, was destined to spell the end of autocracy in the emerging nations. In words that Frost might have adapted from the canons of absolutism, "autocracy has no rights."

Frost is careful in the following verse to signal to these wards that such a burdensome tutelage will be undertaken only if they agree to such a steerage journey toward democracy.

> They are our wards to some extent
> For the time being *and with their consent*,
> to teach them how Democracy is meant. [emphasis added]

Consent, to be sure, is the sticking point of America's imperialism of virtue. From the earliest days of the republic, when Jefferson resolved to purchase and annex the Louisiana Territories, he was tortured by the contradiction between his intended acquisition of control over large numbers of people by the exchange of gold and his generation's earlier successful revolution, fought in the cause of government by consent. As early as 1803, when President Jefferson proposed to double the extent of the new republic by the Louisiana Purchase, John Quincy Adams, senator from Massachusetts, protested that Jefferson had no constitutional authority to add citizens to the republic by an exchange of cash without their consent. There was no power in the Constitution that allowed either Congress or the executive to govern a people without their consent.[33] But congressional agreement with Jefferson's initiative swiftly overwhelmed Adams's constitutional and moral objections, setting a precedent for a diplomacy of purchase.

Jefferson himself had resolved this quandary on the grounds of the imperatives of national security.[34] It was not the last time the conflict between political consistency and the imperatives of national interest was resolved with an uneasy conscience after vigorous ethical debate.

Jefferson's Louisiana Purchase later proved decisive in approving a diplomacy of conquest as well. For in 1899, when the Senate took up McKinley's proposal to annex the Philippines, the senators were stirred by Kipling's poem "The White Man's Burden," drafted for this uncertain occasion. They paused to consider the constitutional challenges hurled at this new initiative to acquire dominion over foreign peoples without their consent. Senator George Vest took up the role that John Adams had played in 1803, insisting that the Constitution made no provision for the acquisition of colonies. The United States, he argued, would betray its unique political heritage by annexing territories against the will of their people: the Philippines bill would impose government without consent of the governed. Senator Orville Platt easily countered that this principle had already been set aside by the Louisiana Purchase (and acquisition of New Mexico and Alaska) and had no further relevance to American diplomacy.[35]

By 1963 senators were no longer debating the constitutional propriety of the exercising of colonial power by the United States. The absolution for such an anomalous American policy in the 1960s had been granted by the inaugural poet, who presumed that leaders such as Diem would be Kennedy's wards only "[f]or the time being and with their consent." Unfortunately, Frost had not inquired of any actual "wards" about their consent to such a passing state of servitude. Indeed, Diem had explicitly withheld his consent from any such protectorate status for Vietnam, as Kennedy had been brusquely informed by cables from Saigon, relaying Diem's uncompromising conditions for U.S. assistance. After Diem had prohibited any U.S. intrusion into South Vietnam's politics, Kennedy had accepted this demand for complete national autonomy.

That solemn agreement came undone when chief of mission William

Trueheart lashed out at Diem about his policy toward the Buddhists. Trueheart's rage in turn sparked Diem's rage. By the summer of 1963 some Americans seemed to have forgotten the genesis of their own revolution, which had been a demand for autonomy, that is, "government by consent of the governed." No matter how enlightened the rule of British colonies might have been in 1776, or might have become after reform in London, that rule was by then alien and thus intolerable to the colonists. At the time, Jefferson's fellow Virginian Patrick Henry had demanded "liberty or death." But when an equally unnegotiable ultimatum was delivered by Diem, it was unrecognizable in Washington. For the American imagination could not concede autonomy for autocracy. To his American interlocutors, Diem in his demand for independence offered a chimera: the freedom to be nondemocratic. The American national experience rebelled against this retreat into the dense past. Blinded by the brilliance of its own historical achievement, Washington had in turn succumbed to an ancient-enough failing: self-adulation. Kennedy's America had become a Narcissus among nations.

Unlike Narcissus of old, Kennedy's America was activist. It fed on reforming others in its own image, although no one was asking for this particular blessing. Foolishly, perhaps, nations stubbornly cling to their own identity. Being robbed of one's identity, even in the name of progress, has the smell of death about it. No nation has yet been willing to surrender its inner self freely to the outsider.

This universal attachment of nations to the particularities of their own histories and cultures was lost on many in Washington. But they might have been alerted to the inescapable hazards of the efforts to refashion Diem's Vietnam in an American mold if they had paid even scant attention to the niceties of old-fashioned diplomacy, including the moral and legal prerogative of all nations, no matter how "backward," to pursue their own vision of the good life. That prerogative is known as sovereignty. It was this prerogative to which Diem clung as a shield against the American-style modernization being foisted on him by Washington. It was this shield that Diem had raised, and Kennedy acknowledged, in their first correspondence about the deployment of U.S. forces.

Sovereignty is defined by the political theorist Hans Morgenthau as "the supreme legal authority of the nation to give and enforce the law within a certain territory, and in consequence, independence from the authority of any other nation and equality with it under international law. Hence, the nation loses its sovereignty when it is placed under the authority of another nation, so that it is the latter which exercises supreme authority to give and enforce the laws within the former's territory."[36] Such a traditional constraint on the coercion of smaller nations by the powerful was operative in Kennedy's White House only selectively. It was scrupulously, if unenthusiastically, observed in Washington's relations with European capitals, but routinely ignored in the developing world generally, and most brutally in Vietnam.[37] In the case of the Kennedy-Diem alliance, its obvious import would be the right of Diem to negotiate freely with Ho about the possibly joint future of their peoples.

Such an American insensitivity is historically puzzling. For the principle had already emerged as the signature of the United Nations.[38] The American blindness to the universal legal constraint of sovereignty is thus especially ironic. For it was officials in Washington who had, in the first half of the twentieth century, championed the principle of sovereignty as the basis of relations among the nations of the Western Hemisphere. As Robert Klein demonstrates in his study of the evolution of the principle of sovereign equality among nations, it was the gradual acceptance by the United States of constant diplomatic pressure from Latin American states that led the Organization of American States to structure hemispheric relations around the principle of nonintervention, a corollary of sovereignty.[39]

Klein's reading of the hemispheric prehistory of the UN Charter principle of sovereignty is persuasive. He attributes the growing salience of this principle in international relations to the bitter experience by weak Latin American and Caribbean nations of Washington's "benevolent" intervention. Such muscled benevolence appeared in the region from the Spanish-American War, through the seizure of Panama from Colombia, to the cyclical American effort to install democracy at the point of a bayonet.[40]

The United States accepted the articulation of the principle of nonintervention in the documents of the Second Hague Conference (1907), the Montevideo Conference (1933), and the Inter-American Conference on Peace (1936), all leading up to the Dumbarton Oaks Conference (1944), which laid the groundwork for the UN Charter.[41] Klein summarizes the resigned acceptance by Washington of the Latin American demand for sovereign immunity from intervention in these words: "Each attempt by the United States to insure a particular form of government has had evil consequences far outweighing the intended good. No doubt the wisest maxim is to leave the choice of government to the people who must live under it."[42]

Klein attributes the origin of the Latin American diplomatic demand for recognition of the inviolable independence of their nations to their own contemporary experience of U.S. intervention during the first third of the American century. But it is equally probable that the prehistory of Latin resistance to intervention is of much longer duration, extending back to 1492, or shortly thereafter. For it was not originally North Americans' meddling in their southern neighbors' politics that sounded the alarm against intervention in the hemisphere but the arrival of the Spaniards in the wake of Columbus's four voyages.

The Spanish assault on these lands had, however, been almost instantaneously challenged in Europe on moral grounds, both in university lecture halls at Salamanca and elsewhere, including at the Spanish court itself. The most renowned of these advocates of the autonomy of independent peoples in the "Indies" was Francisco de Vitoria, the Spanish Dominican professor of theology and dean of faculty at Salamanca. It is almost certain that the twentieth-century Latin American diplomats and jurists who challenged U.S. intervention in their region were intellectually nourished by the natural law tradition in ethics, which Vitoria helped to shape in Spain.[43]

This natural law tradition, to which the Spaniards made a distinctive intellectual contribution in response to the rapacious "age of discovery," is itself rooted in the same classical Greek tradition whose characteristic literary form was the dramatic tragedy.[44] Sophocles, for example, had warned that human choice needs to take cognizance of the inherent structure of reality, which can be violated only at the violator's own peril. As Sophocles traced Creon's downfall to his violation of the imperatives of human affection and familial loyalty, so Vitoria warned the Spanish crown about any colonial policies that would seek to constrain the religious or cultural independence of the recently "discovered" races in the "Indies."[45] Empire, the theologian Vitoria had warned at the time, was ephemeral because the fire of independence is eternal.

But the caution of the European tradition of natural law, argued still later in the Americas by twentieth-century Latin American jurists and diplomats schooled in the continental legal tradition, rang hollow to the men shaping Vietnam policy in 1963. For these overburdened officials shared with most Americans a deep disinterest in the inherited legal and philosophical views of Europeans.[46]

These officials seemed unaware of the deep moral transgression embodied in their dismissal of Diem's plans for Vietnam: they conscientiously undertook the rape of Vietnamese independence in the name of freedom. That rape was innocent enough. For the inviolability of national independence, the "Old World" notion of sovereignty, is an anachronism for many Americans. Like autocracy, it is a value embedded in older cultures, as a result of forgotten experiences, which is no longer relevant to international affairs. For such Americans, sovereignty is a legal obsession that spokesmen for developing nations treasure irrationally. For the United States, legitimacy, shielded by the prerogatives of sovereignty, is a title earned by the merit of virtue, not simply as a matter of de facto rule.

This condescension by Americans for ancient cultures that cling to their independence at the cost of "progress" was articulated by Robert Frost in another much earlier poem, "Mending Wall," which can stand as a folk emblem of American culture. A thoughtful reading of "Mending Wall" will explain the dynamics of American self-confidence in the face of recalcitrant ancient cultures, "old-stone savages" clinging anachronistically to claims of the right of sovereignty.

> I let my neighbor know beyond the hill;
> And on a day we meet to walk the line
> And set the wall between us once again.
>
> .   .   .   .
>
> There where it is we do not need the wall:
> He is all pine and I am apple orchard.
> My apple trees will never get across
> And eat the cones under his pines, I tell him.
> He only says, "Good fences make good neighbors."
>
> .   .   .   .
>
> "Why do they make good neighbors? Isn't it
> Where there are cows? But here there are no cows.
> Before I built a wall I'd ask to know

What I was walling in or walling out,
And to whom I was like to give offense.

.   .   .   .

... I see him there,
Bringing a stone grasped firmly by the top
In each hand, like an old-stone savage armed.
He moves in darkness as it seems to me,
Not of woods only and the shade of trees.
He will not go behind his father's saying,
And he likes having thought of it so well
He says again, "Good fences make good neighbors."[47]

Although Frost wrote "Mending Wall" early in his career, before World War I, he seems to have captured here timelessly the characteristic American confidence that our nation can act wisely with a slate wiped clean of inherited wisdom. It is unsurprising how easily Diem can be matched to Frost's harsh image

... like an old-stone savage armed.
He moves in darkness as it seems to me,

.   .   .   .

He will not go behind his father's saying.

EPILOGUE: THE MIRROR OF THE WALL

By early morning light, the Vietnam Memorial on the Mall serves as a mirror of the Washington Monument, rising to its east. The dark luster of the catalog of the fallen is brightened by this obelisk, the curiously alien symbol selected as the national memorial to the first president. As long as tourists continue to find Washington worthy of a journey, the Vietnam Memorial will remind them of the lengths to which American leaders were driven in seeking to escape the hazards of a nuclear showdown at the height of the Cold War that might have left Washington a modern-day, manmade Pompeii. When the ominous nuclear alternative to the war in Vietnam will finally have been seen in greater historical perspective, these young Americans who were caught in the tidal wave of independence in Southeast Asia will be recognized as unfortunate sentinels of democracy, stationed implausibly in the Vietnamese heartland of Confucian autocracy.

Visitors will likely still look in vain for statues of the military or political leaders who directed the energy of American containment strategies in Vietnam. For nothing that this generation of leaders did in Vietnam is worthy of a memorial. The monument is appropriately raised to those who followed and fell, not to those who led and lived. The only American leaders to be seen at the Wall are those reflected there, George Washington in all seasons and Abraham Lincoln from December to May. But the soldiers' cause was earnest enough, even if it was doomed by its design to co-opt the Vietnamese prerogative of self-determination. In time, foreign tourists will see in the Wall, with its hallowed names and its fleeting reflections of earlier American leaders, an image of soldierly self-determination, the grassroots veterans groups' successful campaign to erect a monument to themselves when they were shunned by many of their fellow citizens and ignored by political leaders who sought solace in amnesia about their war.

But the experience of visitors from abroad will never match the engagement of Americans who pause at the shrine. For one of the unexpected facets of the Wall is its capacity to reflect as well the visitor's own face. In the proper light we see ourselves in the Wall. And well we might. For it was we who, through our choice of leaders, sent the soldiers off on a futile and costly exercise in American self-duplication abroad.

We do well then to reflect on our own role in this doomed crusade. For we must acknowledge that citizens bear the onus for the folly of the Kennedy campaign to superimpose on Saigon the image of Washington. In the proper light, the names of the American victims of that struggle interact with the visitor who sees a self-image superimposed on this catalog of the youthful dead. Now the visitor must ask: What is the lesson written on this wall?

It is a simple lesson. The distinctive American formula of politics, Jefferson's and Madison's writ, which ordered and executed this cruel crusade, is perhaps not, after all, a panacea for the political woes of humanity. Jeffersonian democracy is an idiosyncratic achievement that, like all competing forms of government, is human and therefore vulnerable to human failings.

The foregoing hour-by-hour narration of U.S. government deliberations occurring during the Year of the Hare and culminating in the ouster and assassination of Ngo Dinh Diem offers a mirror in which the United States can contemplate itself without pretense. The folly, complacency, and reckless ambition of many distinguished officials of Kennedy's government are no mere exceptions to America's vaunted "exceptionalism" as a society, but the blemished images of democracy at work. These officials' decisions carried our authority, conferred by democratic elections.

Perhaps the steady meditation on the reality of democracy in the United States, 1963, will shake some of us awake from our self-complacent intolerance of nations that cling to alien and outdated philosophies of government. Perhaps a close study of our own unvarnished national image in this sad narrative will allow us to ask, as Arthur Schlesinger Jr. wisely urged in the mid-1960s, "whether this country is a chosen people, uniquely righteous and wise, with a moral mission to all mankind; or whether it is one of many nations in a multifarious world, endowed with traditions and purposes, legitimate but not infallible, as other nations have legitimate and fallible traditions and purposes of their own."[1]

In this passage, registering the first tremors of the Vietnam crisis in 1966, Schlesinger stresses the limitations of the American heritage, which should lead us to be more modest in setting ourselves up as a transnational paradigm of political wisdom. He notes our capacity for error as one such wholly normal human limitation. A few pages earlier, he had questioned vigorously the logic of the American campaign in Southeast Asia, which he described as "the preposterous adventure in the seventh decade of the twentieth century [of] the salvation of Asia."[2] We have noted Schlesinger's even more trenchant criticism, written a decade later, of Kennedy's romantic and reckless illusion of America's reforming the world in its own image.[3]

Each reader, reflecting on the ominous path of Kennedy's Vietnam policies, will single out one or another root of this tragedy. My own inclination is to attribute these choices to a deep and high-minded intolerance, which lashes out uncontrollably at foreign leaders who refuse to conform to our expectations. However one chooses to evaluate U.S. policies in Southeast Asia during the Year of the Hare, the primary question posed by our reflections on the Wall is this: Do we now feel that we are so above reproach in our political legacy that we are justified in coercing other nations to adopt the political system that crafted and executed this crusade?

Schlesinger's own answer to that question, written in 1972 near the collapse of the soaring mission to Vietnam, addresses directly the urgency of tolerance: "The assumption that other nations have traditions, interests, values, rights, and obligations of their own is the beginning of a true morality of states. . . . But an intelligent regard for one's own national interest joined to unremitting respect for the interests of others seems more likely than the invocation of moral absolutes to bring about greater restraint, justice, and peace among nations."[4] Without appealing explicitly to the moral and international legal principle of sovereignty, Schlesinger here invokes its salutary content of mutual recognition and nonintervention.

This seems to be the lesson of Vietnam: there are no grounds to justify another American campaign to change the face of the world in our image. If the officials of the Kennedy administration had observed this simple principle, there might not now be a Vietnam Wall to recall for the ages the scars of the Cold War. There would be only the small open space in Berlin where once another wall loomed over an entire generation.

NOTES

PROLOGUE

1. The Vietnam Veterans Memorial in Washington was dedicated on November 11, 1982.

2. Frances FitzGerald, *Fire in the Lake: The Vietnamese and the Americans in Vietnam* (1972; New York: Random House, 1989), 325.

3. Kennedy's acceptance of responsibility for the coup plan is recorded in Message from the President to the Ambassador in Vietnam, August 29, 1963, in United States Department of State, *The Foreign Relations of the United States, 1961–1963*, vol. 1, *Vietnam, 1961*, vol. 2, *Vietnam, 1962*, vol. 3, *Vietnam, January–August 1963*, vol. 4, *Vietnam, August–December 1963* (Washington, D.C.: GPO, 1988–91), 4:35 (these volumes are hereinafter cited as *FRUS, 1961–1963*). Testimony of Kennedy's personal continuous monitoring of the coup was offered in the author's interview with Michael V. Forrestal on December 11, 1987. Ellen Hammer is the commentator who underlines this puzzlement most decisively; see Hammer, *A Death in November: America in Vietnam, 1963* (New York: E. P. Dutton, 1987), 35.

4. Senator Mike Mansfield, in a letter to the author dated October 24, 1989, confirms the account of this admission by Kenneth P. O'Donnell and David F. Powers in *"Johnny, We Hardly Knew Ye": Memories of John Fitzgerald Kennedy* (Boston: Little, Brown, 1972), 16. Robert S. McNamara adds his personal authority to the evidence suggesting that Kennedy was only waiting for the 1964 reelection victory to begin withdrawing from Vietnam, although he admits that the president never said this to him personally. See Robert S. McNamara with Brian VanDeMark, *In Retrospect: The Tragedy and Lessons of Vietnam* (New York: Times Books, 1995), 95–96.

5. Author's interviews with Dean Rusk, Roswell Gilpatric, and McGeorge Bundy, February–July 1988. All of them vigorously challenged Mansfield's views. Dean Rusk, for example, denied any such intention on the part of Kennedy. Rusk made the same skeptical statements on a BBC Radio Three broadcast, recorded in December 1976 and published subsequently in Michael Charlton and Anthony Moncrieff, *Many Reasons Why: The American Involvement in Vietnam* (London: Scolar Press, 1978), 82. In several interviews, McNamara claims to have shared knowledge of Kennedy's intention to withdraw. See Deborah Shapley, *Promise and Power: The Life and Times of Robert McNamara* (Boston: Little, Brown, 1993), 262–63. As indicated in the previous note, McNamara's own memoir denies such a personal communication from Kennedy to McNamara.

6. Memorandum from the Deputy Director of the Bureau of Intelligence and Research to the Acting Secretary of State, Washington, January 29, 1964, in United States Department of State, *The Foreign Relations of the United States, 1964–1968*, vol. 1, *Vietnam, 1964* (Washington, D.C.: GPO, 1992), 40–41 (this volume is

hereinafter cited as *FRUS, 1964–1968*). See also Memorandum from Michael V. Forrestal of the National Security Council Staff to the President, Washington, January 30, 1964, in *FRUS, 1964–1968* 1:42–43.

On the governments that succeeded Diem, see George C. Herring, *America's Longest War: The United States in Vietnam, 1950–1975*, 2d ed. (New York: Alfred A. Knopf, 1979), 108–43.

7. Robert Shaplen, "A Reporter at Large: Saigon Exit," *New Yorker*, May 19, 1975, 94–110.

8. Author's interview with Dean Rusk, February 26, 1988.

9. Rusk recounted the same decisive moment in the moral calculations of the Kennedy administration to Thomas Schoenbaum, who records it in *Waging Peace and War: Dean Rusk in the Truman, Kennedy, and Johnson Years* (New York: Simon and Schuster, 1988), 33. Cf. Dean Rusk, *As I Saw It: As Told to Richard Rusk*, edited by Daniel S. Papp (New York: W. W. Norton, 1990), 246–47; and Richard Reeves, *President Kennedy: Profile of Power* (New York: Simon and Schuster, 1993), 230. Reeves dates this briefing on nuclear strategy at September 13, 1961. Rusk himself suggested that it occurred much earlier; author's interview with Rusk, February 26, 1988.

10. For a more comprehensive account of the several effective Kennedy responses to threats in Berlin and Cuba, see chapter 10 below.

11. James Reston, *Deadline: A Memoir* (New York: Times Books, 1992), 299–300. Cf. R. Reeves, *President Kennedy*, 172–76, 411.

12. Michael Beschloss, *The Crisis Years: Kennedy and Khrushchev, 1960–1963* (New York: HarperCollins, 1991), 224–25, 337.

13. The implausibility of this link between Berlin and Saigon may be one reason why its salience is overlooked by some Southeast Asian specialists. For example, the Berlin crisis stimulus to Kennedy's Vietnam engagement is virtually ignored in the standard work by George C. Herring, *America's Longest War*, 79.

Herring's silence on this link between the nuclear risks in Europe and the "colonial war of liberation" in Vietnam is by no means exceptional. In his magisterial historiographical essay, "The Unending Debate: Historians and the Vietnam War," *Diplomatic History* 18 (1994): 239–64, Gary R. Hess fails to indicate that any of the historians whose work he has examined (especially between 1982 and 1994) have taken note of this link between Europe and Vietnam in Kennedy's mind. Moreover, in his own 1993 essay, Hess completely overlooks the same connection; see Hess, "Commitment in the Age of Counterinsurgency: Kennedy's Vietnam Options and Decisions, 1961–1963," in *Shadow on the White House: Presidents and the Vietnam War, 1945–1975*, edited by David L. Anderson (Lawrence: University Press of Kansas, 1993), 63–86.

The uniform silence of U.S. specialists on the Vietnam War concerning this claim made by Dean Rusk (*As I Saw It*), Michael Beschloss (*Crisis Years*), James Reston (*Deadline*), and Richard Reeves (*President Kennedy*) about the link between European security problems and Vietnam is somewhat puzzling. It may be partially attributable to the dominant style in the monographs surveyed by Hess, which tend to study U.S.-Vietnamese relations on a strictly bilateral basis. To ensure a satisfactory account of the foreign policy of a global power, such as the United States during the Cold War, such bilateral historical perspectives obviously require some more intense consideration of the global factors affecting decision makers in Washington. The paradox here seems to be that a historian who focuses exclusively on developments in Southeast Asia can probably never fully plumb the reality of the U.S. war in Vietnam.

14. David Holloway, *Stalin and the Bomb: The Soviet Union and Atomic Energy, 1939–1956* (New Haven, Conn.: Yale University Press, 1994), 339.

15. Holloway, *Stalin and the Bomb*, 336–40.

16. Holloway, *Stalin and the Bomb*, 342.

17. Holloway, *Stalin and the Bomb*, 343, 344, 369.

18. Adam Ulam, *Expansion and Coexistence: Soviet Foreign Policy, 1917–1973*, 2d ed. (New York: Holt, Rinehart and Winston, 1974), 630–31, 636–37. Ulam emphasizes Khrushchev's desire to respond to Chinese pressures on the Soviet Union not to abandon the Marxist doctrine of the struggle against capitalism.

19. Beschloss, *Crisis Years*, 60, 61. Cf. Arthur M. Schlesinger Jr., *Robert Kennedy and His Times* (Boston: Houghton Mifflin, 1978), 422–23; and R. Reeves, *President Kennedy*, 40–41.

20. Hammer, *Death in November*, 275.

21. Hammer, *Death in November*, 301. Schlesinger writes that President Kennedy "said that 'Diem had served his country for twenty years and it shouldn't have ended like this'" (*Robert Kennedy*, 721). Cf. R. Reeves, *President Kennedy*, 650–51.

22. On the antiforeign animus energizing Diem's resistance to U.S. demands for reform, see Gary R. Hess, *Vietnam and the United States: Origins and Legacy of War* (Boston: Twayne, 1990), 75. Just after the coup, Diem's former American political consultant, Major General Edward G. Lansdale, evoked the legacy of the Magna Carta as the goal of the U.S. effort in Vietnam; Lansdale, "Viet Nam: Do We Understand Revolution?" *Foreign Affairs* 43, no. 1 (October 1964): 75–86.

23. Memorandum of a Conversation, Department of State, July 5, 1963, in *FRUS, 1961–1963* 3:466–67.

24. Herring, *America's Longest War*, 46. Cf. Stanley Karnow, *Vietnam: A History* (New York: Viking Press, 1983), 218. George McT. Kahin remarks, however, that by Vietnamese standards Diem's rule was vindicated by the 1946 invitation from Ho Chi Minh to share with him the government of all Vietnam. Kahin, *Intervention: How America Became Involved in Vietnam* (New York: Alfred Knopf, 1986), 79.

25. Herring, *America's Longest War*, 7–8. See Karnow, *Vietnam*, 136, for a slightly different interpretation, attributing more ambivalence to Roosevelt's posture. Rusk claims that Roosevelt had given up the cause of Indochinese independence by 1945 (*As I Saw It*, 112).

26. Guenter Lewy, *America in Vietnam* (Oxford: Oxford University Press, 1978), 4. Cf. Herring, *America's Longest War*, 8–11; and Arthur M. Schlesinger Jr., *The Bitter Heritage: Vietnam and American Democracy, 1941–1966* (Boston: Houghton, Mifflin, 1967), 2–5.

27. Lewy, *America in Vietnam*, 5. Cf. Herring, *America's Longest War*, 9–19, 21–24; and Hess, *Vietnam and the United States*, 38–41.

28. Karnow, *Vietnam*, 223–24. Cf. Hess, *Vietnam and the United States*, 61.

29. Jean Lacouture and Simonne Lacouture, *Vietnam: Voyage à travers une victoire* (Paris: Editions du Seuil, 1976), 20. The Lacoutures observe that the provision for such elections was mere face-saving for the French. Pham Van Dong, later the North Vietnamese foreign minister, predicted at Geneva in 1954: "These elections will never be held." Cf. Hess, *Vietnam and the United States*, 47–49; P. J. Honey, *Genesis of a Tragedy: The Historical Background to the Vietnam War* (London: Ernest Benn, 1968), 67; Hammer, *Death in November*, 93–95; and Henry Kissinger, *Diplomacy* (New York: Simon and Schuster, 1994), 634–36.

30. Herring, *America's Longest War*, 41–45; Lewy, *America in Vietnam*, 7; Karnow, *Vietnam*, 199–204; Kahin, *Intervention*, 52–65. Cf. Robert Scigliano, *South Vietnam: Nation under Stress* (Boston: Houghton Mifflin, 1964), 134. Donald Lancaster estimates that North Vietnam had three million more residents than the South; Lancaster, *The Emancipation of French Indochina* (New York: Octagon Books, 1974), 339n1.

31. Frederick Nolting, *From Trust to Tragedy: The Political Memoirs of Frederick Nolting, Kennedy's Ambassador to Diem's Vietnam* (New York: Praeger, 1988), 2, 19–22.

32. Author's interview with Michael V. Forrestal, December 11, 1987.

33. Truong Vinh-Le, *Vietnam, où est la vérité?* (Paris: Lavauzelle, 1989), 92. Cf. Hammer, *Death in November*, 269–70; Herring, *America's Longest War*, 94; Mieczyslaw Maneli, *War of the Vanquished*, translated by Maria de Gorgey (New York: Harper and Row, 1971), 112–31; Schlesinger, *Robert Kennedy*, 720; and author's interview with Tran Van Dinh, October 1988.

34. Jean Lacouture, *Vietnam: Between Two Truces*, translated by Konrad Kellen and Joel Carmichael (New York: Random House, 1966), 126–29. Schlesinger wrote, "An opportunity of some sort [for American exit with honor] was perhaps missed in the autumn of 1963" (*Robert Kennedy*, 720).

35. Telegram from the Department of State to the Embassy in Vietnam, October 5, 1963, in *FRUS, 1961–1963* 4:371–79.

36. Schlesinger, *Robert Kennedy*, 466, 715. Cf. Kissinger, *Diplomacy*, 638–55.

37. Schlesinger stresses the irony of this missed opportunity in *Robert Kennedy*, 717.

38. Herring, *America's Longest War*, 279. The same sense of inevitability, or foreordained doom, seems to be implied in the title of Herring's first chapter, "A Dead-End Alley: The United States, France, and the First Indochina War, 1950–1954." Interestingly, this thesis of inevitability seems to have softened slightly in the intervening decade, as Herring seems obliquely to suggest in his review of McNamara's *In Retrospect:* "It was a logical, if not inevitable, outgrowth of a worldview and a policy—the policy of global containment"; George C. Herring, "The Wrong Kind of Loyalty: McNamara's Apology for Vietnam," *Foreign Affairs* 74, no. 3 (May–June 1995): 157. At the conclusion of the review essay, however, Herring seems to revert to the conclusion that the tragic outcome was inevitable: "The ideology of a generation of policymakers and a flawed set of policies . . . explain why the United States intervened in Vietnam and ultimately failed" (158).

39. Herring, *America's Longest War*, 279.

40. Summary Record of the 519th Meeting of the National Security Council, White House, October 2, 1963, 6:00 P.M., in *FRUS, 1961–1963* 4:350–52.

CHAPTER 1: "SAUVE QUI PEUT"

"Sauve qui peut": Every man for himself, and the devil take the hindmost.

1. Scigliano, *South Vietnam*, 224. Cf. Daniel C. Hallin, *The "Uncensored War": The Media and Vietnam* (Berkeley: University of California Press, 1989), 39. Hallin is relying here principally on the coverage in the *New York Times*. The optimistic assessment of the American–South Vietnamese alliance progress in 1962 is shared by Barbara W. Tuchman: "Nineteen sixty-two was Saigon's year, unsuspected to be its last. American optimism swelled"; Tuchman, *The March of Folly: From Troy to Vietnam* (New York: Alfred A. Knopf, 1984), 299.

2. The gift from Ho to Diem is mentioned by Truong Vinh-Le, president of the South Vietnamese National Assembly at that time, in his memoirs, *Vietnam, où est la vérité?* 92.

3. Memorandum from the Director of the Bureau of Intelligence and Research (Hilsman) and Michael V. Forrestal of the National Security Council Staff to the President, January 25, 1963, in *FRUS, 1961–1963* 3:49–62.

4. Congressional Research Service, Library of Congress, *The U.S. Government and the Vietnam War: Executive and Legislative Roles and Relationships, Part II, 1961–1964*, prepared for the Committee on Foreign Relations, United States Senate, 98th Congress, 2d session (Washington, D.C.: GPO, 1985), 131–34. The CRS account relies on a 1979 interview with David Halberstam, who recalled a five-hour "lunch" on this visit at which the resident reporters poured out their enmity toward Diem and U.S. ambassador Frederick Nolting.

Mansfield's prescient analysis was shaped as well, and doubtless more decisively, by the senator's own Wilsonian perspective on U.S. diplomacy. He insists that the standard by which to measure Diem's government is Jeffersonian: "a diffusion of political power, essentially in a democratic pattern." Report by Senate Majority Leader (Mansfield), Washington, December 18, 1962, Southeast Asia — Vietnam, in *FRUS, 1961–1963* 2:782.

5. Author's interview with Dean Rusk, February 26, 1988. A review of Mansfield's analysis of December 18, 1962, reveals that his own perspective, and his proposed definition of national interests, were exclusively regional. That is, his view encompassed only Asia. He had apparently no awareness of the global (especially European) perception of strategic interests that animated Kennedy and Rusk.

6. United States Senate, *Vietnam and Southeast Asia, Report of Senator Mike Mansfield to the Committee on Foreign Relations*, 93d Congress, 1st session (Washington, D.C.: GPO, 1963).

7. Report on South Vietnam, Memorandum from the Director of the Bureau of Intelligence and Research (Hilsman) and Michael V. Forrestal of the National Security Council Staff to the President, January 25, 1963, in *FRUS, 1961–1963* 3:57–58.

The salience of U.S. press complaints against Diem in Forrestal's recommendation for a more aggressive policy is revealing. Dean Rusk believes that Forrestal and Hilsman ("I think in cahoots with the press") later led Averell Harriman and Ball to encourage a coup. Author's interview with Rusk, February 26, 1988.

8. Author's interview with Michael V. Forrestal, December 11, 1987.

9. Memorandum from Michael V. Forrestal of the National Security Council Staff to the President, February 4, 1963, in *FRUS, 1961–1963* 3:97.

10. Letter to the author from Ambassador Mike Mansfield, October 24, 1989. Cf. Congressional Research Service, *U.S. Government and the Vietnam War*, 137, 137n1.

Many historians dismiss the claim of Kennedy's intention to withdraw from Vietnam in 1965. Representative of the historians' skepticism is an observation by George C. Herring: "The record suggests otherwise" (*America's Longest War*, 106). Herring then cites an aggressive speech about third world conflicts that the president was scheduled to deliver in Dallas the day of his death, November 22, 1963.

This argument by Herring is not wholly convincing. He does not claim that Mansfield had manufactured the statement about Kennedy's intentions. The case being made then seems to be that the Mansfield-Kennedy conversation is nowhere found in official records. This observation is accurate. The absence of such a document would presumably constitute for Herring conclusive proof that the conversation never took place only on the premise that what has not been officially recorded about a president was never said by him. Such a claim is scarcely serious. The only remaining explanatory assumption is that what is not recorded is historically irrelevant, that is to say, that such statements cannot be used to understand or interpret historical developments. This epistemological premise is less self-evident to the present author than to Herring.

It is noteworthy that Herring obliquely suggests some credulity in the Mansfield thesis about Kennedy's intentions in his recent review of McNamara's *In Retrospect*. "Despite his doubts, Kennedy refused even to consider withdrawal from Vietnam until he had been safely reelected"; Herring, "Wrong Kind of Loyalty," 157.

11. Arthur M. Schlesinger Jr., *A Thousand Days: John F. Kennedy in the White House* (New York: Fawcett World Library, 1967), 301.

12. Memorandum from the Director of the Bureau of Intelligence and Research (Hilsman) and Michael V. Forrestal to the President, January 25, 1963, in *FRUS, 1961–1963* 3:59.

13. Memorandum from Michael V. Forrestal of the National Security Council Staff to the President, February 4, 1963, in *FRUS, 1961–1963* 3:97.

14. Memorandum from Michael V. Forrestal of the National Security Council Staff to the Assistant Secretary of State for Far Eastern Affairs (Harriman), February 8, 1963, in *FRUS, 1961–1963* 3:105–6.

15. Letter from the Ambassador in Vietnam to the Assistant Secretary of State for Far Eastern Affairs, Saigon, February 27, 1963, in *FRUS, 1961–1963* 3:126–28.

16. Editorial Note, in *FRUS, 1961–1963* 3:133.

17. Telegram from the Department of State to the Embassy in Vietnam, February 25, 1963, in *FRUS, 1961–1963* 3:122–24, 122n3.

18. Hammer, *Death in November*, 77. Cf. William Colby, *Lost Victory* (Chicago: Contemporary Books, 1989), 35, 72.

19. Truong Vinh-Le, *Vietnam*, 54.

20. Hammer, *Death in November*, 47, citing the authority of Paul Mus, the leading French scholarly and political authority on Vietnam.

21. Stanley Karnow, ed., *Vietnam, A History*, Public Broadcasting System series, part 3, "America's Mandarin," interview with Madame Ngo Dinh Nhu, 1985. Cf. Truong Vinh-Le, *Vietnam*, 55.

22. Truong Vinh-Le, *Vietnam*, 92–93, 316–17.

23. Ironically, Diem had made substantial contributions to the Xa Loi Pagoda, which was the center of manifestations in 1963 (Lacouture, *Vietnam: Between Two Truces*, 110). Diem pointed out in a conversation with McNamara and Taylor on September 29, 1963, that, because of his decisions as president, official assistance to the Buddhists had doubled the number of temples in the country during his administration; Memorandum of a Conversation, Gia Long Palace, Saigon, September 29, 1963, in *FRUS, 1961–1963* 4:319.

24. Nolting, *From Trust to Tragedy*, 115. Cf. Airgram from the Embassy, Vietnam, to the Department of State, October 28, 1963, reporting on the close cooperation between South Vietnamese government officials and the Buddhist leadership in Ba Xuyen and Vinh Binh provinces:

"The ethnic Cambodians are primarily small-plot rice farmers with a deep attachment to their Theravada Buddhist religion and to the pagodas and religious leaders of their community, and local GVN officials have been particularly adept at building trust on this level. Important Buddhist religious figures are not only included in all significant GVN ceremonies, but they are consulted regularly on virtually all matters—secular as well as religious—affecting the Cambodian community. GVN officials openly admit they often work directly through the religious hierarchy and claim good results. Local GVN officials (many of whom are Catholic) always participate in Buddhist festivities and contribute money and other resources to pagoda activities.

"Main pagodas are allowed their own full-time *religious* schools where Pali and Cambodian are the language of instruction; the GVN itself pays the salaries of many of the teachers. In Vinh Binh, for example, the GVN reportedly built the new school for monks at the province's central pagoda and provides money for 7 full-time teachers in Pali (plus 4 other lower-level instructors) there and at other pagoda schools in the province. Pagodas are also permitted to provide religious instruction to lay Buddhists in Pali and/or Cambodian, but all secular primary education, even at schools on pagoda grounds, must follow the regular GVN curriculum in Vietnamese, for which the GVN provides the teachers." U.S. Department of State, RG 59, container 4048, National Archives II.

25. Hammer, *Death in November*, esp. 83–85 and 139–41. Cf. Truong, *Vietnam*, 83; and Thich Nhat Hanh, *Vietnam: Lotus in a Sea of Fire*, with a foreword by Thomas Merton and an afterword by Alfred Hassler (New York: Hill and Wang, 1967), 12.

26. Wilfred G. Burchett, *Vietnam: Inside Story of the Guerilla War* (New York: International Publishers, 1965), 216–19.

27. Memorandum from the Counselor and Public Affairs Officer of the Embassy in Vietnam (Mecklin) to the Public Affairs Adviser in the Bureau of Far Eastern Affairs (Manell), March 15, 1963, in *FRUS, 1961–1963* 3:152–56.

28. Telegram from the Embassy in Vietnam to the Department of State, April 5, 1963, in *FRUS, 1961–1963* 3:206–13.

29. Nolting, *From Trust to Tragedy*, 40–41.

30. Telegram from the Embassy in Vietnam to the Department of State, April 5, 1963, in *FRUS, 1961–1963* 3:212–13.

31. With this inflexible position, Diem was seeking to safeguard his strongest claim to nationalist credentials, which was accepted by all observers, even those opposed to his regime. He had succeeded in a mere two-year interval in ejecting the (French) foreigners after more than a century of control in Vietnam. He was well aware that tolerating a substitute colonial presence would be his undoing. Jeffrey Race, *War Comes to Long An: Revolutionary Conflict in a Vietnamese Province* (Berkeley: University of California Press, 1972), 182 and notes.

32. Telegram from the Embassy in Vietnam to the Department of State, April 7, 1963, in *FRUS, 1961–1963* 3:213–14. Nolting suggested a reduction in U.S. support from 7.5 billion to 6.2 billion piasters.

33. Telegram from the Department of State to the Embassy in Vietnam, April 8, 1963, in *FRUS, 1961–1963* 3:215–16.

34. Editorial Note, in *FRUS, 1961–1963* 3:221.

35. Memorandum for the Record of a Conversation with the Presidential Counselor (Ngo Dinh Nhu), Saigon, April 12, 1963, in *FRUS, 1961–1963* 3:222–25.

36. Telegram from the Embassy in Vietnam to the Department of State, April 13, 1963, in *FRUS, 1961–1963* 3:225–26.

37. Telegram from the Embassy in Vietnam to the Department of State, April 17, 1963, in *FRUS, 1961–1963* 3:227–29.

38. Telegram from the Embassy in Vietnam to the Department of State, April 26, 1963, in *FRUS, 1961–1963* 3:254–55. Diem's own words were: "Y souscrire serait porter atteinte au principe intangible de la sourverainete [sic] nationale." Text of letter, April 23, 1963, forwarded by Ambassador Nolting with airgram A-718 from Saigon to Department of State, RG 59, container 4049, National Archives II.

39. Geoffrey Warner, "The United States and the Fall of Diem, Part I, The Coup That Never Was," *Australian Outlook* 28, no. 3 (December 1974): 245.

40. Telegram from the Embassy in Vietnam to the Department of State, Saigon, April 5, 1963, in *FRUS, 1961–1963* 3:207–13, esp. 210.

CHAPTER 2: "WHO ARE THESE PEOPLE?"

On the occasion of the disturbance at Hue, President Kennedy asked Michael Forrestal, "Who are these people?"

1. Hammer, *Death in November*, 83–85.

2. Hammer, *Death in November*, 116; Telegram from the Consulate at Hue to the Department of State, May 9, 1963, in *FRUS, 1961–1963* 3:277–778; Telegram

from the Consulate at Hue to the Department of State, May 10, 1963, in *FRUS, 1961–1963* 3:284–85; Telegram from the Consulate at Hue to the Department of State, May 10, 1963, in *FRUS, 1961–1963* 3:285–86; "Manifesto of Vietnamese Buddhist Clergy and Faithful," Hue, May 10, 1963, in *FRUS, 1961–1963* 3:287–88.

3. Author's interviews with Roger Hilsman, June 1987 and December 1992.

4. Author's interviews with Roger Hilsman, June 1987 and December 1992.

5. Ellen Hammer, *The Struggle for Indochina, 1940–1955* (Stanford, Calif.: Stanford University Press, 1966), 11. Cf. Hammer, *Death in November*, 104; Lancaster, *Emancipation of French Indochina*, 87n19; R. B. Smith, *An International History of the Vietnam War*, vol. 2, *The Kennedy Strategy* (New York: St. Martin's, 1985), 149; Lacouture, *Vietnam: Between Two Truces*, 71–72; and Honey, *Genesis of a Tragedy*, 5. This consensus among Western authors is confirmed by the two Vietnamese Buddhist authors Thich Nhat Hanh and Mai-Tho-Truyen, who were friends, colleagues, and, in the case of Mai, fellow activists with Thich Tri Quang. Cf. Thich Nhat Hanh, *Vietnam*, 12; and Mai-Tho-Truyen, *Le Bouddhisme au Vietnam; Buddhism in Vietnam; Phat-Giao Viet-Nam* (Saigon: Xa Loi Pagoda, 1962), 51, 61. Mai fails to mention the earliest stratum, namely, animism.

Mai's book contains the same text in three languages. The English text is occasionally seriously deficient, for example, in suggesting that people who practice Buddhism constitute a minority of the population. The original (French) text says rather that those practicing Buddhism or Taoism, to the exclusion of the other creed, are a minority (16, 51).

The late Japanese-American scholar Joseph M. Kitagawa broadens this analysis by arguing that Buddhism played an ancillary and complementary role in all the Asian cultures with which it came in contact, for example, in Burma, Tibet, China, and Japan. Vietnamese religious syncretism is thus not an exception but representative of a broad pattern. Kitagawa, "Buddhism and Asian Politics," *Asian Survey* 2, no. 5 (July 1962): 3.

6. André Masson, *Histoire du Vietnam* (Paris: Presses Universitaires de France, 1967), 56; Thich Nhat Hanh, *Vietnam*, 7, 8, 10–11. Cf. Mai, *Bouddhisme*, 64.

7. Thich Nhat Hanh, *Vietnam*, 12. Mai, however, estimates that the number of Buddhists recognized by the General Association of Buddhists in Vietnam is about one million, though there are additional adherents (*Bouddhisme*, 53).

8. William J. Duiker, *The Rise of Nationalism in Vietnam, 1900–1941* (Ithaca, N.Y.: Cornell University Press, 1976), 186–87.

9. Duiker, *Rise of Nationalism*, 13. Diem, who was inspired by the utopian project of a Confucian renaissance in Vietnam, had excelled in the penultimate examinations offered under this Confucian culture in 1918.

10. Thich Nhat Hanh, *Vietnam*, 21–22, 14, 26n17, 45–46. Cf. Mai, *Bouddhisme*, 47; and Smith, *International History* 2:149.

11. Author's interview with Ben Read, May 12, 1988.

12. Author's interviews with Roger Hilsman, June 8, 1987, and December 12, 1992.

13. Author's interviews with Roger Hilsman, June 8, 1987, and December 12,

1992. Hilsman made the same curious argument in his oral history interview for the Kennedy Library files.

14. Author's interview with Michael V. Forrestal, December 11, 1987. Lacouture identifies Minh's unusual height and size as a factor in his appeal to American decision makers (*Vietnam: Between Two Truces*, 127).

15. Telegram from the Department of State to the Embassy in Vietnam, May 13, 1963, in *FRUS, 1961–1963* 3:294–96.

16. Memorandum from the Deputy Director of the Vietnam Working Group (Heavner) to the Assistant Secretary of State for Far Eastern Affairs (Hilsman), May 15, 1963, in *FRUS, 1961–1963* 3:303–6.

17. Doan-Them, *Hai Muoi Nam Qua: Viec tung ngay (1945–1964)* (N.p.: Nam-Chi Tung-Thu, 1966), 348; selections translated for the author by Son Vu.

18. Author's interview with Frederick E. Nolting, October 21, 1989.

19. Letter from the Chargé in Vietnam (Trueheart) to the Assistant Secretary of State for Far Eastern Affairs (Hilsman), May 25, 1963, in *FRUS, 1961–1963* 3:327–30.

20. Telegram from the Embassy in Vietnam to the Department of State, June 11, 1963, in *FRUS, 1961–1963* 3:375–76.

21. Author's interview with John R. Burke, July 1, 1988. Truong Vinh-Le's estimates that South Vietnam was 30 percent Buddhist, 10 percent Catholic, and 60 percent animist, including those who belonged to the Cao-Dai sect and those of the Hoa Hao group (*Vietnam*, 83n1). Thich Nhat Hanh adds: "A Vietnamese who professes to be a Confucian does not deny his belief in Buddhism. . . . This is why we cannot say with accuracy how many Vietnamese are Buddhists" (*Vietnam*, 12).

22. Marguerite Higgins, *Our Vietnam Nightmare* (New York: Harper and Row, 1965), 27.

23. Author's interview with William Trueheart, April 26, 1988.

24. Telegram from the Embassy in Vietnam to the Department of State, June 11, 1963, in *FRUS, 1961–1963* 3:376–78.

25. Telegram from the Department of State to the Embassy in Vietnam (not seen by Rusk), June 11, 1963, in *FRUS, 1961–1963* 3:381–83.

26. Cf. Memorandum from Michael V. Forrestal of the National Security Council Staff to the President, Washington, February 4, 1963, in *FRUS, 1961–1963* 3:97–98.

27. Telegram from Trueheart to the Department of State, June 12, 1963, in *FRUS, 1961–1963* 3:385–87. Harriman to Trueheart, cable no. 1207, June 11, 1963, is at 3:381. Author's interview with Trueheart, April 26, 1988: "This was a dramatic démarche."

28. Hallin, *"Uncensored War,"* 45–46.

29. Quoted in Hallin, *"Uncensored War,"* 45–46.

30. Telegram from the Department of State (Hilsman) to the Embassy in Vietnam (Trueheart), June 14, 1963, in *FRUS, 1961–1963* 3:393–94.

31. Telegram from the Embassy in Vietnam (Trueheart) to the Department of State, June 16, 1963, in *FRUS, 1961–1963* 3:398–99. The departmental telegram, no. 1219, June 14, 1963 (in *FRUS, 1961–1963* 3:394–95), discussed U.S. policies

to assure Vice President Tho that the United States would support him as successor to Diem.

32. Chester V. Clifton Series, President's Intelligence Checklist, National Security Files, Kennedy Library, as cited in *FRUS, 1961–1963* 3:386n5. Almost certainly Kennedy also read Max Frankel's version of the leaked cable in the *New York Times* on June 14.

33. "[If Diem] cannot genuinely respect a majority, then he is not the man to be President." Editorial quoted in Congressional Research Service, *U.S. Government and the Vietnam War*, 144n15.

34. Congressional Research Service, *U.S. Government and the Vietnam War*, 144, 144n16. (The ad appeared on June 27; see *FRUS, 1961–1963* 3:510n6.) Trueheart sent the text of the advertisement to Diem's residence, as he noted in Telegram from the Embassy in Vietnam to the Department of State, June 29, 1963, in *FRUS, 1961–1963* 3:430n5.

35. Telegram from the Embassy in Vietnam to the Department of State, June 16, 1963, in *FRUS, 1961–1963* 3:396–97, and Editorial Note, 3:397–98.

36. Telegram from the Department of State to the Embassy in Vietnam (not cleared by Rusk), June 19, 1963, in *FRUS, 1961–1963* 3:402–4.

37. *FRUS, 1961–1963* 3:414n3. For his promise to return to Saigon, see Telegram from the Embassy in Vietnam to the Department of State, April 17, 1963, in *FRUS, 1961–1963* 3:227.

38. Telegram from the Embassy in Vietnam to the Department of State, June 25, 1963, in *FRUS, 1961–1963* 3:413–14. On the same day a CIA contact reported that Nhu had vigorously criticized his brother's regime, and on August 16 the CIA warned Hilsman not to rule out the possibility of a coup by Nhu against Diem; see *FRUS, 1961–1963* 3:569–74, esp. 572.

39. Telegram from the Embassy in Vietnam to the Department of State, June 27, 1963, in *FRUS, 1961–1963* 3:422–23. Also on June 27, the State Department asked Trueheart to investigate the hypothesis that the Buddhist activists were only one faction of the Buddhist population and to comment on the significance of such a division among Buddhists. No trace of such studies by Trueheart is recorded (*FRUS, 1961–1963* 3:423n4).

40. Nolting, *From Trust to Tragedy*, 111.

41. Author's interview with Dean Rusk, February 26, 1988.

42. Author's interview with Michael V. Forrestal, December 11, 1987.

43. From 1912 to 1914 Lodge attended a French-language lycée in Paris. Anne Blair, *Lodge in Vietnam: A Patriot Abroad* (New Haven, Conn.: Yale University Press, 1995), 4.

44. The unanimity of this unflattering assessment of Lodge was a surprisingly salient feature of many of the interviews by the author with principals of Kennedy's Vietnam policies, such as the interviews with George A. Ball, Ben Read, William Sullivan, George Allen, and Frederick E. Nolting. For a more lengthy profile of Lodge, see chapter 12, below.

45. "Vietnam Reappraisal," *New York Times*, July 2, 1963.

46. Obituary, *Washington Post*, December 25, 1992.

47. Telegram from the Embassy in Vietnam to the Department of State, June 27, 1963, in *FRUS, 1961–1963* 3:422.

48. Author's interview with William Trueheart, April 26, 1988. Trueheart confirmed this promised reward in an interview with William Prochnau; see Prochnau, *Once upon a Distant War: Young War Correspondents and the Early Vietnam Battles* (New York: Times Books, 1995), 321.

CHAPTER 3: "SLEEPING IN THE SAME BED,
DREAMING DIFFERENT DREAMS"

This proverb is used by Bui Diem, Vietnam's ambassador to Washington (1966–73), in his memoirs, *In the Jaws of History* (Boston: Houghton Mifflin, 1987), 108. The proverb appears to have a Chinese origin. Sarah Ann Smith, sinologist and former U.S. State Department Chinese-language officer, suggests that the Chinese four-character idiom (Tong Chuang Yi Meng) was adopted in the Korean and Vietnamese cultures. Smith, letter to the author, July 15, 1992.

1. Telegram from the Embassy in Vietnam to the Department of State, June 29, 1963, in *FRUS, 1961–1963* 3:429. Cf. CIA Information Report, July 8, 1963, in *FRUS, 1961–1963* 3:477.

2. Telegram from the Embassy in Vietnam to the Department of State, June 29, 1963, in *FRUS, 1961–1963* 3:431.

3. Memorandum of Conversation, White House, July 4, 1963, in *FRUS, 1961–1963* 3:451–53.

4. On Kennedy's relish for irony, see R. Reeves, *President Kennedy*, 19.

5. As cited in Catherine Bowen, *John Adams and the American Revolution* (Boston: Little, Brown, 1950), 606–7.

6. Hilsman said: "There was thus an element of truth in Diem's view that the Buddhists might push their demands so far as to make his fall inevitable." Memorandum of a Conversation, White House, July 4, 1963, in *FRUS, 1961–1963* 3:452.

7. Memorandum of a Conversation, White House, July 4, 1963, in *FRUS, 1961–1963* 3:453.

8. Memorandum of Conversation, Department of State, July 5, 1963, in *FRUS, 1961–1963* 3:466–67. Nolting had himself privately urged Diem to respond to Washington's directions.

9. *New York Times*, July 3, 1963, cited in Hammer, *Death in November*, 156.

10. An editorial note in *Foreign Relations of the United States, 1961–1963* (1:644), on Galbraith's two cables to Kennedy concerning Diem, refers the reader to volume 11 of the original *Pentagon Papers* (United States-Vietnam Relation, 1945–67, book 11, pp. 406–9, 410–18). The same materials are found in *The Pentagon Papers: The Defense Department History of United States Decisionmaking on Vietnam*, Senator Gravel Edition, vol. 2 (Boston: Beacon Press, 1971), 121–25.

11. Author's interview with John Kenneth Galbraith, June 5, 1987.

12. The basis of Galbraith's judgment was supposedly a pessimistic assessment he received from the CIA chief of station, John H. Richardson, who subsequently has

attested that he never met Galbraith. Author's interview with Richardson, March 12, 1987. The other authority he has cited for his negative assessment of Diem is William Trueheart, who in November 1961 was still a Diem supporter. In a letter to Averell Harriman dated September 10, 1962, Galbraith corroborates this assessment of Trueheart's 1961 views: "Trueheart impressed me very unfavorably when I was there a year ago as a young and belligerent character with strong pro-Dulles convictions. Indeed, I would regard him . . . as a menace"; Averell Harriman Papers, Manuscript Division, Library of Congress, container 463. Cf. Nolting, *From Trust to Tragedy*, 116.

13. *Pentagon Papers*, Gravel Edition, 2:122–25.

14. Author's interview with John Kenneth Galbraith, June 5, 1987. Galbraith used the same wording a decade earlier, in an interview with the BBC.

15. Author's interview with John Kenneth Galbraith, June 5, 1987. Galbraith made essentially the same point in an interview with William J. Rust; see Rust and the editors of U.S. News Books, *Kennedy in Vietnam* (New York: Charles Scribner's Sons, 1985), 56.

16. By June 29 Trueheart was convinced that elements among the Buddhist activists were engaged in an exclusively political campaign to replace the government in Saigon. Telegram from the Embassy in Vietnam (Trueheart) to the Department of State, June 29, 1963, in *FRUS, 1961–1963* 3:431.

17. Telegram from the Embassy in Vietnam to the Department of State, July 9, 1963, in *FRUS, 1961–1963* 3:480nn2,5. See Hammer, *Death in November*, 154.

18. Hammer, *Death in November*, 154–55. Tam, a leader of the Dai Viet brotherhood, had been Ho Chi Minh's foreign minister in 1946.

19. Hammer, *Death in November*, 157.

20. Hammer, *Death in November*, 223–24, based on Hammer's interviews with the principals. The same record of inaugural negotiations between Diem and Ho is narrated by Truong Vinh-Le, in *Vietnam*, 91, 316–17.

21. Hammer, *Death in November*, 223. Maneli's firsthand account of the negotiations is in *War of the Vanquished*, 112–52.

22. Nolting, *From Trust to Tragedy*, 112.

23. Hammer, *Death in November*, 222. Cf. Truong Vinh-Le, *Vietnam*, 92, 316; and *FRUS, 1961–1963* 4:85n3.

24. Telegram from the Embassy in Vietnam to the Department of State, July 7, 1963, in *FRUS, 1961–1963* 3:470–71.

25. Telegram from Malcolm Browne of the Associated Press, David Halberstam of the *New York Times*, Peter Kallisher of CBS News, and Neil Sheehan of United Press International to the President, July 7, 1963, in *FRUS, 1961–1963* 3:472–73.

26. Telegram from the Embassy in Vietnam to the Department of State, July 7, 1963, in *FRUS, 1961–1963* 3:472n.

27. CIA Information Report, July 8, 1963, in *FRUS, 1961–1963* 3:473, 476, 477, 478.

28. Memorandum from Michael V. Forrestal of the National Security Council Staff to the President's Special Assistant for National Security Affairs, July 9, 1963, in *FRUS, 1961–1963* 3:481.

29. The account of the session is found in United States Senate, *Executive Sessions*

of the Senate Foreign Relations Committee (Historical Series), XV, 88th Congress, First Session, 1963 (Washington, D.C.: GPO, 1987), 377–98.

30. United States Senate, *Executive Sessions*, 383, 382, 396. Cf. Nolting, *From Trust to Tragedy*, 108; and Nolting interview in Karnow, ed., *Vietnam*, PBS series, part 3, "America's Mandarin."

31. United States Senate, *Executive Sessions*, 385–86.

32. United States Senate, *Executive Sessions*, 398.

33. Nolting, *From Trust to Tragedy*, 117.

34. Nolting, *From Trust to Tragedy*, 108, 112, 116.

35. It was only a quarter century later that Nolting discovered this missing piece in the puzzle of Trueheart's tergiversation. Author's interviews with Nolting (October 21, 1989) and Trueheart (April 26, 1988). Trueheart had been offered a spot as deputy assistant secretary of state.

36. Telegram from the Embassy in Vietnam to the Department of State, July 15, 1963, in *FRUS, 1961–1963* 3:487–88.

37. Nolting, *From Trust to Tragedy*, 118. For a discussion of the *New York Times*'s interpretation of the "religious" crisis, see chapter 13 below.

38. Higgins, *Our Vietnam Nightmare*, 167–75.

39. R. Reeves, *President Kennedy*, 18: "Kennedy often carried a piece of paper with the size of his majority in 1960: 118,574 votes."

40. Author's interview with Charles Bartlett, June 21, 1988.

41. FitzGerald, *Fire in the Lake*, 45–46, 47–48.

42. Higgins, *Our Vietnam Nightmare*, 174, 166.

43. Telegram from the Embassy in Vietnam to the Department of State, August 12, 1963, in *FRUS, 1961–1963* 3:562–64. By the time Nolting composed his memoir of this period, he had apparently forgotten the uncompromising notice he had dutifully served on Diem; cf. Nolting, *From Trust to Tragedy*, 118–19.

44. Telegram from the Department of State to the Embassy in Vietnam, August 13, 1963, in *FRUS, 1961–1963* 3:564–65.

45. Doan-Them, *Hai Muoi Nam Qua*, 358; translated for the author by Son Vu.

46. Telegram from the Embassy in Vietnam to the Department of State, August 14, 1963, in *FRUS, 1961–1963* 3:565–66.

47. In fact, Nolting had long been candid in disagreeing with Diem. See Telegram from the Embassy in Vietnam to the Department of State, April 17, 1963, in *FRUS, 1961–1963* 3:227.

48. For Trueheart's views, see Telegram from the Embassy in Vietnam to the Department of State, June 29, 1963, in *FRUS, 1961–1963* 3:430–31. For Robert Manning's views, see Report from the Assistant Secretary of State for Public Affairs (Manning) to the President, Washington, undated (sent to McGeorge Bundy on July 26, from the Office of the Secretary of State), *FRUS, 1961–1963* 3:538.

49. Memorandum of a Conversation, Department of State, Washington, July 5, 1963, in *FRUS, 1961–1963* 3:466–67.

50. Averell Harriman Papers, Manuscript Division, Library of Congress, container 467.

51. CIA Information Report, Washington, July 8, 1963, in *FRUS, 1961–1963* 3:473–74, confirms Trueheart's earlier conclusions.

52. Report from the Assistant Secretary of State for Public Affairs (Manning) to the President, undated, in *FRUS, 1961–1963* 3:537–38.

53. Higgins, *Our Vietnam Nightmare*, 28.

54. Lacouture, *Vietnam: Between Two Truces*, 75. Cf. Jerrold Schecter, *The New Face of Buddha: Buddhism and Political Power in Southeast Asia* (London: Victor Gollancz, 1967), 145–252; and Smith, *International History* 2:149.

55. Lacouture, *Vietnam: Between Two Truces*, 109–10. Mai boasted to Lacouture that he had, tucked in his monastic robes, a list of ten additional suicide volunteers. Cf. Thich Nhat Hanh, *Vietnam*, 45.

56. Smith concludes that the Buddhist activism of May–October 1963 was essentially political. He also suggests that this new strategy of *urban* warfare may have been explicitly suggested to Ho Chi Minh by Chinese officials visiting Hanoi in May 1963. Smith, *International History* 2:147–52. Smith indicates in the same passage that the Buddhist demonstrations were confined to Saigon and the cities of Central Vietnam and did not extend to the Mekong Delta. This narrow delineation of the range of demonstrations was confirmed for the author in interviews with George Allen, renowned CIA Vietnamese affairs analyst, on March 7 and April 18, 1988. When asked whether there had been Buddhist demonstrations outside this small number of towns, Allen paused and then replied: "One doesn't recall other demonstrations. One would have to do more research. One would have to talk to David Halberstam."

57. Memorandum of Discussion at White House Staff Meeting, November 22, 1963, in *FRUS, 1961–1963* 4:625.

58. Doan-Them, *Hai Muoi Nam Qua*, 358–59; translated for the author by Son Vu.

59. Memorandum of Conversation, Department of State, August 15, 1963, RG 59, container 4047, National Archives II.

60. Telegram from the Embassy in Vietnam to the Department of State, August 21, 1963, in *FRUS, 1961–1963* 3:595–97. Cf. Nolting, *From Trust to Tragedy*, 121.

61. Memorandum of Conversation, Department of State, October 14, 1963, RG 59, container 4046, National Archives II. The memorandum adds that the low-level U.S. Department of State officials who agreed to meet with Cox "confined their remarks to expressions of interest in the views expressed by Mr. Cox."

62. *FRUS, 1961–1963* 3:606n3.

63. Memorandum from the Acting Secretary of State (Ball) to the Undersecretary of State for Political Affairs (Harriman), August 26, 1963, in *FRUS, 1961–1963* 3:604.

CHAPTER 4: "DOING BUSINESS ON THE WEEKEND"

The phrase captures McGeorge Bundy's analysis of the lessons of Vietnam in 1963 (author's interview with Bundy, July 6, 1988). He believes the August 24 cable and subsequent coup were well advised but that "one shouldn't do business on the weekend."

1. According to Gordon H. Chang, Kennedy's keen interest in the test ban treaty was originally generated by a personal concern of his, dating at least from July 1962, about the risk of nuclear proliferation in China. In this initiative Harriman was a willing negotiator with the Soviets because he had followed closely the emergence of the Sino-Soviet split, which the August treaty agreement between the United States and the Soviet Union helped to accelerate. Chang, *Friends and Enemies: The United States, China, and the Soviet Union, 1948–1972* (Stanford, Calif.: Stanford University Press, 1990), 232, 234, 241, 249.

2. Author's interview with U. Alexis Johnson, May 17, 1988.

3. Author's interview with Dean Rusk, February 26, 1988. Rusk clarified the influence of Forrestal and Hilsman in this initiative.

4. Telegram from the CIA Station in Saigon to the Agency, August 24, 1963, in *FRUS, 1961–1963* 3:618.

5. Telegram from the Embassy in Vietnam to the Department of State, August 24, 1963, 11:00 A.M., in *FRUS, 1961–1963* 3:611–12.

6. Telegram from the Embassy in Vietnam to the Department of State, August 24, 1963, 6:00 P.M., in *FRUS, 1961–1963* 3:613–14.

7. Telegram from the CIA Station in Saigon to the Agency, August 24, 1963, in *FRUS, 1961–1963* 3:614–20.

8. Telegram from the Embassy in Vietnam to the Department of State, August 24, 1963, 11:00 P.M., in *FRUS, 1961–1963* 3:620–21. A summary of Lodge's warnings about the risks of a coup was sent to Kennedy on August 24 with the Intelligence Checklist. Editorial Note, in *FRUS, 1961–1963* 3:626.

9. Author's interview with George A. Ball, October 14, 1988.

10. Forrestal, Memorandum to President for Weekend Reading, August 24, 1963, in *FRUS, 1961–1963* 3:625.

11. Author's interview with George A. Ball, October 14, 1988. Asked later in the same interview why he had concluded "it has to be done," Ball said that he feared that Diem's government would collapse of its own weight and that blame would fall on Kennedy during his next campaign. Cf. Ball's interview in Gerald S. Strober and Deborah H. Strober, *"Let Us Begin Anew": An Oral History of the Kennedy Presidency* (New York: HarperCollins, 1993), 417.

12. Author's interview with Dean Rusk, February 26, 1988.

13. Author's interview with Roswell Gilpatric, July 6, 1988. McNamara disagrees that this was an "end run," as Taylor and Gilpatric believed; see McNamara with VanDeMark, *In Retrospect,* 55.

14. Author's interview with Roswell Gilpatric, July 6, 1988.

15. Author's interview with Richard Helms, March 4, 1988.

16. Telegram from the Department of State (Ball) to the Embassy in Vietnam, August 24, 1963, in *FRUS, 1961–1963* 3:628–29.

17. Author's interview with George A. Ball, October 14, 1988.

18. Author's interviews with William E. Colby, December 14, 1987, and June 27, 1988.

19. Author's interview with Walt Elder, May 13, 1988.

20. Author's interviews with William E. Colby, December 14, 1987, and June 27, 1988.

21. Lacouture, *Vietnam: Between Two Truces*, 207–22. Cf. Thich Nhat Hanh, *Vietnam*, 101.

22. Higgins, *Our Vietnam Nightmare*, 28.

23. Ho Chi Minh liquidated these bureaucrats' contemporaries in North Vietnam in 1956. Frederick Dupont, *Mission de la France en Asie* (Paris: Edition France-Empire, 1956), 335.

24. Author's interviews with William E. Colby, December 14, 1987, and June 27, 1988.

25. Author's interview with Roswell Gilpatric, July 6, 1988. Gilpatric had been the acting secretary of defense on August 24, 1963.

26. Hammer, *Death in November*, 220–21. Cf. Maneli, *War of the Vanquished*, 136–39.

27. Telegram from Forrestal to the President, at Hyannisport, August 25, 1963, reporting a CIA-channel cable from Lodge (August 25), in *FRUS, 1961–1963* 3:634–35.

28. Message from the Acting Secretary of State to the Ambassador in Vietnam, August 25, 1963, in *FRUS, 1961–1963* 3:635n.

29. Author's interview with John H. Richardson, March 12, 1987.

30. Telegram from the CIA Station in Saigon to the Agency, August 25, 1963, in *FRUS, 1961–1963* 3:633–34.

31. Author's interview with William Sullivan, March 13, 1987. Sullivan translated for Harriman at this 1962 Geneva meeting.

32. Author's interview with Nolting, October 21, 1989. But this delayed effort at seeking accommodation with Ho Chi Minh now alarmed Rusk. At Rusk's instigation, Roger Hilsman launched a preemptive bureaucratic strike at Diem later in the week (August 30).

Hilsman reacted to a sudden spurt of U.S. intercepts of Diem's contacts with Ho Chi Minh by a catalog of eleven possible anti-U.S. initiatives by Diem, with recommendations for U.S. response to each. One of the possible Diem démarches was a "political move [of Diem-Nhu] toward Hanoi, such as the opening of neutralization negotiations and indirect threats of such a move." Hilsman's recommendations for a response to such illegitimate initiatives by the government of South Vietnam included: "[E]ncourage the generals to move promptly with a coup." Memorandum from the Assistant Secretary of State for Far Eastern Affairs to the Secretary of State, August 30, 1963, in *FRUS, 1961–1963* 4:49–52.

33. Telegram from the Embassy in Vietnam to the Department of State, August 26, 1963, in *FRUS, 1961–1963* 3:644–45.

34. Blair, *Lodge in Vietnam*, 21.

35. Blair, *Lodge in Vietnam*, 54–55.

36. Memorandum for the Record of a Meeting at the White House, August 26, 1963, in *FRUS, 1961–1963* 3:638–641.

37. Memorandum for the Record of a Meeting at the White House, August 26, 1963, in *FRUS, 1961–1963* 3:640–41.

38. Telegram from the Embassy in Vietnam to the Department of State, August 27, 1963, in *FRUS, 1961–1963* 3:650–51. Lodge was responding to Rusk's

cable of August 26 asking whom the generals planned to place in charge. Lodge rejected Rusk's question as "pointless and dangerous."

39. Memorandum of a Conference with the President, White House, August 27, 1963, in *FRUS, 1961–1963* 3:659–66. Cf. Message from the Acting Secretary of State (Ball) to the Ambassador in Vietnam, August 25, 1963, in *FRUS, 1961–1963* 3:635n1.

40. Memorandum of a Conference with the President, White House, August 27, 1963, in *FRUS, 1961–1963* 3:659–65.

CHAPTER 5: SELMA AND SAIGON

1. Schlesinger, *Thousand Days*, 887.

2. Schlesinger, *Thousand Days*, 883.

3. Author's interviews with William E. Colby, December 14, 1987, and June 27, 1988. Truong Vinh-Le, president of the National Assembly, shared this estimate, calling Big Minh naive, shallow, lazy, and empty-headed. He was principally interested in tennis as well as his orchid garden and aquarium. Truong Vinh-Le claims he spoke no English, which contradicts Forrestal's catalog of his many talents. Truong Vinh-Le, *Vietnam*, 319–20; and author's interview with Forrestal, December 11, 1987.

4. Telegram from the CIA Station in Saigon to the Agency, August 28, 1963, in *FRUS, 1961–1963* 3:671–72.

5. Hammer judges that Richardson betrayed the Ngos (*Death in November*, 189). Many years later Richardson explained the cable equally reasonably: the arrival of the August 24 orders (with the subsequent, approved modification) to launch a coup, along with the overt participation in the plotting by the third-ranking Vietnamese official in Saigon, Nguyen Dinh Thuan, "had changed everything" in Saigon. The United States could not turn the clock back to August 23, since Diem and Nhu were very likely aware of Richardson's role. All the potential military commanders of successor governments would be treated as traitors if Diem were restored to power. Once the coup opened, it would have to succeed. Author's interview with John H. Richardson, March 12, 1987. The cable text itself, however, points to August 21 as a turning point, not August 24, the date of the coup cable.

6. Memorandum of Conference with the President, White House, August 28, 1963, in *FRUS, 1961–1963* 4:3.

7. *Flexible response* was a phrase that conveyed the Kennedy administration's resolve to shift the Cold War struggle from Europe (where the United States and NATO were unprepared for any military action below the apocalyptic nuclear level) to the third world. For the military logic behind "flexible response," see Maxwell D. Taylor, *Responsibility and Response* (New York: Harper and Row, 1967), 2–4.

8. Nolting, *From Trust to Tragedy*, 40–41.

9. Karnow, *Vietnam*, 62–79.

10. Nolting, *From Trust to Tragedy*, 40–41. Cf. Hammer, *Death in November*, 37.

11. Memorandum of a Conference with the President, White House, August 28, 1963, in *FRUS, 1961–1963* 4:2–6.

12. David McCullough, *Truman* (New York: Simon and Schuster, 1992), 569–70. Richard Reeves adds that Kennedy had in fact declined an invitation to address the marchers (*President Kennedy*, 581).

13. Taylor Branch, *Parting the Waters: America in the King Years, 1954–1963* (New York: Simon and Schuster, 1988), 886.

14. Branch, *Parting the Waters*, 880.

15. Schlesinger, *Thousand Days*, 875.

16. Doan-Them, *Hai Muoi Nam Qua*, 346, 360; translated for the author by Son Vu. Schlesinger points out that 250,000 marchers appeared on the Mall (*Thousand Days*, 887).

17. Schlesinger, *Thousand Days*, 880.

18. *Public Papers of the Presidents of the United States: John F. Kennedy, 1963* (Washington, D.C.: GPO, 1964), 468–71, 615.

19. Richard Reeves accentuates the link in Kennedy's mind between these two crises (*President Kennedy*, 490, 527, 622).

20. Memorandum of a Telephone Conversation between the Secretary of State and the President's Special Assistant for National Security Affairs, August 28, 1963, in *FRUS, 1961–1963* 4:12.

21. Telegram from the Department of State to the Embassy in Vietnam, August 28, 1963, in *FRUS, 1961–1963* 4:15–16.

22. Telegram from the Embassy in Vietnam to the Department of State, August 29, 1963, in *FRUS, 1961–1963* 4:20–22. In this cable, "last Sunday's telegram" refers to Ball's unauthorized revision of the August 24 cable, which required Lodge to negotiate with Diem.

23. Memorandum of a Conference with the President, August 29, 1963, in *FRUS, 1961–1963* 4:26–31.

24. Telegram from the Department of State to the Embassy in Vietnam, August 29, 1963, 8:17 P.M., in *FRUS, 1961–1963* 4:33–34.

25. Message from the President to the Ambassador in Vietnam, August 29, 1963, in *FRUS, 1961–1963* 4:35–36.

26. Telegram from the Embassy in Vietnam to the Department of State, August 31, 1963, in *FRUS, 1961–1963* 4:66–68.

27. Telegram from the Embassy in Vietnam to the Department of State, October 5, 1963, p. 2, and Telegram from the Embassy in Vietnam to the Department of State, November 21, 1963, p. 17, U.S. Department of State, RG 59, containers 4046, 4047, National Archives II.

28. Telegram from the Embassy in Vietnam to the Department of State, November 21, 1963, pp. 4, 8, RG 59, container 4047, National Archives II.

29. Telegram from the Embassy in Vietnam to the Department of State, October 7, 1963, pp. 1, 3, RG 59, container 4047, National Archives II.

30. Telegram from the Embassy in Vietnam to the Department of State, November 21, 1963, pp. 4, 14, RG 59, container 4047, National Archives II. Tri Quang (Venerable Enlightened Wisdom) was the religious name adopted by Pham Van Bong; Schecter, *New Face of Buddha*, 148–54.

CHAPTER 6: THE PRESIDENTIAL SEAL

1. Telegram from the Embassy in Vietnam to the Department of State, August 30, 1963, in *FRUS, 1961–1963* 4:38–39.

2. Telegram from the Embassy in Vietnam to the Department of State, August 30, 1963, in *FRUS, 1961–1963* 4:58–59.

3. Geoffrey Warner, "The United States and the Fall of Diem, Part II, The Death of Diem," *Australian Outlook* 29, no. 1 (April 1975): 8.

4. Memorandum of a Conversation, Department of State, August 30, 1963, in *FRUS, 1961–1963* 4:59–61.

5. Telegram from the CIA Station in Saigon to the Agency, August 31, 1963; and Telegram from the Embassy in Vietnam to the Department of State, August 31, 1963, both in *FRUS, 1961–1963* 4:64, 66–68.

6. Memorandum of a Conversation, Department of State, August 31, 1963, in *FRUS, 1961–1963* 4:69–74.

7. Memorandum of a Conversation, Department of State, August 31, 1963, in *FRUS, 1961–1963* 4:69–74.

8. Author's interview with Dean Rusk, February 26, 1988.

9. Author's interview with Dean Rusk, February 26, 1988.

10. Author's interview with Dean Rusk, February 26, 1988.

11. Memorandum of a Conversation, Department of State, August 31, 1963, in *FRUS, 1961–1963* 4:74.

12. Telegram from the Department of State to the Embassy in Vietnam, August 31, 1963, in *FRUS, 1961–1963* 4:76–79.

13. Telegram from the President's Special Assistant for National Security Affairs to the President at Hyannisport, Massachusetts, September 1, 1963, in *FRUS, 1961–1963* 4:82.

14. Interview with the President, Hyannisport, Massachusetts, September 2, 1963, in *FRUS, 1961–1963* 4:93–94.

15. Interview with the President, Hyannisport, Massachusetts, September 2, 1963, in *FRUS, 1961–1963* 4:93–94. Cf. Pierre Salinger, *With Kennedy* (New York: Doubleday and Co., 1966), 114.

16. Author's interview with George A. Ball, October 14, 1988. Ball stressed Kennedy's personal endorsement, through the Labor Day broadcast, of the message in the August 24 cable authorized by Ball.

17. Reported by Lodge to State, September 2, 1963, in *FRUS, 1961–1963* 4:84–85, 85n3 (on Ho interview before May 29). Cf. Maneli, *War of the Vanquished*, 115, 117, 121, 127, 128. At the meeting between Lodge and Nhu, Nhu told Lodge he would leave Saigon as soon as U.S. agents who were plotting a coup left. Nhu said that "everybody knows who they are."

18. Memorandum of a Conference with the President, White House, September 3, 1963, in *FRUS, 1961–1963* 4:100–103.

19. Telegram from the Department of State to the Embassy in Vietnam, September 3, 1963, in *FRUS, 1961–1963* 4:104–6.

20. Telegram from the Embassy in Vietnam to the Department of State, September 4, 1963, in *FRUS, 1961–1963* 4:107–8.

21. Telegram from the Embassy in Vietnam to the Department of State, September 5, 1963, in *FRUS, 1961–1963* 4:109–10.

22. Telegram from Department of State to U.S. Embassies in India, Vietnam, France, and the U.K., September 5, 1963, RG 59, container 4047, National Archives II.

23. Telegram from Department of State to the Embassy in Sweden and the Embassy in Portugal, September 5, 1963, RG 59, container 4049, National Archives II.

24. Memorandum of a Conference with the President, White House, September 6, 1963, in *FRUS, 1961–1963* 4:117–20.

25. Telegram from the Department of State to the Embassy in Vietnam, September 6, 1963, in *FRUS, 1961–1963* 4:128–29.

26. Telegram from the Embassy in Vietnam to the Department of State, September 9, 1963, in *FRUS, 1961–1963* 4:140–43.

27. Memorandum of a Conversation, White House, September 10, 1963, in *FRUS, 1961–1963* 4:162.

28. John M. Newman, *JFK and Vietnam: Deceptions, Intrigue, and the Struggle for Power* (New York: Warner Books, 1992), 371.

29. Phillips had earlier worked for the CIA and had been closely associated with Edward Lansdale. See Blair, *Lodge in Vietnam*, 39.

30. The decisive importance of this signal to the seditious Vietnamese officers is emphasized in two official U.S. government studies of the coup: United States Senate, *U.S. Involvement in the Overthrow of Diem, 1963*, Study no. 3, staff study directed by Robert Biles, Robert Blum, and Ann Hollick for the use of the Committee on Foreign Relations (Washington, D.C.: GPO, 1972), 11, quoting the authority of George Ball; and Congressional Research Service, *U.S. Government and the Vietnam War*, 189. Both studies point out that the rebel leaders had settled on this symbol as a test of Kennedy's bona fides.

31. Memorandum of a Conversation, White House, September 10, 1963, in *FRUS, 1961–1963* 4:166.

32. Memorandum of a Conversation at the Department of State, September 10, 1963, in *FRUS, 1961–1963* 4:170–71, 177n1.

33. Memorandum of a Conference with the President, White House, September 11, 1963, in *FRUS, 1961–1963* 4:190–93.

34. Telegram from the Department of State to the Embassy in Vietnam, September 12, 1963, in *FRUS, 1961–1963* 4:195–196.

35. Telegram from the Embassy in Vietnam to the Department of State, September 13, 1963, in *FRUS, 1961–1963* 4:203. On the basis of the official record, then, Arthur M. Schlesinger Jr. can easily defend his claim that, at least after September 11, Lodge was operating autonomously, imperiling the White House efforts to limit its risks in Vietnam. Author's interview with Schlesinger, December 11, 1987.

36. Telegram from the Embassy in Vietnam to the Department of State, September 16, 1963, in *FRUS, 1961–1963* 4:215–16.

37. Telegram from the Embassy in Vietnam to the Department of State, September 18, 1963, in *FRUS, 1961–1963* 4:255.

38. Telegram from the Embassy in Vietnam to the Department of State, September 19, 1963, in *FRUS, 1961–1963* 4:258–59.

39. Memorandum of a Telephone Conversation between the Under-secretary of State for Political Affairs and Michael V. Forrestal of the National Security Council Staff, Washington, September 17, 1963, 4:20 P.M., in *FRUS, 1961–1963* 4:251.

40. Memorandum of a Telephone Conversation between the Under-secretary of State for Political Affairs and the President's Special Assistant for National Security Affairs, Washington, September 18, 1963, 10:05 A.M., in *FRUS, 1961–1963* 4:256.

41. Letter from the Assistant Secretary of State for Far Eastern Affairs to the Ambassador in Vietnam, September 23, 1963, in *FRUS, 1961–1963* 4:282–83. Hilsman explicitly links the cutoff to the morale and resolve of "middle grade officers" against Diem. Forrestal hand-delivered the letter to Lodge.

42. Congressional Research Service, *U.S. Government and the Vietnam War*, 189. Cf. *FRUS, 1961–1963* 4:373–74.

43. Telegram from the Embassy in Vietnam to the Department of State, October 7, 1963, in *FRUS, 1961–1963* 4:385–86.

44. Telegram from the Embassy in Vietnam to the Department of State, October 7, 1963, in *FRUS, 1961–1963* 4:385–86.

45. Nolting, *From Trust to Tragedy*, 128–29.

46. Rudy Abramson recounts Harriman's pursuit of appointment as secretary of state, beginning on January 1, 1959, the day he left office as governor of New York; Abramson, *Spanning the Century: The Life of W. Averell Harriman, 1891–1986* (New York: William Morrow, 1992), 572, 599, 613, 624. Arthur M. Schlesinger Jr. continues to believe that Harriman would have been Kennedy's shrewdest choice for secretary of state. He several times urged this on the president-elect and on his brother Robert during the transition period in 1960. Schlesinger, *Robert Kennedy*, 223–24.

47. Author's interview with Dean Rusk, February 26, 1988. Richard Reeves (*President Kennedy*, 26) recalls that in January 1961, after a telephone call from President-elect Kennedy, the Rockefeller brothers had put together a financial aid package that matched Rusk's earlier salary as president of the Rockefeller Foundation (sixty thousand dollars). His salary as secretary of state was twenty-five thousand. Reeves claims that Harriman already knew in August 1963 that Kennedy was planning to replace Rusk (561).

48. Joseph Alsop, "The Crusades," *Washington Post*, September 23, 1963.

49. Report by the Secretary of Defense, Saigon, September 26, 1963, in *FRUS, 1961–1963* 4:293–95.

50. On Lodge's effort to remove Richardson, see Letter from the Ambassador in Vietnam to the Secretary of State, September 13, 1963, in *FRUS, 1961–1963* 4:205–6.

51. Report by the Secretary of Defense, Saigon, undated, in *FRUS, 1961–1963* 4:301–3.

52. Editorial Note, in *FRUS, 1961–1963* 4:303–5.

53. Telegram from the Department of State (Ball) to the Embassy in Vietnam, September 28, 1963, in *FRUS, 1961–1963* 4:308–10.

54. Telegram from the Embassy in Vietnam to the Department of State, September 30, 1963, in *FRUS, 1961–1963* 4:321–23.

55. Memorandum for the Record by the Chairman of the Joint Chiefs of Staff (Taylor), Saigon, October 1, 1963, in *FRUS, 1961–1963* 4:326–27.

56. Telegram from the Embassy in Vietnam to the Department of State, September 27, 1963, in *FRUS, 1961–1963* 4:300–301.

57. Blair, *Lodge in Vietnam*, 61.

58. Memorandum from the Chairman of the Joint Chiefs of Staff (Taylor) and the Secretary of Defense to the President, Washington, October 2, 1963, in *FRUS, 1961–1963* 4:336–46, esp. 338 and 341. The supporting analysis provided in favor of such cuts in the financing of Colonel Tung's forces is provided in an Annex to the Draft Report Prepared for the Executive Committee of the National Security Council, drafted by William Bundy, October 4, 1963, in *FRUS, 1961–1963* 4:360–64.

59. Memorandum to Roger Hilsman from William Sullivan, October 3, 1963, in Averell Harriman Papers, Manuscript Division, Library of Congress, container 467. In 1991 Sullivan himself would judge this decision to unleash a coup as "imperialism," that is, "attempting to order other peoples' lives in a way that we thought would be better for them and better for the world as a whole. I guess if that be imperialism, one has to make the most of it. . . . We seemed to know better what was good for people. That surely was pretty pronounced in the whole question in dealing with Diem and Nhu" (Strober and Strober, *"Let Us Begin Anew,"* 402–3). Sullivan's alarm about the imminence of a possible volte-face by Diem and Nhu in favor of an alliance with Ho Chi Minh arose during his trip to Vietnam in interviews with the French chargé d'affaires, the Canadian ICC commissioner, and the Indian ICC commissioner, all of whom reiterated the salience of rumors concerning North-South Vietnamese negotiations. See Memorandum by the Under-secretary of State for Political Affairs' Special Assistant, Sullivan, September 30, 1963, in *FRUS, 1961–1963* 4:325–26.

60. Memorandum of a Conversation, Gia Long Palace, Saigon, September 29, 1963, in *FRUS, 1961–1963* 4:310–21, esp. 320.

61. Letter from the Chairman of the Joint Chiefs of Staff (Taylor) to President Diem, Saigon, October 1, 1963, in *FRUS, 1961–1963* 4:328–30.

62. Summary of National Security Council Meeting, October 2, 1963, in *FRUS, 1961–1963* 4:350–52.

63. Hammer, *Death in November*, 256.

64. Memorandum of a Conversation, Mission at the United Nations, New York, October 2, 1963, in *FRUS, 1961–1963* 4:347–49.

CHAPTER 7: WHO WILL KOWTOW?

1. Telegram from the Department of State to the Embassy in Vietnam, October 5, 1963, in *FRUS, 1961–1963* 4:371–79; emphasis added.

2. Telegram from the President's Special Assistant for National Security Affairs to the Ambassador in Vietnam, October 5, 1963, in *FRUS, 1961–1963* 4:379.

3. Letter from the Ambassador in Vietnam to the Secretary of State, September 13, 1963, in *FRUS, 1961–1963* 4:205–6.

4. *FRUS, 1961–1963* 4:205n4.

5. Telegram from the Department of State to the Embassy in Vietnam, October 4, 1963, in *FRUS, 1961–1963* 4:364–65.

6. Author's interview with John H. Richardson, March 12, 1987.

7. Editorial Note, in *FRUS, 1961–1963* 4:364n2.

8. United States Senate, *Executive Sessions*, 736–39.

9. United States Senate, *Executive Sessions*, 736–39.

10. United States Senate, *Executive Sessions*, 741, 743.

11. United States Senate, *Executive Sessions*, 734. It seems unfortunate that McNamara failed to record these illuminating remarks on the dilemma of Vietnam in *In Retrospect*.

12. United States Senate, *Executive Sessions*, 779, 768.

13. United States Senate, *Executive Sessions*, 767.

14. Hugh Sidey with Cecil Houghton and Chester Clifton, *The Memories of JFK, 1961–1963* (New York: W. W. Norton, 1973), 25.

15. President's news conference, October 9, 1963, in *Public Papers*, 767–75.

16. President's news conference, October 9, 1963, in *Public Papers*, 767–75.

17. United States Senate, *Executive Sessions*, 790.

18. United States Senate, *Executive Sessions*, 803–4.

19. Doan-Them, *Hai Muoi Nam Qua*, 365; translated for the author by Son Vu.

20. Telegram from the Department of State (Ball) to the Embassy in Vietnam, October 25, 1963, in *FRUS, 1961–1963* 4:437–39.

21. Telegram from the Embassy in Vietnam to the Department of State, September 20, 1963, in *FRUS, 1961–1963* 4:272; emphasis added.

22. Telegram from the Ambassador in Vietnam to the President's Special Assistant for National Security Affairs, October 25, 1963, in *FRUS, 1961–1963* 4:434–36; emphasis added.

23. Telegram from the Ambassador in Vietnam to the President's Special Assistant for National Security Affairs, October 25, 1963, in *FRUS, 1961–1963* 4:434–36.

24. Telegram from the Ambassador in Vietnam to the Department of State, October 28, 1963, in *FRUS, 1961–1963* 4:449.

25. Telegram from the Embassy in Vietnam to the Department of State, October 28, 1963, in *FRUS, 1961–1963* 4:442–46.

26. Telegram from the Embassy in Vietnam to the Department of State, October 28, 1963, in *FRUS, 1961–1963* 4:441–42.

27. Telegram from the Embassy in Vietnam to the Department of State, October 28, 1963, in *FRUS, 1961–1963* 4:442–47; emphasis added.

28. Telegram from the Embassy in Vietnam to the Department of State, October 28, 1963, in *FRUS, 1961–1963* 4:441–46.

29. Hammer, *Death in November*, 269–70; and author's interview of Tran Van Dinh, October 1989. Cf. Stanley Karnow, "Lost Chance in Vietnam," *New Republic*, February 2, 1974, 17–19.

CHAPTER 8: LAST RITES AND FINAL JUDGMENTS

1. Briefing Paper Prepared in the White House, October 29, 1963, in *FRUS, 1961–1963* 4:465–66n1.

2. Memorandum of a Conference with the President, White House, October 29, 1963, 4:20 P.M., in *FRUS, 1961–1963* 4:468–71.

3. Memorandum of a Conference with the President, White House, October 29, 1963, 4:20 P.M., in *FRUS, 1961–1963* 4:468–71.

4. For the fulfillment of this dire prophecy, see Memorandum from Michael V. Forrestal of the National Security Council Staff to the President, December 11, 1963, in *FRUS, 1961–1963* 4:699. Cf. Airgram from Embassy in Vietnam to Department of State, December 16, 1963, RG 59, container 4046, National Archives II.

5. Memorandum of a Conference with the President, White House, October 29, 1963, 4:20 P.M., in *FRUS, 1961–1963* 4:468–71.

6. Telegram from the President's Special Assistant for National Security Affairs to the Ambassador in Vietnam, October 29, 1963, in *FRUS, 1961–1963* 4:473–75.

7. Telegram from the Embassy in Vietnam to the Department of State, October 30, 1963, in *FRUS, 1961–1963* 4:477–79.

8. Telegram from the Embassy in Vietnam to the Department of State, November 1, 1963, in *FRUS, 1961–1963* 4:516–17. On October 29 Diem had instructed a close ally, Tran Van Dinh, to travel to Washington, where Harriman and Hilsman were blocking the appointment of Diem's new ambassador, and to hold a press conference on November 1 to announce the implementation of needed governmental reforms in Saigon, "changes in both personnel and policies." Secretary Thuan was about to be appointed prime minister. See Hammer, *Death in November*, 269.

9. Telegram from the Commander, Military Assistance Command, Vietnam (Harkins), to the Chairman of the Joint Chiefs of Staff (Taylor), October 30, 1963, in *FRUS, 1961–1963* 4:499–500.

10. Telegram from the President's Special Assistant for National Security Affairs to the Ambassador in Vietnam, October 29, 1963; and Telegram from the Ambassador in Vietnam to the Department of State, October 30, 1963, both in *FRUS, 1961–1963* 4:473–75, 484–88.

11. Telegram from the Ambassador in Vietnam to the Department of State, October 30, 1963, in *FRUS, 1961–1963* 4:486–87 (no. 8).

12. Telegram from the President's Special Assistant for National Security Affairs to the Ambassador in Vietnam, October 30, 1963, in *FRUS, 1961–1963* 4:500–501; emphasis added.

13. Telegram from the Embassy in Vietnam to the Department of State, November 1, 1963, 6:00 P.M., in *FRUS, 1961–1963* 4:513.

14. Blair, *Lodge in Vietnam*, 69.

15. Zalin Grant, *Facing the Phoenix* (New York: W. W. Norton, 1991), 210–14.

16. This entire account rests on two apparently authoritative accounts by Vietnamese politicians: Truong Vinh-Le, *Vietnam*, 106–10; and Nguyen Ngoc Huy, "Ngo Dinh Diem's Execution," *Worldview* 33 (1976): 39–41.

17. The Latin text of the Sequence is reprinted from the *Rituale Romanum* (New York: Benziger Brothers, 1960), 120. This Sequence was dropped from the liturgy for the Feast of All Souls after the Second Vatican Council in 1965. The English translation is from the Reverends F. X. Lasance and Francis A. Walsh, eds., *The New Roman Missal in Latin and English* (New York: Benziger Brothers, 1937).

18. Memorandum for the Record of Discussion at the Daily White House Staff Meeting, Washington, November 1, 1963, 8:00 A.M., in *FRUS, 1961–1963* 4:518.

19. Kennedy's attendance at the All Saints' liturgy is noted in *FRUS, 1961–1963* 4:519n1.

20. Feast of All Saints, *Rituale Romanum*, 718–21; Matthew 5.1–12, Jerusalem Bible.

21. Telegram from the Department of State to the Embassy in Vietnam, November 1, 1963, in *FRUS, 1961–1963* 4:519n1.

22. Telegram from the Department of State to the Embassy in Vietnam, November 1, 1963, 10:50 A.M.; and Memorandum of a Telephone Conversation between the Secretary of State and Senator J. William Fulbright, November 1, 1963, both in *FRUS, 1961–1963* 4:519–20, 520–21.

23. Telegram from the Department of State to the Embassy in Vietnam, November 1, 1963, in *FRUS, 1961–1963* 4:525–26.

24. Telegram from the Department of State to the Embassy in Vietnam, November 2, 1963; and Telegram from the Embassy in Vietnam to the Department of State, November 2, 1963, both in *FRUS, 1961–1963* 4:527, 531–33.

25. Editorial Note, in *FRUS, 1961–1963* 4:533.

26. Telegram from the President's Special Assistant for National Security Affairs to the Ambassador in Vietnam, November 2, 1963, in *FRUS, 1961–1963* 4:537.

27. Memorandum for the Record of Discussion at the Daily White House Staff Meeting, November 4, 1963, in *FRUS, 1961–1963* 4:555–56.

28. The *Evening Star*, the *Washington Post*, and the *Chicago Tribune* pieces were reprinted in the *New York Times* on November 4, 1963.

29. *Wall Street Journal*, November 4, 1963.

30. Warren Unna, "Brighter Outlook," *Washington Post*, November 5, 1963. See also *FRUS, 1961–1963* 3:294.

31. Joseph Alsop, "Farewell to Diem," *Washington Star*, November 4, 1963.

32. Joseph Buttinger, *Vietnam: A Political History* (New York: Praeger, 1968), 476.

33. Author's interview with U. Alexis Johnson, May 17, 1988.

34. *Washington Star*, November 4, 1963.

35. Telegram from the Embassy in Vietnam to the Department of State, November 3, 1963, in *FRUS, 1961–1963* 4:546–49.

36. Telegram from the Embassy in Vietnam to the Department of State, November 6, 1963, 5:00 P.M., in *FRUS, 1961–1963* 4:575–78.

37. Telegram from the Embassy in Vietnam to the Department of State, November 6, 1963, 5:00 P.M., in *FRUS, 1961–1963* 4:575–78.

38. Telegram from the Department of State to the Embassy in Vietnam, November 6, 1963, 7:50 P.M., in *FRUS, 1961–1963* 4:579–80.

39. Memorandum for the Record of Discussion at the Daily White House Staff

Meeting, November 4, 1963, in *FRUS, 1961–1963* 4:555–56. Richard Reeves comments that Bundy's "cool objectivity . . . unmoved by moral argument" appealed to Kennedy (*President Kennedy*, 467).

40. Telegram from the Embassy in Vietnam to the Department of State, November 4, 1963, in *FRUS, 1961–1963* 4:560–62. On Can's fate, see Hammer, *Death in November*, 306–7.

41. Telegram from the Embassy in Vietnam to the Department of State, November 8, 1963, in *FRUS, 1961–1963* 4:586–88.

42. Averell Harriman Papers, Manuscript Division, Library of Congress, container 463.

43. United States Senate, *Executive Sessions*, 896.

44. Burchett, *Vietnam*, 216–19; Truong Vinh-Le, *Vietnam*, 111.

45. Truong Vinh-Le, *Vietnam*, 111. Cf. Colby, *Lost Victory*, 167.

46. Hammer, *Death in November*, 309–10.

47. Hammer, *Death in November*, 310. For still more extensive documentation of assessments by the Liberation Front of the windfall of the November coup, see Burchett, *Vietnam*, 216–19.

48. Hammer, *Death in November*, 310.

49. Memorandum of a Discussion at the Special Meeting on Vietnam, Honolulu, November 20, 1963, in *FRUS, 1961–1963* 4:608–11.

50. Memorandum of a Discussion at the Special Meeting on Vietnam, Honolulu, November 20, 1963, in *FRUS, 1961–1963* 4:610. Lodge had reported this apathy in the countryside on November 9; Telegram from Vietnam to Department of State, November 9, 1963, RG 59, container 4046, National Archives II.

51. Memorandum for the Record of a Conversation between the Assistant Director for Rural Affairs of the United States Operations Mission (Phillips) and President Minh, Saigon, November 18, 1963, in *FRUS, 1961–1963* 4:602–7. Phillips, perhaps hoping to lighten the atmosphere, suggested that this tactic would be most impressive if the executed official were a relative of some high official in Minh's government. Minh gave no sign of being amused (605).

52. Memorandum of a Discussion at the Special Meeting on Vietnam, Honolulu, November 20, 1963, in *FRUS, 1961–1963* 4:616–17.

53. Hammer, *Death in November*, 309.

CHAPTER 9: AFTERSHOCKS

1. Hammer, *Death in November*, 312.

2. During Diem's lifetime three Vietnamese emperors lived in exile: "Two of the three had led rebellions against France. Only when the Americans decided to intervene in Vietnamese affairs was a Vietnamese chief of state who stood up to them murdered, in 1963" (Hammer, *Death in November*, 50, 50n).

3. FitzGerald, *Fire in the Lake*, 328.

4. Lacouture, *Vietnam: Between Two Truces*, 99, 121. Lacouture's account of the junta's curious sense of government priorities is confirmed by Lodge; Telegram

from Vietnam to Department of State, November 13, 1963, RG 59, container 4046, National Archives II.

5. "The President asked that we try to find out who these key people are." Memorandum of a Conference with the President, White House, October 29, 1963, 4:20 P.M., in *FRUS, 1961–1963* 4:469.

6. Memorandum for the Record of a Meeting, Executive Office Building, Washington, November 24, 1963, 3:00 P.M., in *FRUS, 1961–1963* 4:635–37.

7. Memorandum for the Record of a Meeting, Executive Office Building, Washington, November 24, 1963, 3:00 P.M., in *FRUS, 1961–1963* 4:635–37.

8. Memorandum for the Record of a Meeting, Executive Office Building, Washington, November 24, 1963, 3:00 P.M., in *FRUS, 1961–1963* 4:635.

9. Memorandum of a Telephone Conversation between Harriman and Bundy, Washington, December 4, 1963, 10:40 P.M., in *FRUS, 1961–1963* 4:665–66.

10. Blair, *Lodge in Vietnam*, 86, 99–100, 112–13. On the Eisenhower influence, Blair cites Theodore H. White, *The Making of the President, 1964* (London: Jonathan Cape, 1965), 84.

11. Memorandum from the Chairman of the CIA's Working Group on Vietnam (Cooper) to the Director of Central Intelligence, Washington, December 6, 1963, in *FRUS, 1961–1963* 4:681.

12. Hammer, *Death in November*, 314.

13. Memorandum from Michael V. Forrestal of the National Security Council Staff to the President, December 11, 1963, in *FRUS, 1961–1963* 4:699, 698–700. Cf. Airgram from Embassy of Vietnam to Department of State, December 16, 1963, RG 59, container 4046, National Archives II. As Kissinger observed: "Ultimately, every revolutionary war is about governmental legitimacy; undermining it is the guerrillas' principal aim. Diem's overthrow handed that objective to Hanoi for free. As a consequence of Diem's feudal style of government, his removal affected every tier of civil administration down to the village level. Authority now had to be rebuilt from the ground up" (*Diplomacy*, 655).

14. CIA Information Report, Washington, December 16, 1963, in *FRUS, 1961–1963* 4:711–13.

15. Memorandum of a Conversation, Saigon, December 20, 1963, 3:45 P.M., in *FRUS, 1961–1963* 4:716–19.

16. Memorandum from the Secretary of Defense (McNamara) to the President, Washington, December 21, 1963, in *FRUS, 1961–1963* 4:732–35.

17. Highlights of Discussions in Saigon, December 18–20, 1963, drafted by McCone, in *FRUS, 1961–1963* 4:736–38.

18. Telegram from the Embassy in Vietnam to the Department of State, December 31, 1963, in *FRUS, 1961–1963* 4:748.

19. Message from the President to the Ambassador in Vietnam (Lodge), December 30, 1963, in *FRUS, 1961–1963* 4:744.

20. Telegram from the Embassy in Vietnam to the Department of State, January 10, 1964, in *FRUS, 1964–1968* 1:16–22.

21. Telegram from the Embassy in Vietnam to the Department of State, January 10, 1964, in *FRUS, 1964–1968* 1:16, 16n2.

22. Telegram from the Ambassador in Vietnam to the Department of State,

January 21, 1964, in *FRUS, 1964–1968* 1:28–31.

23. Telegram from the Embassy in Vietnam to the Department of State, January 21, 1964, in *FRUS, 1964–1968* 1:32–33.

24. FitzGerald, *Fire in the Lake*, 295.

25. Truong Vinh-Le, *Vietnam*, 124–25.

26. FitzGerald, *Fire in the Lake*, 312–16.

27. Hammer, *Death in November*, 294.

28. Author's interview with Stephen Young, January 1989.

29. Burchett, *Vietnam*, 219. In his memoirs, McNamara explains this folly by insisting that he acted this way, promoting Khanh to his own people, at President Johnson's explicit orders; McNamara with VanDeMark, *In Retrospect*, 112.

30. Author's interview with Lucien Conein, March 4, 1988.

31. Letter from Averell Harriman to Henry Cabot Lodge Jr., January 27, 1964, in Averell Harriman Papers, Manuscript Division, Library of Congress, container 484.

32. Averell Harriman Interview, p. 109, Kennedy Administration Oral History Series, April 1964, Kennedy Library. Cf. Blair, *Lodge in Vietnam*, 85.

33. Telegram from the Embassy in Vietnam to the Department of State, May 4, 1964, in *FRUS, 1964–1968* 1:284–87.

34. Telegram from the Embassy in Vietnam to the Department of State, May 22, 1964, in *FRUS, 1964–1968* 1:346. On the incursions of the Vietnamese into Cambodia, see *FRUS, 1964–1968* 1:330n3.

35. Telegram from the Ambassador in Vietnam to the Department of State, June 18, 1964; and Editorial Note, both in *FRUS, 1964–1968* 1:521–22, 523–24.

36. Kahin, *Intervention*, 227.

37. FitzGerald, *Fire in the Lake*, 321. Cf. Lacouture, *Vietnam: Between Two Truces*, 135.

38. Telegram from the Embassy in Saigon to the Department of State, September 29, 1964. This text, in the possession of the author, was declassified on August 25, 1989.

39. Kahin, *Intervention*, 233. Cf. Robert Hopkins Miller, ed., *Inside an Embassy: The Political Role of Diplomats Abroad* (Washington, D.C.: Congressional Quarterly, 1992), 20–22; and FitzGerald, *Fire in the Lake*, 322. Stanley Karnow describes Phan Khac Suu and Tran Van Huong as "decrepit characters" (*Vietnam*, 356).

40. Kahin, *Intervention*, 256–58. Khanh was permanently exiled from Vietnam on February 22, 1965 (Karnow, *Vietnam*, 385).

41. Kahin, *Intervention*, 274, 344–45.

42. McNamara with VanDeMark, *In Retrospect*, 321.

43. Johnson quoted in *Vietnam: A Television History*, Public Broadcasting System series, part 3, "LBJ Goes to War."

44. Nolting, *From Trust to Tragedy*, 135.

45. General Maxwell Taylor, Address at Georgetown University, April 1976. Taylor had been using this formula since September 1964; McNamara with VanDeMark, *In Retrospect*, 154.

46. Higgins, *Our Vietnam Nightmare*, 169.

47. Author's interview with Dean Rusk, February 26, 1988.

48. Averell Harriman Interview, p. 106, Kennedy Administration Oral History

Series, April 1964, Kennedy Library. Under Johnson, Harriman returned to a significant role in U.S.-Vietnamese affairs, from December 1965 until Johnson's final day in the White House. See Abramson, *Spanning the Century*, 639–74.

49. Author's interview with U. Alexis Johnson, May 17, 1988. Cf. Strober and Strober, *"Let Us Begin Anew,"* 419.

50. Author's interview with Henry Brandon, June 28, 1988.

51. Rudyard Kipling, *Rudyard Kipling's Verse, Inclusive Edition, 1885–1926* (Garden City, N.Y.: Doubleday, Doran, 1931), 373–74.

CHAPTER 10: DEAN RUSK

1. Kennedy had been urged by Eisenhower, on January 19, 1961, to prepare to make a stand against Asian communism in Laos. For military and political reasons, however, Kennedy had decided that Vietnam would be a more propitious place to fight. William Sullivan interview in Strober and Strober, *"Let Us Begin Anew,"* 405.

2. Theodore H. White, "Does He Drive or Is He Driven?" *Life*, June 8, 1962, reprinted in Edward T. Thompson, ed., *Theodore H. White at Large: The Best of His Magazine Writing, 1939–1986* (New York: Pantheon, 1992), 63.

3. Rusk, *As I Saw It*, 246–47.

4. Robert J. McCloskey, "Dean Rusk: Reflections on Alliances," *Mediterranean Quarterly* 1, no. 1 (Fall 1989): 14. Cf. Rusk, *As I Saw It*, 246–47.

5. Rusk, *As I Saw It*, 502; cf. Dean Rusk, in an interview in Karnow, ed., *Vietnam*, PBS series, part 3, "America's Mandarin." Rusk said that "our policies must have made them think: 'We'd better be careful. Those damn-fool American might do something about it.'" Rusk articulated this linkage between Berlin and Vietnam in a conversation with the French ambassador to the United States on July 1, 1964. Herring, *America's Longest War*, 115.

6. R. Reeves, *President Kennedy*, 552–54.

7. McCloskey, "Dean Rusk," 18.

8. Author's interview with Dean Rusk, February 26, 1988. One of the enlightening facets of *In Retrospect* is McNamara's marked disagreement with Rusk on this capital issue of the meaning of the Vietnam tragedy. For McNamara, this war had no merit or meaning. See McNamara with VanDeMark, *In Retrospect*, 319.

9. McNamara with VanDeMark, *In Retrospect*, 345, 345n.

10. McNamara has recently indicated that in October 1962 the Soviet forces had at their disposal in Cuba 162 nuclear warheads, including 90 tactical (short-range, battlefield) nuclear warheads, which might have been used against conventionally armed U.S. invasion forces. Such an invasion might likely have been launched by Kennedy shortly after October 29, if the Soviet leader had not announced the dismantling and removal of the missiles on that date. Three days earlier, such Soviet warheads had, with the approval of Khrushchev, been moved closer to their delivery vehicles. McNamara with VanDeMark, *In Retrospect*, 337–42.

11. In addition to McNamara's useful summary of the crisis (McNamara with VanDeMark, *In Retrospect*, 337–42), see McGeorge Bundy, *Danger and Survival: Choices about the Bomb in the First Fifty Years* (New York: Random House, 1990),

391–462. See also Beschloss, *Crisis Years*, 379–545; and R. Reeves, *President Kennedy*, 368–425.

12. Beschloss, *Crisis Years*, 272–87.

13. John Lewis Gaddis, *Strategies of Containment: A Critical Appraisal of Postwar American National Security Policy* (New York: Oxford University Press, 1982), 197, 207.

14. Gaddis, *Strategies of Containment*, 238; cf. 231, 237. Gaddis's luminous and learned analysis seems not to consider here whether it was the theory of "flexible response" that failed in Vietnam or whether it was its misapplication by the Kennedy administration. Specifically, Gaddis passes over virtually without comment the Kennedy decision to overthrow Diem, implying thereby either that the coup was historically inconsequential or that this option was a preordained outcome of the administration's strategic theories (246). This assumption seems not wholly convincing; the fact that one historical test of a strategic theory failed woefully does not necessarily establish the invalidity of the theory itself, but only its failure in a specific crisis, which may have been due to other (nonstrategic) constraints, in this case including domestic political, and powerful bureaucratic, pressures on Kennedy to dump the despot Diem. The historical record of Kennedy's deliberations about Vietnam, available since 1991 in *The Foreign Relations of the United States*, defies the effort to reconstruct Kennedy's deliberations under the rubric of a "Charles River strategic seminar," primarily concerned with examining comparative strategic models of intervention in a politically neutral atmosphere.

Gaddis's reconstruction of the operational behavior of the Kennedy White House in its Vietnam deliberations under this rubric of unencumbered cerebration seems to verify the general evaluation of American academic treatments of these events offered recently by the British scholar Ralph Smith. Including Robert McNamara's recent *In Retrospect* in his second category of (civilian authors') fatalistic judgments, in which the 1975 denouement stemmed irrevocably from earlier choices, Smith remarks of this entire genre of studies:

"American writing about the Vietnam War tends to follow two paths. . . .

"Civilian officials and political scientists . . . more frequently take for granted the eventual U.S. defeat—regarding the involvement as a disastrous mistake from the start. . . .

". . . [T]he book describes in alarming detail the fumblings of the Kennedy administration in the second half of 1963, which led to the overthrow of the Ngo Dinh Diem regime, without consideration of what would replace it. But in complaining about South Vietnam's subsequent failure to re-establish stability and to fight its own war in 1964–67, McNamara overlooks the fact that Saigon's difficulties stemmed directly from that American miscalculation." Ralph Smith, "Biting the Dust," *Far Eastern Economic Review*, August 3, 1995, 38.

15. Author's interview with Dean Rusk, February 26, 1988.

16. McCloskey, "Dean Rusk," 14. For an account of Khrushchev's recoiling from the responsibility for waging nuclear war, see the Prologue, above.

17. John Kenneth Galbraith, likely unaware of the logic of "flexible response," judged Rusk a statesman imprisoned by Cold War clichés. Strober and Strober, *"Let Us Begin Anew,"* 116–17, 180.

18. For Defense Secretary McNamara's recollection of the Kennedy administration's abandonment of "first use" policy, see Robert S. McNamara, "The Military Role of Nuclear Weapons: Perceptions and Misperceptions," *Foreign Affairs* 62, no. 1 (Fall 1983): 59–80. McNamara wrote:

"Nuclear weapons serve no military purpose whatsoever. They are totally useless — except only to deter one's opponent from using them.

"This is my view today. It was my view in the early 1960s.

"At that time, in long private conversations with successive presidents—Kennedy and Johnson—I recommended, without qualification, that they never initiate, under any circumstances, the use of nuclear weapons. I believe they accepted my recommendation" (79).

See also McNamara with VanDeMark, *In Retrospect*, 354.

19. Bundy, *Danger and Survival*, 604–6.

20. A notable exception was George F. Kennan, whose four-decade campaign against nuclear deterrence is chronicled in Kennan, *The Nuclear Delusion: Soviet-American Relations in the Nuclear Age* (New York: Pantheon, 1982).

21. McNamara with VanDeMark, *In Retrospect*, 51. See Kissinger, *Diplomacy*, 656–57.

22. Rusk, *As I Saw It*, 441; author's interview with Dean Rusk, February 26, 1988.

23. Rusk, *As I Saw It*, 441–42.

24. Telegram from the Department of State to the Embassy in Vietnam, August 29, 1963, in *FRUS, 1961–1963* 4:33–34.

25. In a 1989 interview Rusk went so far as to wonder aloud whether the creation of SEATO was not a mistake. See McCloskey, "Dean Rusk," 11. For a longer account of his critical views on the SEATO treaty, see Rusk, *As I Saw It*, 427. Rusk recalled his own opposition to SEATO as early as 1949, when he was serving as assistant secretary of state under Acheson; author's interview with Rusk, February 26, 1988.

26. Rusk, *As I Saw It*, 436; cf. 439–40.

27. Author's interviews with Ben Read, U. Alexis Johnson, William E. Colby, and Frederick E. Nolting. Cf. Nolting, *From Trust to Tragedy*, 12, 29.

28. Author's interview with U. Alexis Johnson, May 17, 1988.

29. Memorandum of a Conversation, Department of State, Washington, August 31, 1963, in *FRUS, 1961–1963* 4:69–72.

30. Rusk had earlier written a letter of resignation, which he submitted to Kennedy on his first day in office for use at the president's discretion. Cf. Rusk, *As I Saw It*, 296.

31. Forrest C. Pogue, *George C. Marshall: Statesman, 1945–1959* (New York: Viking Press, 1987), 373. Rusk, apparently almost alone in the State Department, seems to have favored recognition of Israel and objected only to the timing of Truman's decision. Cf. Warren I. Cohen, *Dean Rusk*, vol. 19 of *The American Secretaries of State and Their Diplomacy*, edited by Robert H. Ferrell (Totowa, N.J.: Cooper Square, 1980), 26, 323.

32. Message from the President to the Ambassador in Vietnam, August 29, 1963, in *FRUS, 1961–1963* 4:35–36.

33. Memorandum of a Conference with the President, White House, October 29,

1963, 4:20 P.M., in *FRUS, 1961–1963* 4:468–71. A cable was drafted to present this question to Lodge and was circulated at a meeting with the president an hour later. It was discarded and replaced by a cable from Bundy insisting that Lodge discourage any coup that *risked failure.* An exchange of cables on the point of avoiding support for any risky coup initiatives continued between Saigon and Washington until the coup was actually under way. Memorandum of a Conference with the President, White House, October 29, 1963, 6:00 P.M.; Telegram from the President's Special Assistant for National Security Affairs to the Ambassador in Vietnam, October 29, 1963, 7:22 P.M.; Telegram from the Ambassador in Vietnam to the Department of State, October 30, 1963, 6:30 P.M.; Telegram from the President's Special Assistant for National Security Affairs to the Ambassador in Vietnam, October 30, 1963, 5:49 P.M., all in *FRUS, 1961–1963* 4:472–75, 484–88, 500–502.

34. Rusk, *As I Saw It*, 440–41. Both Kennedy and Lodge, however, saw the American role as indispensable to the instigation of the coup. See chapter 8, above.

35. Rusk, *As I Saw It*, 439–40.

36. Rusk, *As I Saw It*, 436–39. Rusk made the same point to White in 1962: "What kinds of governments are they: do they speak for their people?" (Thompson, ed., *Theodore H. White*, 64).

37. Thompson, ed., *Theodore H. White*, 64.

38. Rusk, *As I Saw It*, 616–17; emphasis added.

39. Dean Rusk, an Address to the Hebrew Union College—Jewish Institute of Religion, Cincinnati, Ohio, October 12, 1963, pp. 2, 7, Averell Harriman Papers, Manuscript Division, Library of Congress, container 499.

40. Rusk, *As I Saw It*, 616–17.

41. Cohen, *Dean Rusk*, ix.

42. Cohen, *Dean Rusk*, 108–9, 320–21, 328–30.

43. Cohen, *Dean Rusk*, 330.

44. Cohen, *Dean Rusk*, 11.

45. See, for example, the interviews with his son that served as the basis for Rusk, *As I Saw It*; Schoenbaum, *Waging Peace and War*; and McCloskey, "Dean Rusk."

46. Cf. Michael Walzer, *Just and Unjust Wars: A Moral Argument with Historical Illustrations* (New York: Basic Books, 1977), esp. chap. 6, pp. 86–108, where Walzer relies on the political philosophy of John Stuart Mill.

47. Rusk, *As I Saw It*, 432, 437.

48. Wilson's willingness to impose the blessings of liberty by force of arms was most evident in Haiti and the Dominican Republic. See Harley Notter, *The Origins of the Foreign Policy of Woodrow Wilson* (New York: Russell and Russell, 1965), 303–4; and Arthur S. Link, *Wilson the Diplomatist: A Look at His Major Foreign Policies* (Baltimore: Johns Hopkins University Press, 1957), 14–15. Similar views of Wilson concerning the U.S. role in the Philippines are discussed in Notter, *Origins*, 143.

49. Rusk, *As I Saw It*, 440.

50. This mood of a U.S. mandate to rebuild the postwar world was captured by William Sullivan (Harriman's special assistant in 1963) in a 1991 interview: "It was not imperialism in the sense of wanting to have territory. It was imperialism in the sense that you were manipulating lesser breeds. Probably all of us were guilty of the hubris that carried from our success in World War II, and from several other

arrangements that we had made around the world in attempting to order other peoples' lives in a way that we thought would be better for them and better for the world as a whole" (Strober and Strober, *"Let Us Begin Anew,"* 402–3).

51. Graham Greene, *The Quiet American* (London: Penguin Books, 1977), 20. Anne Blair indicates that Lodge's wife, Emily, was startled and bewildered by reading *The Quiet American*. Blair offers no indication that the ambassador had time for this light reading (Blair, *Lodge in Vietnam*, 58).

52. Greene, *Quiet American*, 23–25, 28–32, 74, 94–95, 124, 156–57.

53. See chapter 15, below.

54. Greene, *Quiet American*, 163.

CHAPTER 11: NGO DINH DIEM

1. McNamara with VanDeMark, *In Retrospect*, 41–42.

2. United States Senate, *Executive Sessions*, 739.

3. Gary Hess takes note, however, of several recent studies that conclude that the U.S. decision to remove Diem was the primordial mistake of the war. Hess, "Unending Debate," 243–46.

4. Thich Nhat Hanh, *Vietnam*, 55, 57, 60.

5. Joseph Buttinger, *Vietnam: The Unforgettable Tragedy* (New York: Horizon Press, 1977), 50, 35. Cf. Joseph Buttinger, *Vietnam: A Dragon Embattled*, vol. 2, *Vietnam at War* (New York: Praeger, 1967), 941.

6. Buttinger, *Vietnam: A Dragon Embattled* 2:924, 1129.

7. Scigliano, *South Vietnam*, 91.

8. Cited in Buttinger, *Vietnam: A Dragon Embattled* 2:1187.

9. Buttinger, *Vietnam: A Dragon Embattled* 2:1009.

10. Duiker, *Rise of Nationalism*, 174–75.

11. Scigliano, *South Vietnam*, 16–17.

12. Buttinger, *Vietnam: A Dragon Embattled* 2:849.

13. Scigliano, *South Vietnam*, 17.

14. Scigliano, *South Vietnam*, 14. Scigliano cites similar views of Ellen Hammer (*Struggle for Indochina*, 86, 48, 254, 286).

15. John T. McAlister Jr., *Viet Nam: The Origins of Revolution* (New York: Alfred A. Knopf, 1969), 167–68.

16. McAlister, *Viet Nam*, 177.

17. Hess, *Vietnam and the United States*, 11.

18. Duiker, *Rise of Nationalism*, 26–27. In another royalist rebellion, the emperor Duy Tan, who had replaced his father, Thanh Tai, in 1907, consented to lead a revolt, which was aborted in April 1916. Duy Tan was then deposed in favor of Khai Dinh, son of the former emperor Dong Khanh (74–75).

19. Duiker, *Rise of Nationalism*, 42–44, 32–33. Cf. Scigliano, *South Vietnam*, 71.

20. Hess, *Vietnam and the United States*, 12. Cf. Duiker, *Rise of Nationalism*, 85, 143.

21. Hess, *Vietnam and the United States*, 12–13. Cf. Scigliano, *South Vietnam*, 70.

22. Duiker, *Rise of Nationalism*, 116–27.

23. FitzGerald, *Fire in the Lake*, 14, 15, 18, 21, 137–42. See Hammer, *Death in November*, 51–53; and Hess, *Vietnam and the United States*, 2.

24. Higgins, *Our Vietnam Nightmare*, 166.

25. Jacques Dalloz, *The War in Indo-China: 1945–1954*, translated by Josephine Bacon (Dublin: Gill and Macmillan, 1990), 4ff. Cf. Hess, *Vietnam and the United States*, 12–13.

26. Thich Nhat Hanh, *Vietnam*, 58.

27. Buttinger, *Vietnam: A Dragon Embattled* 2:906–61, 1156, 1248. Cf. Lancaster, *Emancipation of French Indochina*, 108, 348; and Duiker, *Rise of Nationalism*, 184–88.

28. Hess, *Vietnam and the United States*, 10–11; Scigliano, *South Vietnam*, 70, 107; Lancaster, *Emancipation of French Indochina*, 214; and Buttinger, *Vietnam: A Dragon Embattled* 2:928.

29. Buttinger, *Vietnam: A Dragon Embattled* 2:899. Cf. Scigliano, *South Vietnam*, 16.

30. Buttinger, *Vietnam: A Dragon Embattled* 2:982–83. Kissinger points to this terrorist strategy as a cardinal factor in Diem's failure:

"Their [Viet Cong guerrillas'] favorite targets are the worst and the best government officials. They attack the worst in order to win popular sympathies by 'punishing' corrupt or oppressive officials; and they attack the best because it is the most effective way of preventing the government from achieving legitimacy and of discouraging an effective national service.

"By 1960, some 2,500 South Vietnamese officials were being assassinated each year. Only a small number of the most highly motivated, and a much larger percentage of the most corrupt, would run such risks. In the contest between nation-building and chaos, between democracy and repression, the guerrilla enjoyed a huge advantage" (*Diplomacy*, 639–40).

31. Bernard B. Fall, *Last Reflections on a War* (Garden City, N.Y.: Doubleday and Co., 1967), 219.

32. McAlister, *Viet Nam*, 208. Cf. Duiker, *Rise of Nationalism*, 279; and Thich Nhat Hanh, *Vietnam*, 54.

33. Denis Warner, *The Last Confucian* (New York: Macmillan, 1963), 67.

34. Buttinger, *Vietnam: A Dragon Embattled* 2:912–15. Cf. Lancaster, *Emancipation of French Indochina*, 376–78.

35. Jean Lacouture, *Ho Chi Minh*, translated by Peter Wiles (London: Penguin, 1968), 57. For a brief account of Ho's training, teaching, and organizing in the USSR and China, see Duiker, *Rise of Nationalism*, 271–75.

36. Lacouture, *Ho Chi Minh*, 96, 100; Lacouture and Lacouture, *Vietnam: Voyage*, 251. On the brutalities of Mao's career, see Harrison E. Salisbury, *The New Emperors: China in the Era of Mao and Deng* (New York: Avon, 1992), citing an authority who attributed four million deaths to Mao's Red Guards (249). Estimating the fatalities as a consequence of "the great leap forward," Salisbury indicates that the toll was thirty million or more (166).

37. Dupont, *Mission*, 335.

38. Lacouture, *Ho Chi Minh*, 208–9.

39. FitzGerald, *Fire in the Lake*, 282.

40. FitzGerald, *Fire in the Lake*, 283. Cf. Hess, *Vietnam and the United States*, 18.

41. FitzGerald, *Fire in the Lake*, 124–25.

42. For an analysis of the distinctive priority of village life in Vietnam, see Fitz-Gerald, *Fire in the Lake*, 12, 53–56, 135–37. See, likewise, John T. McAlister Jr. and Paul Mus, *The Vietnamese and Their Revolution* (New York: Harper and Row, 1970), 31–37, 46–54, 90–94, 111–18, 160–62.

43. Dalloz, *War in Indo-China*, 5.

44. *The Times of Vietnam*, October 7, 1963, 1–5.

45. Masson, *Histoire du Vietnam*, 52, 58.

46. McAlister and Mus, *Vietnamese and Their Revolution*, 17, 94. Jean and Simonne Lacouture are uncertain about Mus's claim that Ho Chi Minh had won the mandate of heaven by his successful challenge to the French. Indeed, they seem to question the accuracy of Mus's interpretation of the mandate of heaven in Vietnamese culture. Lacouture and Lacouture, *Vietnam: Voyage*, 250.

47. McAlister and Mus, *Vietnamese and Their Revolution*, 1–28.

48. Paul Mus, *Viet-Nam: Sociologie d'une guerre* (Paris: Edition du Seuil, 1952). John T. McAlister Jr., a student of Mus's at Yale, after endeavoring to have Mus's classic study translated into English, eventually decided that a cooperative work between himself and Mus would be more serviceable. References to Mus's studies are here derived from McAlister and Mus, *Vietnamese and Their Revolution*.

49. McAlister and Mus, *Vietnamese and Their Revolution*, 24, 33, 66, 68.

50. McAlister and Mus, *Vietnamese and Their Revolution*, 3, 78–79, 80, 31, 32, 44, 52, 55.

51. McAlister and Mus, *Vietnamese and Their Revolution*, 36, 37, 53, 79, 94, 161, 80, 88–89, 94–97, 118, 156, 164, 165.

52. Nolting, *From Trust to Tragedy*, 87–88.

53. This quotation comes from Richard Attenborough, dir., *Gandhi* (1982).

54. For a further discussion of the recent literature on the village as the symbol of conflicting theories of Vietnamese revolution, see Hue-Tam Ho Tai, *Radicalism and the Origins of the Vietnamese Revolution* (Cambridge, Mass.: Harvard University Press, 1992), 259; and Thich Nhat Hanh, *Vietnam*, 48. On the salience of the village in Vietnamese culture and on Ho Chi Minh's village-centered revolution, see Hess, *Vietnam and the United States*, 3, 16.

55. Karnow, *Vietnam*, 269.

56. Hans J. Morgenthau, "Vietnam—Another Korea?" *Commentary* 33 (1962): 369–74.

57. John P. Roche, "Unquiet Americans in Saigon," *Wall Street Journal*, June 22, 1987, 24.

CHAPTER 12: HENRY CABOT LODGE JR.

1. Blair, *Lodge in Vietnam*, 14–15.

2. Telegram from the Embassy in Vietnam to the Department of State, October 28, 1963, in *FRUS, 1961–1963* 4:441–42.

3. Blair, *Lodge in Vietnam*, 4 and notes. The "Confidential Journal" is unpublished. It is found in the Massachusetts Historical Society Archives.

4. Blair, *Lodge in Vietnam*, 4, 7.

5. Blair, *Lodge in Vietnam*, 2–7.

6. Blair, *Lodge in Vietnam*, 4.

7. Blair, *Lodge in Vietnam*, 1.

8. Blair, *Lodge in Vietnam*, 21. For Nolting's cables and the response from Washington, see Telegram from the Embassy in Vietnam to the Department of State, April 5, 1963; Telegram from the Embassy in Vietnam to the Department of State, April 7, 1963; Telegram from the Embassy in Vietnam to the Department of State, April 9, 1963; Telegram from the Embassy in Vietnam to the Department of State, April 17, 1963; and Editorial Note, all in *FRUS, 1961–1963* 3:207–29; Editorial Note on 221.

9. Author's interview with Frederick Flott, May 12, 1988.

10. Blair, *Lodge in Vietnam*, 24, 34.

11. Blair, *Lodge in Vietnam*, 154.

12. For Forrestal's initiation of this inversion of diplomacy and public relations, see Memorandum from Michael V. Forrestal of the National Security Council to the President, February 4, 1963, in *FRUS, 1961–1963* 3:97–98.

13. Author's interview with Michael V. Forrestal, December 11, 1987.

14. On the imperialistic vision and policies of Senator Henry Cabot Lodge Sr., see Stanley Karnow, *In Our Image: America's Empire in the Philippines* (New York: Ballantine Books, 1990), esp. 79. Blair develops extensively the impact of the elder senator on his eldest grandson, Henry Cabot Lodge Jr. The death of Lodge's father when he was only seven led to his being raised in the patrician ambience of his grandfather, who seemed to transfer his own ambitions for his deceased son, Bay, onto his grandson, who adopted the "Jr." after his name in deference to his grandfather. See Blair, *Lodge in Vietnam*, 5–7, 155: "It was to be a nineteenth-century upbringing for the Lodge children in their formative years" (7).

15. *FRUS, 1961–1963* 3:628; 4:4, 16, 34, 105, 128 ("You should negotiate with Diem soonest"), 195, 374. To be fair to Lodge, George Ball had assured Lodge on August 25 that he could dispense with such consultations.

16. Telegram from the Embassy in Vietnam to the Department of State, October 28, 1963, in *FRUS, 1961–1963* 4:441–42.

17. "Lodge was chairman of the efforts to get rid of Diem. Once Lodge got to Saigon, all subsequent initiatives were his. Lodge ran away with the situation." Author's interview with Arthur M. Schlesinger Jr., December 11, 1987.

18. Blair, *Lodge in Vietnam*, 5.

19. Author's interviews with George A. Ball, William Sullivan, Ben Read, George Allen, and Frederick E. Nolting.

20. Karnow, ed., *Vietnam*, PBS series, part 3, "America's Mandarin."

21. Telegram from the Embassy in Vietnam to the Department of State, November 4, 1963, in *FRUS, 1961–1963* 4:559.

22. See Telegram from the Embassy in Vietnam to the Department of State, Saigon, September 13, 1963, in *FRUS, 1961–1963* 4:203.

23. Toward the Neutralization of North Vietnam, October 30, 1963, in *FRUS, 1961–1963* 4:656–58.

24. *FRUS, 1961–1963* 4:656n4.

25. Maneli, *War of the Vanquished,* 126–37.

26. Blair, *Lodge in Vietnam,* 85, 137–38.

27. Blair, *Lodge in Vietnam,* 141, 149–50, 153.

CHAPTER 13: THE *NEW YORK TIMES*

1. *Time,* April 24, 1995, 22, 45. Tillman is a professor at the School of Foreign Service of Georgetown University.

2. Keith Richburg, "Mission to Hanoi," *Washington Post,* November 11, 1995, A23, 25. The participation of General Giap in the Hanoi planning session is mentioned in Tim Larimer, "McNamara in Hanoi, for a 'Dialogue,' Not to 'Tell' Ex-Foe Anything," *New York Times,* November 9, 1995, A4. The Vietnamese spokesman applauded McNamara's admission that the United States was "wrong, terribly wrong," while observing that Vietnam had won a war of independence and was itself therefore innocent of mistakes.

3. Prochnau, *Once upon a Distant War,* 496.

4. Prochnau is here citing approvingly the estimate of John Mecklin, the U.S. embassy press officer in Saigon at the time. Prochnau, *Once upon a Distant War,* 196–97; cf. 483.

5. Memorandum of a Conversation between Assistant Secretary of State (for Public Affairs), Robert J. Manning, and Ngo Dinh Nhu, July 17, 1963, in *FRUS, 1961–1963* 3:497, 510.

6. Report from the Assistant Secretary of State for Public Affairs (Manning) to the President, Washington, undated, in *FRUS, 1961–1963* 3:531–43.

7. Prochnau, *Once upon a Distant War,* 346, 354.

8. Author's interviews with George Allen, March 7 and April 18, 1988, describing the locations of the Buddhist demonstrations.

9. Truong Vinh-Le, *Vietnam,* 317.

10. David Halberstam, *The Powers That Be* (New York: Alfred A. Knopf, 1979), 452. Halberstam repeats this mea culpa about the quality of his political reporting in his commentary on McNamara's *In Retrospect;* Halberstam, "The Story We Never Saw in Vietnam," *Washington Post,* Outlook Section, May 14, 1995.

11. David Halberstam, "The Role of Journalists in Vietnam: A Reporter's Perspective," in *Vietnam Reconsidered: Lessons from a War,* edited by Harrison E. Salisbury (New York: Harper and Row, 1984), 113–16.

12. Michael Emery, *On the Front Lines: Following America's Foreign Correspondents across the Twentieth Century* (Washington, D.C.: American University Press, 1995), 142, 157. Cf. Russ Braley, *Bad News: The Foreign Policy of the New York Times* (Chicago: Regnery Gateway, 1984), 238–39.

13. Hallin, *"Uncensored War,"* 44.

14. Report from the Assistant Secretary of State for Public Affairs (Manning) to the President, Washington, undated, in *FRUS, 1961–1963* 3:531–43.

15. Mohr was angered by the *Time* editors' rewrite of his essay on Madame Nhu,

complaining particularly about their deletion of his opening sentence: "Vietnam is a graveyard for lost hopes, destroyed vanity, glib promises, and good intentions" (Prochnau, *Once upon a Distant War*, 355–57).

16. "Diplomacy by Television," *Time*, September 13, 1963, 21.

17. Memorandum for the Record of a Meeting at the White House, August 26, 1963, in *FRUS, 1961–1963* 3:638–41; emphasis added.

18. Reston, *Deadline*, 323. Richard Reeves adds the information about Reston's veto (*President Kennedy*, 637).

19. Diem informed Lodge on October 29 of the identity of Vann as the press's source. Telegram from the Embassy in Vietnam to the Department of State, November 1, 1963, recording Diem's last meeting with Lodge, in which the president sought to clear his name from false charges in the U.S. press, in *FRUS, 1961–1963* 4:516.

20. Neil Sheehan, *A Bright Shining Lie: John Paul Vann and America in Vietnam* (New York: Random House, 1988), 485–97, 597. Cf. Halberstam, *Powers That Be*, 451.

21. Sheehan, *Bright Shining Lie*, 383–86, 493. Vann avoided court-martial by outwitting a lie detector examiner. He also sought to steal and destroy the official record of his trial on charges of statutory rape (493). He reentered government service as an official of U.S. AID (495). For an unvarnished assault on Vann's credibility as an authentic interpreter of the war, see Hess, "Unending Debate," 254.

22. Prochnau, *Once upon a Distant War*, 279–80.

23. Betsy Wade, *Forward Positions: The War Correspondence of Homer Bigart* (Fayetteville: University of Arkansas Press, 1992), 216.

24. Nolting, *From Trust to Tragedy*, 87–88.

25. Wade, *Forward Positions*, 229. The editors of the *Times* decided against using Bigart's lead.

26. Homer Bigart, "Vietnam Victory Remote Despite U.S. Aid to Diem," *New York Times*, July 25, 1962, 1. Cf. William M. Hammond, *Public Affairs: The Military and the Media, 1962–1968*, United States Army in Vietnam Series (Washington, D.C.: Center of Military History, U.S. Army, 1988), 25.

27. *New York Times*, July 25, 1962, 2, quoted in Emery, *On the Front Lines*, 129–32. Cf. Hammond, *Public Affairs*, 25.

28. Wade, *Forward Positions*, 216; cf. 223–24.

29. As Harrison Salisbury observes, there was no daily coordination between the *Times*'s fiefdoms of news and editorial departments, which were formally segregated by decree of the paper's founder, Adolph S. Ochs. What convergence might appear from time to time between the work of these departments arose from simultaneous and converging judgments by the two groups. Salisbury points out that the editorial writers habitually relied on the AP wire service for their information. Harrison E. Salisbury, *Without Fear or Favor: The New York Times and Its Times* (New York: Times Books, 1980), 41–44.

30. Salisbury, *Without Fear or Favor*, 43.

31. Prochnau, *Once upon a Distant War*, 346.

32. Halberstam, *Powers That Be*, 449; emphasis added.

33. On Ball's championing of Halberstam's views, see Strober and Strober, *"Let Us Begin Anew,"* 410–11.

34. "McNamara's Retreat," *New York Times Book Review*, April 16, 1995, 1ff.

35. Hammer, *Death in November*, 319–20. For Lodge's provision of a landing pad, see Memorandum of a Conversation between the Assistant Secretary of State for Far Eastern Affairs and the Ambassador to Vietnam, Washington, November 24, 1963, 10:00 A.M., in *FRUS, 1961–1963* 4:632.

36. Hammer, *Death in November*, 319–20. Cf. Karnow, *Vietnam*, 668–70.

37. Karnow, *Vietnam*, 669. One of the innumerable ironies of the struggle for Vietnam came to light in the twentieth anniversary issue of *L'Express*, commemorating the "fall" of Saigon. The editors discovered that Bui Tin, now critical of the Communist regime, and Big Minh are currently neighbors and fellow exiles in the same Paris suburb but remain separated by the years of war (*L'Express*, April 27, 1995, 26, 30).

CHAPTER 14: JOHN FITZGERALD KENNEDY

1. For example, George W. Ball, "Kennedy Up Close," *New York Review of Books*, February 3, 1994, 17–20. Cf. Douglas Brinkley, "What He Did for His Country," *New York Times Book Review*, October 24, 1993, 11.

2. R. Reeves, *President Kennedy*, unnumbered page.

3. Thomas C. Reeves, *A Question of Character: A Life of John F. Kennedy* (New York: Free Press, 1991), 414–21; cf. 245, 310.

4. R. Reeves, *President Kennedy*, 651.

5. Inexplicably, McNamara now contends that Kennedy never made any Vietnam-related decisions under pressure from U.S. political exigencies. McNamara with VanDeMark, *In Retrospect*, 115.

6. Memorandum of a Conference with the President, White House, October 29, 1963, 6:00 P.M., in *FRUS, 1961–1963* 4:472.

7. Message from the President to Lodge, August 29, 1963, in *FRUS, 1961–1963* 4:35.

8. Author's interview with Charles Bartlett, June 21, 1988.

9. Author's interview with Charles Bartlett, June 21, 1988.

10. Beschloss, *Crisis Years*, 694–95.

11. Telegram from the Department of State to the Embassy in Vietnam, November 6, 1963, in *FRUS, 1961–1963* 4:579–80 (eyes only for Lodge from the president): "We necessarily faced and accepted the possibility that our position might encourage a change of government. We thus have a responsibility to help this new government to be effective in every way that we can, and in these first weeks we may have more influence and have more chance to be helpful than in any time in recent years."

12. R. Reeves, *President Kennedy*, 175.

13. R. Reeves, *President Kennedy*, 175–76, 177.

14. R. Reeves, *President Kennedy*, 172–73.

15. R. Reeves, *President Kennedy*, 411.

16. Reston, *Deadline*, 299–300.

17. R. Reeves, *President Kennedy*, 220.

18. Schlesinger, *Robert Kennedy*, 440–41, 466. Cf. Schlesinger's interview recorded in Strober and Strober, *"Let Us Begin Anew,"* 182.

19. Schlesinger, *Robert Kennedy*, 467. Schlesinger's endorsement of the critique of American foreign policy is implied in this allusion to *The Quiet American*.

20. Schlesinger, *Robert Kennedy*, 707–8.

21. Jonathan Schell, "Reflections: The Time of Illusion," *New Yorker*, July 7, 1975, 38–62. There is a strikingly parallel interpretation of the impact of nuclear weapons on the judgment of Charles de Gaulle in Jean Lacouture, *De Gaulle, the Ruler, 1945–1970*, translated by Alan Sheridan (New York: W. W. Norton, 1985), 434.

CHAPTER 15: LESSONS OF THE YEAR OF THE HARE

1. Unsigned, *New Yorker*, April 14, 1975, 27–29. Portions of this passage were reprinted in Jonathan Schell, *The Real War: The Classic Reporting on the Vietnam War with a New Essay* (New York: Pantheon, 1987), 1–55.

2. David Fromkin and James Chace, "What *Are* the Lessons of Vietnam?" *Foreign Affairs* 63, no. 4 (Spring 1985): 742–46.

3. See the analysis of Vietnam in Tuchman's *March of Folly*. Tuchman is forthright in her indictment of Kennedy for this egregious violation of the elementary responsibilities of allies: not to overthrow one another (309). She further identifies the coup as the step that tied the United States definitively to the fate of South Vietnam (305).

4. McNamara with VanDeMark, *In Retrospect*, 320.

5. Schlesinger, *Robert Kennedy*, 720. In his memoirs, McNamara virtually ignores Kennedy's deliberate decision to overthrow Diem after a prolonged and bitter debate in the National Security Council. Only in a destined-to-be-forgotten "letter to the editor" in the *New York Times*, dated September 14, 1995, does McNamara make a belated judgment about that decision and accept a share of responsibility for it — factually perhaps too great a share: "As a result, during the period just before and after the overthrow of President Ngo Dinh Diem of South Vietnam, we were flying blind.

"The erroneous decisions were ours, and we must accept the responsibility for them, but the absence of experienced senior advisers helps explain the errors. . . .

". . . I believe that United States support of the overthrow of President Diem was a mistake, but I hold senior officials — the President, Dean Rusk and me — responsible" (A26).

6. Schlesinger, *Robert Kennedy*, 717–18. Kennedy's knowledge of these negotiations is discussed in chapter 10, above.

7. Kissinger, *Diplomacy*, 656–57.

8. Kissinger, *Diplomacy*, 638.

9. Kissinger, *Diplomacy*, 638–40.

10. Kissinger, *Diplomacy*, 653.

11. Stanley Karnow, "Commentary: The Two Vietnams," in *Vietnam as History: Ten Years after the Paris Peace Accords*, edited by Peter Braestrup (Washington, D.C.: University Press of America, 1984), 81, 83.

12. Karnow, "Commentary," 83.

13. Karnow, "Lost Chance in Vietnam," 17–19. Cf. Hammer's account of these imminent negotiations, in *Death in November*, 268–70; and the present author's interview with Tran Van Dinh, October 1988. George C. Herring, the leading academic historian of the war, comes to a similar conclusion about the unexpected (and neglected) opportunities offered to Kennedy by Diem's negotiations with Ho; Herring, *America's Longest War*, 101.

14. Kissinger, *Diplomacy*, 645.

15. H. D. F. Kitto, *Sophocles: Dramatist and Philosopher* (Oxford: Oxford University Press, 1958), 37–63 passim.

16. Kissinger, *Diplomacy*, 667.

17. Kissinger, *Diplomacy*, 699.

18. Kissinger, *Diplomacy*, 668, 653–54, 676. Cf. Loren Birtz, *Backfire: A History of How American Culture Led Us into Vietnam and Made Us Fight the Way We Did* (New York: Ballantine Books, 1985), 15–18.

19. Schlesinger, *Robert Kennedy*, 465–66. Cf. Schlesinger, *Bitter Heritage*, 76–79.

20. Karnow, *In Our Image*, 109.

21. Karnow, *In Our Image*, 80, 227. The theme of American exceptionalism is the leitmotiv of the study of American foreign policy by Louis Hartz, *The Liberal Tradition in America: An Interpretation of American Political Thought since the Revolution* (New York: Harcourt, Brace, 1955).

22. Link, *Wilson the Diplomatist*, 14–15.

23. Notter, *Origins*, 306–7.

24. Link, *Wilson the Diplomatist*, 15–16.

25. Lawrence Thompson and R. H. Winnick, *Robert Frost: The Later Years* (New York: Holt, Rinehart, and Winston, 1976), 277–83.

26. Edward Connery Lathem, ed., *The Poetry of Robert Frost* (New York: Holt, Rinehart, and Winston, 1969), 422–24; emphasis added. Thompson and Winnick record another, perhaps original, version (*Robert Frost*, 277–83).

27. On August 27 or 28, when Nolting objected that authorizing a coup against the government of South Vietnam was a violation of commitments made by the president, Harriman shouted: "Shut up, Nolting. We've heard that before." Roswell Gilpatric later told an interviewer that he had never witnessed such a tongue-lashing in the presence of the president, who finally prevailed upon Harriman to allow Nolting to complete his remarks. Nolting, *From Trust to Tragedy*, 128; cf. Schlesinger, *Robert Kennedy*, 713–14.

28. Madison indeed took up the study of the law precisely in order to earn a livelihood that would "depend as little as possible on the labour of slaves." And Madison was himself the originator of the "federal ratio" stratagem that bypassed an intersectional political struggle over the calculation of population size for the determination of taxes and representation. Madison's proposal to equate five slaves with

three free men was later enshrined in the U.S. Constitution, Madison's proudest achievement. See *Dictionary of American Biography* (New York: Charles Scribner's Sons, 1957), 6:184–193. For the biography of Thomas Jefferson, see *DAB* 5:17–35, which confirms that Jefferson was the holder of between one hundred and two hundred slaves throughout his life.

29. A. A. Lipscomb and A. E. Bergh, eds. *The Writings of Thomas Jefferson*, vol. 14 (Washington, D.C.: Thomas Jefferson Memorial Association, 1903), 143.

30. Peter S. Onuf, "Peerless Tom," review of *Thomas Jefferson, A Life*, by W. S. Randall (1993), *New York Times Book Review*, October 10, 1993, 22.

31. Hannah Arendt, *On Revolution* (New York: Viking Press, 1963), 235–36.

32. Telegram from the Embassy in Vietnam to the Department of State, July 15, 1963, in *FRUS, 1961–1963* 3:487–88.

33. Robert W. Tucker and David C. Hendrickson, *Empire of Liberty: The State-craft of Thomas Jefferson* (New York: Oxford University Press, 1990), 170.

34. Merrill D. Peterson, *The Jefferson Image in the American Mind* (New York: Oxford University Press, 1960), 266–76.

35. Karnow, *In Our Image*, 137.

36. Hans J. Morgenthau, *Politics among Nations: The Struggle for Power and Peace*, 4th ed. (New York: Alfred A. Knopf, 1967), 305.

37. On the Kennedy administration's simultaneous strategy to remove Castro, "Operation Mongoose," see R. Reeves, *President Kennedy*, 335–36, 343, 367.

38. Charter of the United Nations, Chapter 1, Article 2, No. 4.

39. Robert A. Klein, *Sovereign Equality among States: The History of an Idea* (Toronto: University of Toronto Press, 1974), 37, 56, 65, 87–94, 97–102, 111–16, 136, 141.

40. By 1928 Walter Lippmann was able to enumerate thirty U.S. interventions in Latin America; Klein, *Sovereign Equality*, 86.

41. Klein, *Sovereign Equality*, 54–61, 98–99, 101–3, 115.

42. Klein, *Sovereign Equality*, 102.

43. Francis X. Winters, "The Freedom to Resist Coercion: Augustine, Aquinas, Vitoria," *Commonweal* 118, no. 11 (June 1, 1991), 369–72.

44. In the ancient world, analyzed by Thucydides in *The Peloponnesian War*, sovereignty was claimed by the *victims* of Athenian imperialism. The classic formulation of the plea of the weak to retain their independence is put by Thucydides on the lips of the rulers of Melos just before their conquest by Athens. See "The Melian Dialogue," in Thucydides, *The Peloponnesian War*, translated by John H. Finley Jr. (New York: Modern Library, 1951), 330–36. The Athenian response is familiar: "Of the gods we believe, and of men we know, that by a necessary law of their nature they rule wherever they can. And it is not as if we were the first to make this law, or to act upon it when made: we found it existing before us and shall leave it to exist forever after us; all we do is to make use of it, knowing that you and everybody else having the same power as we have, would do the same as we do" (334).

It was the medieval and Renaissance thinkers of Europe who, despite their prominent positions *within* the imperialist nations themselves, spoke on behalf of the victims' violated sovereign rights. It is striking that both the Spanish Renaissance

Catholic moral argument *against* the prerogatives of empire and the contrary Athenian *assertion* of such imperial rights are phrased in terms of a "natural law" that validates certain types of behavior.

45. Kitto, *Sophocles,* 37–63 passim.

46. FitzGerald, *Fire in the Lake,* 9.

47. Lathem, ed., *Poetry of Robert Frost,* 33–34.

EPILOGUE

1. Schlesinger, *Bitter Heritage,* 79. For a cognate critical analysis, see Arthur M. Schlesinger Jr., "National Interests and Moral Absolutes," *Ethics and World Politics: Four Perspectives,* edited by Ernest W. Lefever (Baltimore: Johns Hopkins University Press, 1972), 21–42.

2. Schlesinger, *Bitter Heritage,* 76–77.

3. Schlesinger, *Robert Kennedy,* 441, 467, 707–8; and chapter 14, above.

4. Schlesinger, "National Interests and Moral Absolutes," 42.

SOURCES

ARCHIVAL SOURCES

Averell Harriman Papers. Manuscript Division, Library of Congress, Washington, D.C.

Averell Harriman Interview. Kennedy Administration Oral History Series, April 1964. Kennedy Library, Boston, Massachusetts.

United States Department of State. General Records, Group 59. Declassified documents: "Vietnam: Political, 1963." General Records, Group 59. National Archives II, College Park, Maryland.

INTERVIEWS WITH PRINCIPAL OFFICIALS

Allen, George. DIA/CIA Vietnamese affairs analyst, mid–1963 to 1988. March 7 and April 18, 1988.

Ball, George A. Undersecretary of state. October 14, 1988.

Bartlett, Charles. Personal friend of John F. Kennedy, and syndicated columnist. June 21, 1988.

Brandon, Henry. Friend of W. Averell Harriman, and Washington correspondent for *The Sunday Times* (London). June 28, 1988.

Bundy, McGeorge. National security adviser to President Kennedy. July 6, 1988.

Burke, John R. Vietnamese-language officer and second secretary, embassy, Saigon, June 1963. July 1, 1988.

Colby, William E. Director, Operations/Far East, 1962–63. December 14, 1987, and June 27, 1988.

Conein, Lucien. CIA operative, liaison to coup leaders, November 1, 1963. March 4, 1988.

Cooper, Chester. National Security Council liaison to CIA, Vietnam, 1962–66. December 7, 1987.

Elder, Walt. Executive assistant to John McCone. May 13, 1988.

Flott, Frederick. Personal assistant to Ambassador Henry Cabot Lodge Jr. May 12, 1988.

Forrestal, Michael V. National Security Council official responsible for South Vietnam. December 11, 1987.

Galbraith, John Kenneth. Ambassador to India, and confidant of John F. Kennedy. June 5, 1987.

Gilpatric, Roswell. Deputy secretary of defense. July 6, 1988.

Helms, Richard. Deputy director, CIA, 1963. March 4, 1988.

Hilsman, Roger. Assistant secretary of state (Far East), 1963–64. June 1987 and December 1992.

Johnson, U. Alexis. Deputy undersecretary of state, April 1961–64. May 17, 1988.

Nolting, Frederick E. Ambassador to Saigon, 1961–63. October 21, 1989.

Read, Ben. Executive secretary to Dean Rusk. May 12, 1988.

Richardson, John H. Chief of station, CIA, Saigon, 1962–63. March 12, 1987.

Rusk, Dean. Secretary of state. February 26, 1988.

Schlesinger, Arthur M., Jr. Historian and White House official.
    December 11, 1987.

Sullivan, William. Personal assistant to W. Averell Harriman, 1962–63.
    March 13, 1987.

Tran Van Dinh. South Vietnamese ambassador to India and simultaneously Diem's
    designated personal negotiator with representatives of Ho Chi Minh, 1963.
    October 1988.

Trueheart, William. Chargé d'affaires in Saigon, May–August 1963.
    April 26, 1988.

Young, Stephen. Vietnamese-language officer and specialist on South Vietnamese
    political parties, CIA. January 1989.

GOVERNMENT DOCUMENTS

Congressional Research Service, Library of Congress. *The U.S. Government and the Vietnam War: Executive and Legislative Roles and Relationships. Part II, 1961–1964.* Prepared for the Committee on Foreign Relations, United States Senate, 98th Congress, 2d session. Washington, D.C.: GPO, 1985.

The Pentagon Papers: The Defense Department History of United States Decisionmaking on Vietnam. Senator Gravel Edition. Vol. 2. Boston: Beacon Press, 1971.

Public Papers of the Presidents of the United States: John F. Kennedy, 1963. Washington, D.C.: GPO, 1964.

United States Department of State. *The Foreign Relations of the United States, 1961–1963.* Vol. 1, *Vietnam, 1961.* Washington, D.C.: GPO, 1988.

———. Vol. 2, *Vietnam, 1962.* Washington, D.C.: GPO, 1990.

———. Vol. 3, *Vietnam, January–August 1963.* Washington, D.C.: GPO, 1991.

———. Vol. 4, *Vietnam, August–December 1963.* Washington, D.C.: GPO, 1991.

United States Department of State. *The Foreign Relations of the United States, 1964–1968.* Vol. 1, *Vietnam, 1964.* Washington, D.C.: GPO, 1992. (The editor in chief, John P. Glennon, remarks in the prefaces to the successive volumes that only a small percentage of documents originally selected by the editors for publication has been withheld for reasons of national security: *1961–1963,* volume 3, 1.2 percent; *1961–1963,* volume 4, 1.7 percent; and *1964–1968,* volume 1, 2.5 percent.)

United States Senate. *Executive Sessions of the Senate Foreign Relations Committee (Historical Series), XV, 88th Congress, First Session, 1963.* Washington, D.C.: GPO, 1987.

———. *U.S. Involvement in the Overthrow of Diem, 1963.* Study no. 3. Staff study directed by Robert Biles, Robert Blum, and Ann Hollick for the use of the Committee on Foreign Relations. Washington, D.C.: GPO, 1972.

————. *Vietnam and Southeast Asia. Report of Senator Mike Mansfield to the Committee on Foreign Relations.* 93d Congress, 1st session. Washington, D.C.: GPO, 1963.

SECONDARY SOURCES

Abramson, Rudy. *Spanning the Century: The Life of W. Averell Harriman, 1891–1986.* New York: William Morrow, 1992.
Alsop, Joseph. "The Crusades." *Washington Post,* September 23, 1963.
Arendt, Hannah. *On Revolution.* New York: Viking Press, 1963.
Ball, George W. "Kennedy Up Close." *New York Review of Books,* February 3, 1994.
————. *The Past Has Another Pattern.* New York: W. W. Norton, 1982.
Bassett, Lawrence J., and Stephen E. Pelz. "The Failed Search for Victory: Vietnam and the Politics of War." In *Kennedy's Quest for Victory: American Foreign Policy, 1961–1963,* edited by Thomas G. Paterson, 223–52. New York: Oxford University Press, 1989.
Batchelor, Stephen. *The Awakening of the West: The Encounter of Buddhism and Western Culture.* Berkeley, Calif.: Parallax Press, 1994.
Beschloss, Michael R. *The Crisis Years: Kennedy and Khrushchev, 1960–1963.* New York: HarperCollins, 1991.
Birtz, Loren. *Backfire: A History of How American Culture Led Us into Vietnam and Made Us Fight the Way We Did.* New York: Ballantine Books, 1985.
Blair, Anne. *Lodge in Vietnam: A Patriot Abroad.* New Haven, Conn.: Yale University Press, 1995.
Bowen, Catherine. *John Adams and the American Revolution.* Boston: Little, Brown, 1950.
Braley, Russ. *Bad News: The Foreign Policy of the New York Times.* Chicago: Regnery Gateway, 1984.
Branch, Taylor. *Parting the Waters: America in the King Years, 1954–1963.* New York: Simon and Schuster, 1988.
Bui Diem. *In the Jaws of History.* Boston: Houghton Mifflin, 1987.
Bundy, McGeorge. *Danger and Survival: Choices about the Bomb in the First Fifty Years.* New York: Random House, 1990.
Burchett, Wilfred G. *Vietnam: Inside Story of the Guerilla War.* New York: International Publishers, 1965.
Buttinger, Joseph. *A Dragon Defiant: A Short History of Vietnam.* New York: Praeger, 1972.
————. *Vietnam: A Dragon Embattled.* Vol. 1, *From Colonialism to the Vietminh.* New York: Praeger, 1967.
————. *Vietnam: A Dragon Embattled.* Vol. 2, *Vietnam at War.* New York: Praeger, 1967.
————. *Vietnam: A Political History.* New York: Praeger, 1968.
————. *Vietnam: The Unforgettable Tragedy.* New York: Horizon Press, 1977.
Chang, Gordon H. *Friends and Enemies: The United States, China, and the Soviet Union, 1948–1972.* Stanford, Calif.: Stanford University Press, 1990.

Charlton, Michael, and Anthony Moncrieff. *Many Reasons Why: The American Involvement in Vietnam*. London: Scolar Press, 1978.

Chomsky, Noam. *Rethinking Camelot: JFK, the Vietnam War, and U.S. Political Culture*. Boston: South End Press, 1993.

Church, George J. "Saigon: The Final 10 Days," *Time*, April 24, 1995, 25–35.

Cohen, Warren I. *Dean Rusk*. Vol. 19 of *The American Secretaries of State and Their Diplomacy*, edited by Robert H. Ferrell. Totowa, N.J.: Cooper Square, 1980.

Colby, William. *Lost Victory*. Chicago: Contemporary Books, 1989.

Dalloz, Jacques. *The War in Indo-China: 1945–1954*. Translated by Josephine Bacon. Dublin: Gill and Macmillan, 1990.

de Bary, William T., ed. *The Buddhist Tradition of India, China, and Japan*. New York: Random House, 1972.

DiLeo, David L. *George Ball, Vietnam, and the Rethinking of Containment*. Chapel Hill: University of North Carolina Press, 1991.

Doan-Them. *Hai Muoi Nam Qua: Viec tung ngay (1945–1964)*. N.p.: Nam-Chi Tung-Thu, 1966.

Duiker, William J. *Historical Dictionary of Vietnam*. London: Scarecrow Press, 1989.

———. *The Rise of Nationalism in Vietnam, 1900–1941*. Ithaca, N.Y.: Cornell University Press, 1976.

Dupont, Frederick. *Mission de la France en Asie*. Paris: Edition France-Empire, 1956.

Elegant, Robert. "How to Lose a War." *Encounter*, August 1, 1981. Reprinted in *Major Problems in the History of the Vietnam War: Documents and Essays*, edited by Robert J. McMahon, 528–36. Lexington: D. C. Heath and Co., 1990.

Emery, Michael. *On the Front Lines: Following America's Foreign Correspondents across the Twentieth Century*. Washington, D.C.: American University Press, 1995.

Fall, Bernard B. *Last Reflections on a War*. Garden City, N.Y.: Doubleday and Co., 1967.

FitzGerald, Frances. *Fire in the Lake: The Vietnamese and the Americans in Vietnam*. 1972; New York: Random House, 1989.

Fromkin, David, and James Chace. "What *Are* the Lessons of Vietnam?" *Foreign Affairs* 63, no. 4 (Spring 1985): 722–46.

Gaddis, John Lewis. *The Long Peace: Inquiries into the History of the Cold War*. New York: Oxford University Press, 1987.

———. *Strategies of Containment: A Critical Appraisal of Postwar American National Security Policy*. New York: Oxford University Press, 1982.

———. *The United States and the End of the Cold War: Implications, Reconsiderations, Provocations*. New York: Oxford University Press, 1992.

Gardner, Lloyd C. *Pay Any Price: Lyndon Johnson and the Wars for Vietnam*. Chicago: Ivan R. Dee, 1995.

Giglio, James N. *The Presidency of John F. Kennedy*. Lawrence: University Press of Kansas, 1991.

Grant, Zalin. *Facing the Phoenix*. New York: W. W. Norton, 1991.

Greene, Graham. *The Quiet American*. London: Penguin Books, 1977.

Halberstam, David. *The Powers That Be*. New York: Alfred A. Knopf, 1979.

———. "The Role of Journalists in Vietnam: A Reporter's Perspective." In *Vietnam Reconsidered: Lessons from a War*, edited by Harrison E. Salisbury, 113–16. New York: Harper and Row, 1984.

Hallin, Daniel C. *The "Uncensored War": The Media and Vietnam*. Berkeley: University of California Press, 1989.

Hammer, Ellen. *A Death in November: America in Vietnam, 1963*. New York: E. P. Dutton, 1987.

———. *The Struggle for Indochina, 1940–1955*. Stanford, Calif.: Stanford University Press, 1966.

Hammond, William M. *Public Affairs: The Military and the Media, 1962–1968*. United States Army in Vietnam Series. Washington, D.C.: Center of Military History, U.S. Army, 1988.

Hartz, Louis. *The Liberal Tradition in America: An Interpretation of American Political Thought since the Revolution*. New York: Harcourt, Brace, 1955.

Hatcher, Patrick Lloyd. *The Suicide of an Elite: American Internationalists and Vietnam*. Stanford, Calif.: Stanford University Press, 1990.

Herring, George C. *America's Longest War: The United States in Vietnam, 1950–1975*. 2d ed. New York: Alfred A. Knopf, 1986.

———. "The Wrong Kind of Loyalty: McNamara's Apology for Vietnam." *Foreign Affairs* 74, no. 3 (May–June 1995): 154–58.

Hess, Gary R. "Commitment in the Age of Counterinsurgency: Kennedy's Vietnam Options and Decisions, 1961–1963." In *Shadow on the White House: Presidents and the Vietnam War, 1945–1975*, edited by David L. Anderson, 63–86. Lawrence: University Press of Kansas, 1993.

———. "The Unending Debate: Historians and the Vietnam War." *Diplomatic History* 18 (1994): 239–64.

———. *Vietnam and the United States: Origins and Legacy of War*. Boston: Twayne, 1990.

Higgins, Marguerite. *Our Vietnam Nightmare*. New York: Harper and Row, 1965.

Holloway, David. *Stalin and the Bomb: The Soviet Union and Atomic Energy, 1939–1956*. New Haven, Conn.: Yale University Press, 1994.

Honey, P. J. *Genesis of a Tragedy: The Historical Background to the Vietnam War*. London: Ernest Benn, 1968.

Hue-Tam Ho Tai. *Radicalism and the Origins of the Vietnamese Revolution*. Cambridge, Mass.: Harvard University Press, 1992.

Kahin, George McT. *Intervention: How America Became Involved in Vietnam*. New York: Alfred A. Knopf, 1986.

Karnow, Stanley. "Commentary: The Two Vietnams." In *Vietnam as History: Ten Years after the Paris Peace Accords*, edited by Peter Braestrup, 78–83. Washington, D.C.: University Press of America, 1984.

———. *In Our Image: America's Empire in the Philippines*. New York: Ballantine Books, 1990.

———. "Lost Chance in Vietnam." *New Republic*, February 2, 1974.

———. *Vietnam: A History*. New York: Viking Press, 1983.

———, ed. *Vietnam, A Television History*. Part 3, "America's Mandarin." Part 4, "LBJ Goes to War." Public Broadcasting System series. 1985.

Kennan, George F. "Morality and Foreign Policy." *Foreign Affairs* 64, no. 2 (Winter 1985–86): 205–18.

———. *The Nuclear Delusion: Soviet-American Relations in the Nuclear Age.* New York: Pantheon, 1982.

Kinnard, Douglas. *The Certain Trumpet: Maxwell Taylor and the American Experience in Vietnam.* Washington, D.C.: Brassey's, 1991.

Kipling, Rudyard. *Rudyard Kipling's Verse, Inclusive Edition, 1885–1926.* Garden City, N.Y.: Doubleday, Doran, 1931.

Kissinger, Henry. *Diplomacy.* New York: Simon and Schuster, 1994.

Kitagawa, Joseph M. "Buddhism and Asian Politics." *Asian Survey* 2, no. 5 (July 1962): 1–11.

Kitto, H. D. F. *Sophocles: Dramatist and Philosopher.* Oxford: Oxford University Press, 1958.

Klein, Robert A. *Sovereign Equality among States: The History of an Idea.* Toronto: University of Toronto Press, 1974.

Lacouture, Jean. *De Gaulle, the Ruler, 1945–1970.* Translated by Alan Sheridan. New York: W. W. Norton, 1985.

———. *Ho Chi Minh.* Translated by Peter Wiles. London: Penguin, 1968.

———. *Vietnam: Between Two Truces.* Translated by Konrad Kellen and Joel Carmichael. New York: Random House, 1966.

Lacouture, Jean, and Simonne Lacouture. *Vietnam: Voyage à travers une victoire.* Paris: Editions du Seuil, 1976.

Lake, Anthony, ed. *The Vietnam Legacy: The War, American Society, and the Future of American Foreign Policy.* New York: New York University Press, 1976.

Lancaster, Donald. *The Emancipation of French Indochina.* New York: Octagon Books, 1974.

Lansdale, Edward G. "Viet Nam: Do We Understand Revolution?" *Foreign Affairs* 43, no. 1 (October 1964): 75–86.

Lasance, Reverend F. X., and Reverend Francis A. Walsh, eds. *The New Roman Missal in Latin and English.* New York: Benziger Brothers, 1937.

Lathem, Edward Connery, ed. *The Poetry of Robert Frost.* New York: Holt, Rinehart, and Winston, 1969.

Lewy, Guenter. *America in Vietnam.* Oxford: Oxford University Press, 1978.

Link, Arthur S. *Wilson the Diplomatist: A Look at His Major Foreign Policies.* Baltimore: Johns Hopkins University Press, 1957.

Lipscomb, A. A., and A. E. Bergh, eds. *The Writings of Thomas Jefferson.* Vol. 14. Washington, D.C.: Thomas Jefferson Memorial Association, 1903.

Mai-Tho-Truyen. *Le Bouddhisme au Vietnam; Buddhism in Vietnam; Phat-Giao Viet-Nam.* Saigon: Xa Loi Pagoda, 1962.

Maneli, Mieczyslaw. *War of the Vanquished.* Translated by Maria de Gorgey. New York: Harper and Row, 1971.

Masson, André. *Histoire du Vietnam.* Paris: Presses Universitaires de France, 1967.

McAlister, John T., Jr. *Viet Nam: The Origins of Revolution.* New York: Alfred A. Knopf, 1969.

McAlister, John T., Jr., and Paul Mus. *The Vietnamese and Their Revolution.* New York: Harper and Row, 1970.

McCloskey, Robert J. "Dean Rusk: Reflections on Alliances." *Mediterranean Quarterly* 1, no. 1 (Fall 1989): 9–20.

McCullough, David. *Truman.* New York: Simon and Schuster, 1992.

McNamara, Robert S. "The Military Role of Nuclear Weapons: Perceptions and Misperceptions." *Foreign Affairs* 62, no. 1 (Fall 1983): 59–80.

McNamara, Robert S., with Brian VanDeMark. *In Retrospect: The Tragedy and Lessons of Vietnam.* New York: Times Books, 1995.

Miller, Robert Hopkins, ed. *Inside an Embassy: The Political Role of Diplomats Abroad.* Washington, D.C.: Congressional Quarterly, 1992.

Morgenthau, Hans J. *Politics among Nations: The Struggle for Power and Peace,* 4th ed. New York: Alfred A. Knopf, 1967.

———. "Vietnam—Another Korea?" *Commentary* 33 (1962): 369–74.

Mus, Paul. *Viet-Nam: Sociologie d'une guerre.* Paris: Editions du Seuil, 1952.

Nelan, Bruce W. "Lessons from the Lost War." *Time,* April 24, 1995, 44–45.

Newman, John M. *JFK and Vietnam: Deceptions, Intrigue, and the Struggle for Power.* New York: Warner Books, 1992.

Nguyen Ngoc Huy. "Ngo Dinh Diem's Execution." *Worldview* 33 (November 1976): 39–41.

Nolting, Frederick. *From Trust to Tragedy: The Political Memoirs of Frederick Nolting, Kennedy's Ambassador to Diem's Vietnam.* New York: Praeger, 1988.

Notter, Harley. *The Origins of the Foreign Policy of Woodrow Wilson.* New York: Russell and Russell, 1965.

O'Donnell, Kenneth P., and David F. Powers. *"Johnny, We Hardly Knew Ye": Memories of John Fitzgerald Kennedy.* Boston: Little, Brown, 1972.

Parados, John. *The Hidden History of the Vietnam War.* Chicago: Ivan R. Dee, 1995.

Peterson, Merrill D. *The Jefferson Image in the American Mind.* New York: Oxford University Press, 1960.

Pike, Douglas. *History of Vietnamese Communism, 1925–1976.* Stanford, Calif.: Hoover Institution Press, 1978.

Pogue, Forrest C. *George C. Marshall: Statesman, 1945–1959.* New York: Viking Press, 1987.

Prochnau, William. *Once upon a Distant War: Young War Correspondents and the Early Vietnam Battles.* New York: Times Books, 1995.

Race, Jeffrey. *War Comes to Long An: Revolutionary Conflict in a Vietnamese Province.* Berkeley: University of California Press, 1972.

Reeves, Richard. *President Kennedy: Profile of Power.* New York: Simon and Schuster, 1993.

Reeves, Thomas C. *A Question of Character: A Life of John F. Kennedy.* New York: Free Press, 1991.

Reston, James. *Deadline: A Memoir.* New York: Times Books, 1992.

Rituale Romanum. New York: Benziger Brothers, 1960.

Rusk, Dean. *As I Saw It: As Told to Richard Rusk.* Edited by Daniel S. Papp. New York: W. W. Norton, 1990.

Rust, William J., and the editors of U.S. News Books. *Kennedy in Vietnam.* New York: Charles Scribner's Sons, 1985.

Salinger, Pierre. *With Kennedy*. New York: Doubleday and Co., 1966.

Salisbury, Harrison E. *The New Emperors: China in the Era of Mao and Deng*. New York: Avon, 1992.

————. *Without Fear or Favor: The New York Times and Its Times*. New York: Times Books, 1980.

————., ed. *Vietnam Reconsidered: Lessons from a War*. New York: Harper and Row, 1984.

Schecter, Jerrold. *The New Face of Buddha: Buddhism and Political Power in Southeast Asia*. London: Victor Gollancz, 1967.

Schell, Jonathan. *The Real War: The Classic Reporting on the Vietnam War with a New Essay*. New York: Pantheon, 1987.

————. "Reflections: The Time of Illusion." *New Yorker*, July 7, 1975.

————. "The Talk of the Town." *New Yorker*, April 14, 1975.

Schlesinger, Arthur M., Jr. *The Bitter Heritage: Vietnam and American Democracy, 1941–1966*. Boston: Houghton Mifflin, 1967.

————. "National Interests and Moral Absolutes." In *Ethics and World Politics: Four Perspectives*, edited by Ernest W. Lefever, 21–42. Baltimore: Johns Hopkins University Press, 1972.

————. *Robert Kennedy and His Times*. Boston: Houghton Mifflin, 1978.

————. *A Thousand Days: John F. Kennedy in the White House*. New York: Fawcett World Library, 1967.

Schoenbaum, Thomas. *Waging Peace and War: Dean Rusk in the Truman, Kennedy, and Johnson Years*. New York: Simon and Schuster, 1988.

Scigliano, Robert. *South Vietnam: Nation under Stress*. Boston: Houghton Mifflin, 1964.

Shaplen, Robert. *The Lost Revolution: The U.S. in Vietnam, 1946–1966*. New York: Harper Colophon Books, 1966.

————. "A Reporter at Large: Saigon Exit." *New Yorker*, May 19, 1975.

————. *Road from War: Vietnam, 1965–1970*. New York: Harper and Row, 1970.

Shapley, Deborah. *Promise and Power: The Life and Times of Robert McNamara*. Boston: Little, Brown, 1993.

Sheehan, Neil. *A Bright Shining Lie: John Paul Vann and America in Vietnam*. New York: Random House, 1988.

Sheehan, Neil, Hedrick Smith, E. W. Kenworthy, and Fox Butterfield, eds. *The Pentagon Papers as Published by the New York Times*. New York: Bantam, 1971.

Shen, Michael Koping. "Sowing Instability: U.S. Influences on South Vietnamese Leadership, 1963–1965." Unpublished manuscript. Georgetown University School of Foreign Service Scholars Seminar Thesis, 1991.

Sidey, Hugh, with Cecil Houghton and Chester Clifton. *The Memories of JFK, 1961–1963*. New York: W. W. Norton, 1973.

Smith, Ralph. "Biting the Dust." *Far Eastern Economic Review*, August 3, 1995, 38–39.

Smith, R. B. *An International History of the Vietnam War*. Vol. 1, *Revolution versus Containment, 1955–61*. New York: St. Martin's, 1983.

————. Vol. 2, *The Kennedy Strategy*. New York: St. Martin's, 1985.

————. Vol. 3, *The Making of a Limited War, 1965–66*. New York: St. Martin's, 1991.

Steel, Ronald. *Walter Lippmann and the American Century*. Boston: Little, Brown, 1980.

Strober, Gerald S., and Deborah H. Strober. *"Let Us Begin Anew": An Oral History of the Kennedy Presidency*. New York: HarperCollins, 1993.

Taylor, Maxwell D. *Responsibility and Response*. New York: Harper and Row, 1967.

Thich Nhat Hanh. *Vietnam: Lotus in a Sea of Fire*. With a foreword by Thomas Merton and an afterword by Alfred Hassler. New York: Hill and Wang, 1967.

Thompson, Edward T., ed. *Theodore H. White at Large: The Best of His Magazine Writing, 1939–1986*. New York: Pantheon, 1992.

Thompson, Lawrence, and R. H. Winnick. *Robert Frost: The Later Years*. New York: Holt, Rinehart, and Winston, 1976.

Thucydides. *The Peloponnesian War*. Translated by John H. Finley Jr. New York: Modern Library, 1951.

Truong Vinh-Le. *Vietnam, où est la vérité?* Paris: Lavauzelle, 1989.

Tuchman, Barbara W. *The March of Folly: From Troy to Vietnam*. New York: Alfred A. Knopf, 1984.

Tucker, Robert W. *Nation or Empire? The Debate over American Foreign Policy*. Baltimore: Johns Hopkins Press, 1968.

Tucker, Robert W., and David C. Hendrickson. *Empire of Liberty: The Statecraft of Thomas Jefferson*. New York: Oxford University Press, 1990.

Ulam, Adam. *Expansion and Coexistence: Soviet Foreign Policy, 1917–1973*. 2d ed. New York: Holt, Rinehart and Winston, 1974.

Wade, Betsy. *Forward Positions: The War Correspondence of Homer Bigart*. Fayetteville: University of Arkansas Press, 1992.

Walzer, Michael. *Just and Unjust Wars: A Moral Argument with Historical Illustrations*. New York: Basic Books, 1977.

Warner, Denis. *The Last Confucian*. New York: Macmillan, 1963.

Warner, Geoffrey. "The United States and the Fall of Diem. Part I, The Coup That Never Was." *Australian Outlook* 28, no. 3 (December 1974): 245–58.

————. "The United States and the Fall of Diem. Part II, The Death of Diem." *Australian Outlook* 29, no. 1 (April 1975): 3–17.

West, Morris L. *The Ambassador*. New York: William Morrow, 1965.

Winters, Francis X. "The Freedom to Resist Coercion: Augustine, Aquinas, Vitoria." *Commonweal* 118, no. 11 (June 1, 1991): 369–72.

Woodside, Alexander B. "Historical Essay." In *The Tale of Kieu*, by Du Nguyen. Bilingual edition of *Truyen Kieu*. Translated and annotated by Huynh Sanh Thong. New Haven, Conn.: Yale University Press, 1983.

INDEX

Acheson, Dean, 146
Adams, John Quincy, 217–18
Agrovilles, 59
Allen, George, 241 (n. 56)
Alsop, Joseph, 86, 109
American exceptionalism, 5–6,
  197, 209–11, 225, 268
  (n. 21)
American foreign policy. *See* Foreign
  policy, of United States
Americans for Democratic Action
  (ADA), 164
Animism, in Vietnam, 30, 161
Autocracy, 222; in oriental mandarin
  tradition, 148; American
  intolerance of, 217, 219

Ball, George, 26; moral rationale
  for opposing Diem, 15; orders
  concerning first State Department
  cable to Lodge, 53; role in
  authorizing overthrow of Diem, 56,
  57–58, 60–61, 63, 141; support for
  overthrow of Diem, 68, 86, 242
  (n. 11); rage in reminiscences of
  Diem, 214
Bao Dai: deposal of, 10, 23–24, 157;
  offering of premiership to Diem,
  59, 154–55, 157
Bartlett, Charles, 192, 193
Beech, Keyes, 178–79
Beschloss, Michael, 193
Bigart, Homer, 181–82
Big Minh. *See* Duong Van Minh ("Big
  Minh")
Blair, Anne: on Lodge's first
  conversation with Diem, 62; on
  Lodge's final conversation with
  Diem, 104; on role of Lodge's
  political ambitions in diplomatic

strategy, 166; on Lodge in United
  Nations, 167
Brandon, Henry, 124
"Bravo" nuclear test, 7
Browne, Malcolm, 33, 166, 176
Buddhism, in Vietnam, 24–25, 30–31,
  236 (n. 31)
Buddhist activist movement, 29–30,
  31, 34, 164; self-immolations, 12,
  33, 50, 52, 116; Diem government
  policies toward, 12, 29–30, 36, 59;
  as vehicle of nationalism, 24–25;
  and perception of religious
  persecution in U.S., 29, 33–34;
  Kennedy Administration reaction
  to, 29–30, 34–37, 51–53; political
  goals of, 40, 45–46, 52, 241 (n. 56)
Bui Tin, 188, 266 (n. 37)
Bulganin, Nikolai, 7
Bundy, McGeorge: military rationale
  for opposition to Diem, 15; doubts
  about Lodge's efficacy, 52; support
  for overthrow of Diem, 62, 70, 71,
  91; and proposal to cut aid to Tung,
  81; cable to Lodge regarding coup,
  91; misgivings about coup, 100;
  final efforts to stop coup if risk of
  failure, 101, 102–3; satisfaction with
  coup, 105; reaction to assassination
  of Diem, 107; coping with fallout
  from coup, 110–11; confidence
  in policy of nuclear deterrence,
  137
Burchett, Wilfred, 45, 111, 119
Buttinger, Joseph, 109, 153, 157
Buu Hoi, 73, 89–90

Can Lao Party, 23, 24, 60
Carver, George, 43
Central Intelligence Agency (CIA):